VACATIONS IN
THE MARITIMES

A *YANKEE BOOKS* TRAVEL GUIDE

VACATIONS IN THE MARITIMES

A TOURBOOK OF NOVA SCOTIA, PRINCE EDWARD ISLAND, NEW BRUNSWICK *PLUS* NEWFOUNDLAND AND LABRADOR

BY LAURIE FULLERTON

YANKEE BOOKS

YANKEE is a registered trademark of Yankee Publishing, Inc.
Used by permission.

Printed in the United States of America
on acid-free ∞ paper

Senior Editor: Edward Claflin
Editors: John Feltman, Sarah Dunn
Book Designer: Leslie Waltzer
Cover Designer: Stan Green
Cover Layout: Karen C. Heard
Cover Photographer: Randy Ury

About the cover photo: Peggy's Cove is located on the South Shore of Nova Scotia. It is the most popular stop along the Lighthouse Route (see page 34).

Library of Congress Cataloging-in-Publication Data

Fullerton, Laurie.
    Vacations in the Maritimes : a tourbook of Nova Scotia, Prince Edward Island, New Brunswick plus Newfoundland and Labrador / Laurie Fullerton
        p.   cm.— (A Yankee Books travel guide)
    Includes index.
    ISBN 0–89909–356–6   Paperback
    1. Atlantic Provinces—Tours.   I. Title   II. Series.
F1035.8.F84   1993
917.1504'4—dc20
                                                            92–41441
                                                            CIP

Distributed in the book trade by St. Martin's Press

2   4   6   8   10 9   7   5   3   1   paperback

CONTENTS

ACKNOWLEDGMENTS

The author would like to thank the following people and organizations for their assistance in the research and writing of *Vacations in the Maritimes*. Special thanks to Richard and Carol Fullerton for their endless assistance and support, as well as Pamela Fullerton, Deborah and Daniel McCarthy, Richard Upton, Wendy Upton and Mr. and Mrs. W. C. Upton. Thanks to Sylvia Fullerton for her kind hospitality and insights into bird life in Atlantic Canada; to Mr. and Mrs. Phil Shea for their generosity and information on Brier Island and its famous son, Joshua Slocum. Thanks to Brenda Shesnicky and Isabelle Geraets of Ottawa, David and Nancy Car of Lunenburg, Sally and Upton Brady, Linda Spencer, Ed Karl, Peggy Munro and W. P.

Also thanks to all the helpful and friendly folks at the Nova Scotia, Newfoundland and Labrador, Prince Edward Island and New Brunswick tourism offices. An extended thanks to the friendly and generous people of Atlantic Canada, both on the road and in their homes, who offered insights and impressions of their provinces.

This book is dedicated to the memory of Gladys and Gordon Fullerton.

PREFACE

This guide came to be after a long summer's journey of rediscovery through a region that had captivated my imagination as a child. In 1967, when I was seven years old, my family took the old station wagon north from Massachusetts to visit the places where my grandfather and his brothers and sisters had grown up. Like many other descendants of Scottish immigrants, they had settled in Nova Scotia on the rich farmlands of the Annapolis Basin. During that summer, I wore my first kilt with the tartan colors of Nova Scotia, I swam in the black brooks of Cape Breton and went beachcombing, grabbing stones of unimaginable beauty that I still keep today.

Last summer, finally returning to Atlantic Canada, I visited the places I had dreamed of seeing again. I was not disappointed. My tour of the Maritimes, Newfoundland and Labrador was better than I had hoped, and by walking, cycling, driving and even hitchhiking the backroads, I rediscovered my identity as an American of Canadian-Scottish descent.

On Prince Edward Island, my father and I wandered around the old cemeteries until, in the remote town of Mt. Stewart, he found the grave of his great-grandfather and great-grandmother. As we toured, the people of Prince Edward Island always had a kind word for us. They loved my red hair, calling it Prince Edward Island hair. (It seems that Anne of Green Gables, the fictional heroine of the island and the idol of thousands of visiting Japanese tourists, also sports that hair color.) Being appreciated as not just a redhead but as a Prince Edward Island redhead made me proud of my heritage and my link to this land.

In Nova Scotia, I traveled alone down the coasts of the South Shore towards the rugged beauty of Digby, meeting folks who lived off the sea or struggled in other ways to eke out a living in a tough economy. I eventually reached the Annapolis Basin. At Grand Pré National Historic Park, I spent the day sensing the sadness of the Acadian expulsion but also lost in thoughts about my own relatives, long gone now, who had picnicked at Grand Pré every summer.

On the South Shore of Nova Scotia, visiting a second cousin, I discovered the tasty flavor of the seaweed called Irish moss, ate cream of lobster on toast (a Nova Scotia specialty) and wandered throughout the town of Lunenburg, which captivated me with its seafaring past and its native craftsmen. I always stopped to listen while Edward Tanner rang the ten church bells by hand at 2 P.M. every day. The clear bells rang hymns and tunes like "Danny Boy" and "Amazing Grace" that gave me a lump in my throat. At Mahone Bay, I sought out the home of the late David Stevens, one of the best schooner builders in the world. And I went sailing amidst the islands while hearing yet more stories about Stevens' prowess as a master craftsman and sailor.

In Cape Breton, I found the old Keltic Lodge where I had stayed as a child. And I fell in love with Baddeck, with its pristine Bras d'Or Lake, bald eagles and quiet coastal hideaways.

New Brunswick was full of island-hopping from Grand Manan to Campóbello. I'll never forget watching the fishing fleet at North Harbour on Grand Manan as they raced out one night after the migrating sardines. In their haste, they nearly knocked the cocktails out of the hands of the yachtsmen whose boats were tied up side by side with those of the impatient fishermen. I ate fresh Atlantic salmon, waded along the banks when the Fundy tides depleted the bays of water and watched shark, whales and dolphins follow our ferry as we crossed the Bay of Fundy.

The best surprise of all was Newfoundland. One day the world will discover this land, and by then all that is unique about it may be gone. But for now, it still holds on to many things that we Americans have lost. The people here live simple lives. The men who once fished the Grand Banks have stories of great hardships to pass down to their children, yet they love their beautiful island. Their remoteness makes them the target of many jokes, but they really enjoy a laugh at themselves. I was very sad to leave Newfoundland. With their open, friendly ways and their straightforward philosophies about life, the Newfoundlanders are the sanest of all on an otherwise zany continent.

Labrador, with its icebergs, permafrost and dead-end roads, is really for the rugged. Taking the mail boat trip to its northern villages, I found, was like a forage into one of our last frontiers. Labrador is a place that is untapped and waiting to be discovered.

I think I share the dream of many when I say that after returning from the Maritimes, Newfoundland and Labrador, I'd be happy to live out the rest of my days along the coasts of Atlantic Canada, combing those beaches that already feel like home.

AN INTRODUCTION
TO ATLANTIC CANADA

This guide encompasses four provinces of northeastern Canada, a part of North America that was discovered by Europeans 500 years ago and quite possibly by Vikings 500 years before that. Included are the three Maritime provinces of Nova Scotia, Prince Edward Island and New Brunswick, as well as the province of Newfoundland and Labrador. Together these four are best known as Atlantic Canada.

Having spent many months traveling throughout this region, I feel it is safe to say that there are few vacation destinations on this continent that offer the kind of diversity you can find in Atlantic Canada. The region is steeped in history, culture and a natural beauty that is very inviting, offering adventure for families, couples and individual travelers. There is not only one "must see" attraction here; each county and province offers something new, exciting and unusual around the corner.

Atlantic Canada is really one of the last places in North America where traditional livelihoods like farming and fishing continue to thrive, unfettered by the kind of commercialism that abounds along the coast of Maine and much of the rest of the eastern seaboard. You can meet people with French, Scottish, Irish and English roots that date back to the 1600s. Many who came here were victims of war or famine searching for a new and better life. The Canadians who live here today retell stories of their grandfathers and great-grandfathers who went in schooners to fish along the Grand Banks or who descended into the rich coal mines beneath the ocean floor. This is a region of North America where change is not always welcomed, where independence and proximity to unspoiled natural beauty are top priorities of the inhabitants.

HIGHLIGHTS

Nova Scotia still receives the bulk of the tourism trade, thanks to the drawing power of the Cabot Trail in Cape Breton and the scenic South Shore around Halifax. But traditionally less-visited areas like New Brunswick and Newfoundland are attracting the attention of today's travelers, too. People come from as far away as England and Australia to watch whales off Grand Manan Island in New Brunswick or hike the trails of Gros Morne National Park in Newfoundland, where wild caribou still roam. In Labrador, you can catch a glimpse of icebergs or visit the native Innuit people, who still hunt for seal and polar bear. On Prince Edward Island there are miles of beaches and vast fields speckled with wild lupine. The Lighthouse Route and Evangeline Trail in Nova Scotia are great to explore, and the dramatic Fundy Tides off New Brunswick and Nova Scotia are awe-inspiring. Throughout Atlantic Canada there are ferry boats and scenic drives to take you farther away from the hassles of the twentieth century but closer to what is really important to see and experience.

A BRIEF HISTORY

Atlantic Canada is made up of four very distinct provinces whose common link is their geographical and cultural connection to the sea. For centuries, many Atlantic Canadians have depended on fishing for their livelihood and faced high risks at sea due to severe winter weather, particularly in the icebound northeast regions. The three provinces of Nova Scotia, Prince Edward Island and New Brunswick are commonly called the Maritimes, while Newfoundland and Labrador together form a separate province that remained independent of Canada through much of its history.

It is believed that the first people to see Atlantic Canada, particularly Newfoundland and Labrador, were the Vikings. Sagas of these Norsemen, dating back to the 1300s, tell of a distant land called Vinland, where grapes were plentiful. Some historians claim that Vinland was in Nova Scotia, others say in New Brunswick while still others say it was in New England. In the 1970s, however, a Viking settlement was discovered at L'Anse aux Meadows in Newfoundland. It is believed that this was the first settlement, dating back to around 1000 A.D. Historians believe that the Viking settlers explored the region for about three years, then left for good. Scholars still hope to find more evidence from the Vikings' brief stay and their travels around the Atlantic coast.

During the 1400s, Portuguese, French and English fishermen discovered the rich waters of the Grand Banks off Newfoundland. They spent summers fishing there, returning to Europe each winter. Once word of these rich fishing grounds reached the leaders of Europe, explorers were shipped out to chart this new land. One of the earliest, a scant five years after Columbus, was John Cabot.

In 1497, after 52 days at sea, John Cabot landed on the northern point of Cape Breton and, ceremoniously unfurling a royal banner, took possession of the land for England. Cabot believed that he had reached the northeastern coast of Asia—a gateway to the rich silk, porcelain and tea that were so coveted in Europe. Cabot called this new land St. John, for it was discovered on the festival day of St. John the Baptist. Then, in 1534, Jacques Cartier reached the Gulf of St. Lawrence, claiming the entire region for France. Cartier traded with the Micmac and Maliceet Indians on the northern shore of what is now New Brunswick. These Indians were nomadic tribes who followed the caribou herds throughout Atlantic Canada; they also hunted seal and fished for their livelihood. Evidence from religious artifacts shows that they worshipped the sun.

The French trumped the English in 1605 when the explorers Samuel de Champlain and Sieur de Monts rounded Cape Sable near present-day Yarmouth, Nova Scotia, and reached the Annapolis Basin via the Bay of Fundy. Here they established Annapolis Royal, the first settlement of Europeans on North American soil north of Florida.

As settlement by the French and English progressed, conflicts between the two nations began to divide the new lands of Canada. Before 1713, the newly settled lands of the Maritimes came to be called Acadia. These areas were largely populated by French farmers who cultivated the land and called themselves Acadians. By 1713, the British had muscled their way into the settlements and taken control over much of the region. The French were forced to relinquish their claims on the new land when the Treaty of Utrecht was signed, handing Port Royal over to the English who renamed it Annapolis Royal. The land called Acadia became Nova Scotia, and the early French settlers, the Acadians, were now under British rule.

French and English battles raged from Louisbourg to Annapolis Royal. When the Acadians, who numbered in the thousands, were asked to declare allegiance to either France or England, they refused to take sides. This led to the wide-scale deportation of almost 10,000 Acadians from the Maritime provinces. Three quarters of the deported arrived in the American colonies and were resettled in the swamplands of Louisiana. Descendents of these Acadians are now called Cajuns.

The Acadian lands were taken over by New England planters who, having fled the newly independent colonies of America, were loyal to Britain. These Loyalists, who were generally well educated, were fundamental in the settlement and prosperity of Atlantic Canada. Later settlers included the Scots, who came to Nova Scotia as early as 1773 and in greater numbers throughout the 1800s. The Irish and Welsh came to Atlantic Canada as well, escaping potato famines and joblessness. They settled in Newfoundland, Cape Breton and Prince Edward Island. Some Acadians succeeded in returning to their lands, and many now live along the coast of New Brunswick, on Prince Edward Island and throughout Nova Scotia.

To appreciate the diversity of the settlers of Atlantic Canada, you need only observe the panoply of flags flying from flagpoles in front of people's homes. It is not unusual, during a drive, to see an Acadian flag flying next to a British, Irish, Scottish or French flag. Nova Scotia, New Brunswick and Prince Edward Island each have their own pennants. Ironically, it is rare to see the Maple Leaf, the flag of Canada, in front of people's homes; it is most often found flying above post offices or other government buildings.

GEOGRAPHY

The geography of Atlantic Canada is varied, rugged and unique. This is a region of extremes, characterized by looming icebergs, spectacular coastal fjords and some of the highest tides in the world. But the most common sights—fog permitting—in these remote provinces are of rolling hills dotted with farms and grazing cattle, and of distant coves and bays. Atlantic Canada also has beautiful rivers and lakes, particularly in New Brunswick where sports fishermen congregate to catch trout and salmon. The most important feature, however, remains the ocean, and the many activities centered around it.

TOURISM

Because Atlantic Canada's economy relies on tourism, the provinces are well equipped to handle the seasonal influx. All major cities and most small towns have a tourism office where the staff is prepared to answer just about every question imaginable. The young people who work at these tourism agencies are fun to talk with and you can learn a great deal from them. You can also pick up free literature about each province.

PLANNING YOUR TRIP

Transportation

It would be virtually impossible to travel throughout all of Atlantic Canada in one brief vacation. The most common method of touring Atlantic Canada is by car, camper van, or recreational vehicle. RVs, especially, are everywhere on the roads of Atlantic Canada during the summer.

A valid U.S. driver's license and vehicle registration card are required while traveling in Atlantic Canada.

Before traveling to Canada motorists should obtain a Non-Resident Inter-Province Motor Vehicle Liability Insurance Card. Available through your own insurance agency, this card is accepted by Canadian police as an indication of financial responsibility in the event of an accident.

Speed limits in Canada are posted in kilometers per hour, not miles per hour. Fifty miles per hour is roughly equal to 80 kilometers per hour. Eighty kilometers is the average speed on the Trans-Canada Highway, while 50 kilometers is common in cities and towns.

Many groups and individuals choose to tour Atlantic Canada by bicycle. Cape Breton, in particular, gets hordes of cyclists who come to ride around the Cabot Trail. There are two major drawbacks that cyclists often overlook. Cape Breton is notorious for its strong winds throughout the summer months. And there is an endless stream of vehicles touring Cape Breton as well. For cyclists, a ride around Prince Edward Island or along the South Shore of Nova Scotia may be a more attractive alternative.

Touring by bus is another way to see Atlantic Canada. I rode plenty of buses during my travels in the region and found that it can provide a relaxing change from driving. You can almost always find a friendly local to chat with. Train travel is really no longer an option here, for the tracks are fast disappearing throughout the Maritimes. In places like Newfoundland, Cape Breton or Prince Edward Island, hitchhiking is a reliable means of travel, for those with hitchhiking savvy and enduring patience. People tend to be trusting and extremely hospitable, so it's a great way to meet the locals.

Atlantic Canada is served by an excellent ferry system, with connections between all four provinces. These trips provide an opportunity to relax, spot marine life and meet people. There are also important ferry connections between Yarmouth, Nova Scotia and both Bar Harbor and Portland, Maine. An important point to remember when traveling by ferry is that often you must anticipate long waits to board. Try to arrive early.

Accommodations

Overnight alternatives in Atlantic Canada vary from rustic campgrounds to luxury hotels. Whether you plan to sleep on the ground or in a king-size bed, it's a good idea to make initial reservations in advance, then call ahead from local tourist bureaus as the rest of your itinerary takes shape. The vast majority of hotels, bed & breakfasts, inns and campgrounds are open seasonally, from May to October. The high season is July and August. The tourism boards of each province can be lifesavers, for people in the tourism office will often call ahead and make bookings for you at the hotel or bed & breakfast of your choice.

Budget travelers will find that bed & breakfasts and tourist homes (slightly cheaper versions of the traditional bed & breakfasts) are not cheap. The average bed & breakfast costs $35 to $50 per night, including breakfast. Please note that all prices listed throughout this guide are in Canadian dollars. Room rates may be subject to change. For the latest information, call ahead.

The best alternative for low-budget tourists is to stay at a youth hostel or a campground. While hostels are scattered about Atlantic Canada and are few and far between, campgrounds are everywhere. The average campground charges between $8 and $12 per night. For that price you usually get running water, firewood, showers and a campground canteen selling supplies and necessities. There is usually a warden nearby who can help out during emergencies. If you're planning a lengthy trip to Atlantic Canada during the height of the summer season, bring a tent along. Camping not only saves money, it's fun and a great way to meet fellow travelers and locals. Having a tent also helps if every hotel and bed & breakfast in town turns out to be full—a common occurrence during a festival or at the height of summer.

Food

Atlantic Canada is best known for its seafood, especially scallops, lobster and salmon. In general, Canadian cuisine is fairly unimaginative, though Acadian cooking can be innovative and flavorful. Most Canadian cuisine reflects the British influence. It's generally simple, wholesome and bland. Nonetheless, there are some well-known gourmet restaurants in the larger cities. In my opinion, sitting in the dining room of an inn overlooking the Bay of Fundy, eating boiled potatoes, garden-fresh peas and poached Atlantic salmon is as good as it gets in Canada, and that's pretty good indeed.

If you are on the road, one place to find a quick meal is the Irving Gas Station chain. At the diners inside these stations, there's often a daily special or some homemade pie. Another old standby: the Canadian-Chinese restaurants that abound throughout the Maritimes and Newfoundland. In larger cities, there are a number of ethnic restaurants ranging from Middle Eastern to Vietnamese. Pizza is a favorite throughout the region, and there are the usual fast-food joints that you find in the United States.

Alcoholic Beverages

Anyone over the age of 19 can buy liquor in Atlantic Canada. With the exception of Newfoundland and Labrador, all liquor is sold at government-run Liquor Commission outlets. These are open Monday through Thursday until 6 P.M. and until 10 P.M. on Fridays and Saturdays. All outlets are closed on Sundays. Restaurants that serve wine, beer and spirits are advertised as being "licensed" or "fully licensed." They are authorized to sell drinks, but only if the customer places a food order as well. There are also abundant licensed pubs and lounges where liquor is served without food.

Money

The U.S. dollar generally buys about 15 percent more in Canada, but many places of business do not accept U.S. dollars. There are authorized currency exchange counters throughout Atlantic Canada at the tourist information centers. Traveler's checks are accepted at all banks, which are generally open Monday through Thursday from 10 A.M. to 3 P.M., and from 10 A.M.. to 6 P.M. on Fridays. A few banks are open on Saturdays from 10 A.M. to 3 P.M. The best exchange rates, however, are found at the Irving Gas Stations throughout Atlantic Canada. If you are close to one of those stations, exchange your dollars here.

Travel in Atlantic Canada is expensive. The tax system within Canada takes its pound of flesh from every citizen, as well as visitors. Each restaurant bill and every purchase from a store is accompanied by the dreaded GST, or general sales tax. But non-Canadian visitors get a lucky break—a refund on departure. Whenever you make a purchase, remember to save the sales slip to turn in to the customs office when leaving Canada. Whatever you paid as GST will be reimbursed by the government before you depart from Canada.

Customs Information

Citizens and permanent residents of the United States do not need a passport to enter Canada. Some proof of citizenship or identification, such as a driver's license or birth certificate, is required, however. Visitors may enter the country with up to 40 ounces of spirits, 288 ounces of beer or ale, and 200 cigarettes. Federal regulations forbid bringing firearms into Canada unless they are specifically for hunting.

Measurements

Canada is on the metric system. All weights and measures use the metric equivalent, not the imperial measurement system that prevails in the United States. The following summarizes some important conversions:

1 kilometer = 0.62 mile   *1 centimeter = 0.39 inch*
1 meter = 1.09 yard   *1 square kilometer = 0.38 square mile*
1 meter = 3.28 feet   *1 liter = 0.26 gallon*

Telephones

Telephones in Atlantic Canada accept international calling cards, which do make calling home a great deal easier than using coins. Local calls in Canada cost 25 cents for the first three minutes.

When to Go

The best time to visit Atlantic Canada is during the summer and early autumn. If you travel during off-season, you can beat the tourist crunch. But be advised that many hotels, bed & breakfasts and tourist-related activities operate only from mid-May to late October. Winters can be pretty rough, particularly in Newfoundland. Remember, too, that other less-appealing aspects of Atlantic Canada—including the Fundy fog, the winds of Cape Breton, the summer flies of Labrador and the August humidity of the Annapolis Valley—have become part of local lore for very good reason.

The following are average seasonal daytime high temperatures for Atlantic Canada:

Season	Celsius	Fahrenheit
NOVA SCOTIA		
Spring	10–16	50–61
Summer	20–25	68–77
Autumn	12–15	54–59
Winter	-2–1	28–34
PRINCE EDWARD ISLAND		
Spring	12–17	54–64
Summer	25–30	75–86
Autumn	12–15	54–59
Winter	-2–6	27–44
NEW BRUNSWICK		
Spring	10–16	50–60
Summer	24–30	75–86
Autumn	11–14	54–58
Winter	-7–5	10–40
NEWFOUNDLAND AND LABRADOR		
Spring	9–14	47–58
Summer	20–25	68–77
Autumn	10–13	50–55
Winter	-15–0	3–32

Remember

As mentioned, the Canadian government does not require a passport to enter the country, but you should certainly carry a driver's license or some other kind of identification with you at all times. And, above all, don't forget your camera.

Mileage Chart for Nova Scotia

Amherst to Halifax	130 miles
Halifax to Yarmouth	183 miles
Halifax to Truro	62 miles
Halifax to Lunenburg	57 miles
Halifax to New Glasgow	98 miles
Halifax to Antigonish	130 miles
Halifax to Baddeck	216 miles
Halifax to Sydney	248 miles
Halifax to Louisbourg	290 miles
Halifax to Parrsboro	147 miles
Truro to Port Hawkesbury	115 miles
Port Hawkesbury to Louisbourg	124 miles
Yarmouth to Windsor	155 miles
Yarmouth to Digby	69 miles
Yarmouth to Annapolis Royal	87 miles
Halifax to Saint John, NB	259 miles
Halifax to St. John's, NF*	907 miles
Halifax to Charlottetown, PEI*	203 miles
Calais, ME, to Halifax, NS	325 miles
Bangor, ME, to Halifax, NS	431 miles

*By Ferry

Legend:
- Halifax/Dartmouth Region
- The Lighthouse Route
- The Evangeline Trail
- The Glooscap Trail
- The Sunrise Trail
- The Marine Drive
- The Ceilidh Trail
- The Marconi Trail
- The Cabot Trail
- The Fleur-de-lis Trail

NOVA SCOTIA

Atlantic Ocean

Bay of Fundy

NOVA SCOTIA
LAND OF KILTS AND COVES

Oh we'll heave up our anchor
Along our lee bow
Hooray fare ye well
Goodbye fare ye well
Oh heave up our anchor
Along our lee bow
We're bound homeward bound
For Lunenburg town.
　　　　—NOVA SCOTIA FISHERMEN'S SONG

H undreds of thousands of visitors come to Nova Scotia each
summer. They come to see the *Bluenose*—the famous
schooner depicted on the Canadian dime—and to drive the
scenic Cabot Trail in northern Cape Breton. In some ways,
however, Nova Scotia's "Scottish-ness" is its most important tourist
attraction. The province is known for its Scottish heritage, and many
images of Nova Scotia (New Scotland) show kilt-clad clansmen
swirling their skirts and playing bagpipes. True, there is still a bit of
Gaelic spoken here and many a transported Scotsman has passed
down the culture's love of music, dance and tradition. But most Nova
Scotians don't wear kilts or march around playing bagpipes as portrayed on the front of tourist brochures. Though not as picturesque,
they are definitely welcoming. As any trip to this Maritime province will
reveal, the really wonderful thing about Nova Scotia *is* the people—
so be sure to strike up a conversation whether or not your Nova
Scotian acquaintance is wearing a kilt.

Nova Scotia is a great place for families, nature lovers and seekers of solitude. Each year, particularly in summer, the province draws
sports fishermen, yachtsmen and bird and whale watchers from as far
away as Europe and Australia. Families from the United States and
other provinces of Canada travel here by the carload looking for that

---

ideal picnic spot by the sea. Nova Scotia also attracts artists, photographers and writers to its rocky shores. There is nothing more rewarding than finding a deserted cove or a white, sandy beach to explore in silence.

A BRIEF HISTORY

While there is evidence that the Norsemen or Vikings stayed in Newfoundland, it is still an open question whether or not they came to Nova Scotia. Most likely, they explored the area more than 1,000 years ago but did not settle here. At that time, Nova Scotia was inhabited by Micmac tribes. Described by early settlers as being friendly and intelligent, the Micmacs hunted bears in winter, finding them by their scent and then driving them out of their sleepy dens. They also hunted caribou, killing them with bows and arrows. Those Native Americans aided the early arrivals, but European dominance soon drove them off the best lands, and imported diseases seriously weakened the Micmac nation.

The first record of European discovery of Nova Scotia dates back to 1497, when John Cabot landed on northern Cape Breton Island. Unfurling a royal banner, he claimed the entire region for England. Because he found fertile soil and temperate climate, Cabot concluded that he had reached the northeast coast of Asia.

In 1603, the French explorers Sieur de Monts and Samuel de Champlain secured a spot for France on a rocky bluff on Nova Scotia's South Shore. They named it La Have, for it resembled Cap de la Have in France. They continued on to enter Liverpool Harbour (as it is called today), rounded Cape Sable and entered the Annapolis Basin. They founded Port Royal (called Annapolis Royal today) in 1605, establishing a fort and beginning the first white settlement north of Florida in North America.

The newly discovered region around Port Royal was called Acadia by the French. Three years later, Samuel de Champlain discovered Québec.

By 1607, the English had declared that all of North America should be theirs. Dispatching a ship to Port Royal, the British attacked the settlers, burning homes and destroying crops. This incident sparked a 200-year-long struggle between England and France for supremacy in North America. While the disputes raged on, the original French settlers around Port Royal, the Acadians, were quietly prospering and steadily colonizing the new land.

The English presence in Acadia grew, however—particularly when King James I granted Cape Breton and all the country to the south, including parts of Acadia, to Sir William Alexander in 1621. Alexander changed the land's name to New Scotland and encouraged English settlers to immigrate here, via Port Royal. The growing hostilities between the English and French became increasingly directed at the Acadians. In 1688, 500 men from Massachusetts attacked French settlements around the Annapolis Valley, burning buildings and killing cattle. The New Englanders further enraged the French government by fishing the rich waters around Nova Scotia. To this day, Canadians and Americans argue over these Atlantic waters, and they will most likely continue to do so until all the fish are gone.

By the early 1700s, Port Royal had become a rendezvous spot for French privateers who stalked the coast of New England. They captured vessels, and stole wheat and corn. In 1713, in retaliation, the pirates of Port Royal were ambushed by an assembly of Massachusetts men under the command of Colonel Francis Nicholson. The skirmish was not a complete success for either side, but the keys to the fort were handed to Nicholson, the French flag was lowered and Port Royal became Annapolis Royal. Soon after, an agreement was signed, called the Treaty of Utrecht, which gave "all Nova Scotia, or Acadia, to the Queen of Great Britain and to her crown forever." The island of Cape Breton was allotted to the French as compensation. The French built the Fortress of Louisbourg on the south side of Cape Breton, which became a battleground between the French and English in 1763.

The Treaty of Utrecht put the Acadians under British rule. But threats from the French at Louisbourg and growing hostility among the Acadians created an atmosphere of paranoia among the English rulers. They forced the Acadians to sign an oath of allegiance that would oblige them to fight the French if it came to war. Because the Acadians refused to sign an oath to either side, they were subsequently rounded up and expelled from their lands. As many as 10,000 were sent away in ships, mainly to the American colonies. Many Acadians were sent to the swamplands of Louisiana, whose descendants are called Cajuns. Their former lands were settled by New England Planters who arrived in 1760 from places like Massachusetts, Connecticut, Rhode Island and New Hampshire.

During this same period, the French at Louisbourg were viewed as the instigators of attacks on New England fishermen by Micmac Indians. Outraged New Englanders attacked the fort in 1745, and their success sent shockwaves throughout the world. The fort was given back to the French and again attacked, this time by the British, who destroyed it completely in 1758. By 1763, a peace treaty between the French and English was signed that gave Britain full possession of Nova Scotia and most of eastern Canada.

By 1784, the presence of over 25,000 Loyalists from the United States prompted the creation of two separate provinces: Nova Scotia and New Brunswick. And to add to the diversity of the region, the Highland Scots had begun to arrive in Nova Scotia as early as 1773. The Scottish immigration to Nova Scotia continued throughout the next century as they settled Cape Breton, Antigonish and Pictou. In these areas, it is not uncommon to still hear Gaelic spoken, and many of the traditions of the highlanders, such as clan gatherings and old Scottish festivals, continue to this day.

With immigration providing more manpower to tap the riches of coal mines, forests and fisheries, Nova Scotia became a very powerful British colony. During the War of 1812, the capital city of Halifax was the leading British base in North America.

Beginning in 1758, Nova Scotia was also the first British North American colony to have representative government. In 1848, it became the first province in Canada where a cabinet was elected by the people instead of by appointment to the crown.

Nova Scotia today abounds with historic sites, old stately homes and museums. Its role as a seafaring province and a center for ship-building reflects its former prowess as a center for trade and commerce throughout North America.

GEOGRAPHY AND CLIMATE

Cape Breton Island so resembles the highlands of Scotland that the name "New Scotland" could not be more appropriate for this diverse province. Although there is a geographic similarity to the windswept lands of Scotland, Nova Scotia also has fertile river valleys where a variety of crops grow, as well as marshlands, waterfalls and ponds. But the primary force that has shaped the province is the sea. While the eastern shores of Nova Scotia and the island of Cape

Breton meet the fierce Atlantic directly, the western shores are most affected by the Bay of Fundy and its dramatic tides. The rugged shoreline that so typifies Nova Scotia has claimed many a seafarer's life, during the many strong gales that are so typical of this region.

The inland areas of Nova Scotia are still primarily woodlands. Hunting, fishing and canoeing are common pursuits for nature-oriented visitors as well as Nova Scotians. With an abundance of clean rivers, bays and lakes, there are ample challenges for all types of sports enthusiasts. Hiking and cycling are very popular in the Cape Breton highlands, particularly around the Bras d'Or Lake, which is also a nesting area for the North American bald eagle.

Nova Scotia's climate is comparable to that of the northeast coast of the United States. Summers are beautiful, although the cool waters of the Atlantic keep swimmers from frolicking in the waves as much as they'd like. Autumns are marked by brilliant foliage, which brings plenty of tourists to the region well into October. November through April is a long, wintry stretch, while May brings sure signs of spring and the long-awaited thaw from the grips of winter.

HIGHLIGHTS

A trip through Nova Scotia reveals a land full of diversity. I recall as a child driving across the border from New Brunswick and hearing my first bagpipes. A bagpiper, dressed in tartan colors and a kilt, still plays in a circular garden at the border town of Amherst, beneath the official flag of Nova Scotia, with its Scottish lion and proud cross of St. Andrew's.

Each summer the province is the site of numerous festivals, ranging from pipes and drum concerts to clan gatherings. The Nova Scotia Department of Tourism and Culture can assist visitors of Scottish heritage who want to join their clan in a gathering. The department also offers information on the location of various festivals and when they are happening. Some of the most popular events in addition to the clan gatherings are the Antigonish Highland Games, the Lunenburg Folk Harbour Festival and Fishermen's Reunion, and the Scotia Festival held in Halifax.

You'll enjoy the numerous festivals and clan gatherings, but the abundance of natural beauty makes a trip here equally inviting. The most popular destination in Nova Scotia is Cape Breton Island with its Cabot Trail. Cape Breton is replete with coastal views, dramatic cliffs and a winding road that can take almost two days to traverse. Cape Breton's highlights include the Bras d'Or Lake, the cliffs along the North Shore near Cheticamp, the simple beauty of Baddeck and Ingonish and the Fortress of Louisbourg. From Cape Breton, it is possible to catch a ferry to Newfoundland.

The South Shore of Nova Scotia is an idyllic place to spend a few days camping, swimming or sailing. From Halifax to Yarmouth, you'll find many coastal inlets that are rarely visited by tourists. This stretch, referred to as the Lighthouse Route, includes places like Peggy's Cove, Lunenburg and Mahone Bay.

The Evangeline Trail, running from Yarmouth to Windsor, encompasses the historic Annapolis Valley, sight of the Acadian expulsion. The Evangeline Trail leads to the Bay of Fundy where a visit to Brier Island is a must if you want to go whale-watching. Humpback, minke and fin whales feed just off the shores of the island.

Other routes include the Sunrise Trail, the Glooscap Trail and the Marine Drive along the Fundy Shore, the Northumberland Shore and the Eastern Shore, respectively. You could spend weeks simply traveling the backroads of Nova Scotia.

Although most tourists prefer to either drive to Nova Scotia from New Brunswick or travel north from the Yarmouth ferry, directions of this guidebook will begin in the Halifax/Dartmouth region and follow the coast in a clockwise fashion, first south and then north to Cape Breton.

PRACTICALITIES

Getting There

BY AIR. Air Canada has daily flights to Nova Scotia from New York, Boston, Toronto, Montreal and St. John's, Newfoundland. Other major carriers to Halifax include Delta and Continental Airlines. Air Nova provides scheduled connections within the Atlantic Provinces. Car and motor-home rentals are available at the Halifax, Sydney and Yarmouth international airports.

BY LAND. The Trans-Canada Highway links Nova Scotia with New Brunswick and with all major Canadian and U.S. highways. Greyhound buses from the United States and Voyageur buses from Montreal connect with SMT buses in New Brunswick, which then connect with Acadian Lines in Halifax and Truro. Acadian Lines bus service is fairly good, particularly the run from Halifax to North Sydney (and the Newfoundland ferry), which costs $36 and takes five hours. All roads lead to Halifax, and major bus connections to the rest of Nova Scotia are available here. Train travel around Nova Scotia and the other Maritime provinces is somewhat impractical because passenger service has been greatly reduced all over Canada. However, Halifax is a rail hub, with connecting links to Truro and other points.

BY SEA. Numerous ferries link Nova Scotia to other Maritime provinces and the United States. If you are traveling by car from the United States, taking the ferry provides a good alternative to the long drive through New Brunswick. Schedules are available from the marine terminals or at tourist offices throughout Nova Scotia. Please note that ferry schedules picked up in Canada list Atlantic time for departures and arrivals in Nova Scotia, and prices are in Canadian dollars. Main routes are summarized below:

❖ *Bar Harbor, Maine, to Yarmouth, Nova Scotia*

Daily service is available from mid-June to mid-September. There is off-season service three times a week. Round-trip fare is $70 for individual passengers and $129.50 for vehicles. Prices are subject to change. For the latest information, write to Terminal Supervisor, Marine Atlantic, Bar Harbor, Maine 04609, or call (800) 341-7981. In Canada, write to Marine Atlantic Reservations, P.O. Box 250, North Sydney, Nova Scotia, Canada B2A 3M3. It's important to make vehicle reservations in advance (there is always room for one more passenger, but not so for vehicles) and to pick up tickets one hour before departure time.

❖ *Saint John, New Brunswick, to Digby, Nova Scotia*

There are three trips daily during the peak travel season. This three-hour ride is a pleasant alternative to the longer trip from Bar Harbor to Yarmouth. One-way tickets cost $18 for individuals, $50 for vehicles.

❖ *Portland, Maine, to Yarmouth, Nova Scotia*

From May to October, Prince of Fundy Cruises provides a daily ferry service. You can contact them at Box 4216, Station A, Portland, Maine, or call (800) 341-7540.

This is the most expensive and, for my money, the least desirable ferry crossing. But others love it for the slot machines, roulette wheels and card tables. It is a long crossing, taking 11 hours. One-way tickets for an individual passenger cost $80, for a vehicle $200.

❖ Wood Island, Prince Edward Island, to Caribou, Nova Scotia

This ferry service operates daily from May 1 to December 20. The fare is $7.50 round-trip for individuals, $24.50 round-trip for automobiles. Run by the Northumberland Ferries, Ltd., this route can be very crowded during the high summer season. Try to arrive early in the morning for a crossing. Ferries depart every hour and a half. For more information, write to Northumberland Ferries, Ltd., Box 634, Charlottetown, Prince Edward Island, Canada C1A 7L3. Call toll free at (800) 565-0201.

❖ Newfoundland to Nova Scotia

From mid-June to mid-September, a ferry runs from Argentia, Newfoundland, to North Sydney, Nova Scotia, on Tuesdays, Thursdays and Saturdays. Return trips on Mondays, Wednesdays and Fridays are $41 one way for an individual, $99 for a vehicle. There is also ferry service between Channel Port aux Basques, Newfoundland and North Sydney, leaving twice daily all year round. The fare is $15.25 one way per person, $46.25 for a vehicle.

Tourist Information

The Nova Scotia Department of Tourism offers an excellent information service for tourists from May through October. There are 12 Nova Scotia Tourism Centers, and many local communities run smaller tourist offices. Marine Atlantic offers an on-board tourist information service during ferry crossings.

For more information, write to the Nova Scotia Department of Tourism and Culture, P.O. Box 456, Halifax, Nova Scotia, Canada B3J 2R5 or phone (800) 341-6096 from the United States or (800) 565-6096 from within Nova Scotia.

The Nova Scotia tourism board has a unique service for travelers called the Check In System. It is a free, computerized reservation and travel information network that represents more than 450 hotels, motels, country inns, bed & breakfasts, and campgrounds in the province. You can make reservations from anywhere in Canada or the United States by calling a toll-free number ahead of time. Simply tell them the town or city in which you want to stay, the dates of your visit and your specific accommodation needs. From the United States, call (800) 341-6096; from Canada, call (800) 565-0000.

Language and Population

The primary language of the province is English. But in areas around Cape Breton and the French shore in the south, you will hear the distinct sounds of Acadian French being spoken. The language of Scotland and Ireland, Gaelic, is still spoken in parts of Nova Scotia, particularly in the northwestern part of the province and on Cape Breton island.

More than 850,000 people live in Nova Scotia—primarily descendants of early settlers who came here from France, England, Scotland and Ireland during the eighteenth and nineteenth centuries. There is also a large population of blacks whose forebears came to Halifax during the American Civil War along the underground railway to live here as free men and women.

Time

Nova Scotia is within the Atlantic Time Zone. This puts it one hour ahead of Eastern Time. Daylight Savings Time begins on the last Sunday in April and extends to the last Saturday in October.

Telephones

The area code throughout Nova Scotia is **902.**

Major Entry Points

There are several important entry points by land, sea and air in Nova Scotia. Where you arrive will determine the route for your trip through the province. The following list gives a brief description of each possible entry point. More in-depth detail is provided in the appropriate sections.

❖ *Yarmouth*

The largest community in southern Nova Scotia, Yarmouth, is known as the "Gateway City." It is the terminus for car and passenger ferries operating from Portland and Bar Harbor, Maine. There is a well-stocked Department of Tourism and Culture here. There is regular bus service to Halifax, Digby or the South Shore. The Yarmouth airport has daily flights to Halifax.

From Yarmouth, you can drive north towards Brier Island, Digby and the Evangeline Trail or east towards Halifax along the Trans-Canada Highway or the scenic Lighthouse Route.

❖ Digby

Digby is a busy fishing port on the Bay of Fundy and an entry point to Nova Scotia from Saint John, New Brunswick, by ferry. Far less commercial than Yarmouth, Digby is a great place to get acquainted with Nova Scotia's charms.

❖ Amherst

The major gateway by road to Nova Scotia from the United States, Amherst is at the geographical center of Maritime Canada. There is daily bus service between Amherst and Halifax via Truro. Amherst is the starting point of the Sunrise Trail and the Glooscap Trail, two scenic drives.

❖ Caribou

Caribou is the terminus for the ferry from Wood Island, Prince Edward Island. From here you can head east towards Cape Breton Island or south to Halifax.

❖ North Sydney

This small town on the north side of the vast Sydney Harbour is the terminus for the Marine Atlantic ferries from Channel Port aux Basques and Argentia, Newfoundland. The crossing from Channel Port aux Basques takes only 5 hours, while the trip from Argentia on the Avalon peninsula takes 13 hours.

❖ Halifax

Halifax is the hub of the Maritimes and has a busy international airport. It is an excellent starting point for any trip around the region. There is bus service from here to North Sydney, Digby and the South Shore. Halifax has two tourist offices in the downtown area and one at the airport.

THE HALIFAX/DARTMOUTH REGION

The early days along the Halifax waterfront were rough ones, as press gangs once roamed the streets taking young men away by force to join the British Navy. This practice gave Halifax the reputation of being "the Grey City," and locals recall a time when the waterfront was a very rough place to be. Today, the big schooners are gone, the British and French are at peace and all seems pretty tame around the harborfront's Historic Properties district. The gentrification of this district may explain why some local Nova Scotian cynics call it the Hysterical Properties district, a rebuff to all good citizens who wanted to clean up the place.

HALIFAX

Founded in 1749 by the Honorable Edward Cornwallis, Halifax was the first town in Canada to be settled by the English. Originally built as a fortification against the French, who were seen as a threat to the English colonials in North America, Halifax was once one of the most strongly fortified cities in the world. Rudyard Kipling wrote of Halifax: "Into the mists my guardian prows put forth, Behind the mists my virgin ramparts lie, The warden of the Honour of the North Sleepless and veiled am I."

Halifax is the capital city of Nova Scotia, and has one of the finest deep harbors in the world. In Nova Scotia, all points lead to the city, which was once the hub of trading and commerce during the Golden Age of Sail in the 1800s. Today, Halifax is the Atlantic terminus of the Canadian National Railway and a jumping off point for trips throughout Nova Scotia. Halifax was the home of Canada's first representative government and had two other firsts—the first Protestant church and the first newspaper.

Halifax's military history is ever present, with the clock tower and Citadel looming over the historic waterfront district. The city is surrounded by a vast harbor, and on a summer afternoon, the waterways are busy with sailing yachts and power boats. Halifax is joined to the smaller city of Dartmouth by a bridge, and there is also a ferry service linking the cities. Halifax offers a unique urban environment where one can drive for a mere 20 minutes and be amidst pine trees, coastal views and wide open spaces.

Information

There is ample information for tourists in Halifax both at the International Airport and the Old Red Store on Lower Water Street in the Historic Properties district. There is also an information center in City Hall at the corner of Barrington and Duke Streets.

The Halifax Explosion

The most dramatic and tragic event to occur in this city was the Halifax Explosion of 1917. The explosion happened at 9 A.M. on December 6, 1917. Over 2,000 people were killed and 6,000 were injured. At the time, Halifax Harbour was full of warships participating in World War I. A French munitions ship, the *Mont Blanc*, was at anchor, loaded with 2,750 tons of TNT and other explosives. A Belgian relief ship, the *Imo*, suddenly broke free and collided with the *Mont Blanc*, causing a fire in the ship's interior. Sensing disaster, the sailors fled the ships in lifeboats. The commotion stirred up interest on shore, and the unsuspecting people of Halifax gathered around to watch the action. Some came to their windows to press their faces against glass and watch. While sailors scurried for cover, the resulting fire from the collision caused a tremendous explosion. Hundreds of people were killed instantly while many more were maimed or blinded by flying glass, particularly those standing at their windows. The explosion was heard in Truro, 60 miles away. Parts of the ships were sent careening onto the shores—the anchor of the *Mont Blanc* landed in a field 2 miles away. No man-made explosion, except for Hiroshima and Nagasaki's atom bombs, could match this one for intensity. The day after the explosion, a winter blizzard swept through the exposed city. A film about the blast, called *A Moment in Time*, can be seen at the Maritime Museum of the Atlantic on the Halifax waterfront. A great deal of the city's heritage was lost in the blast, and many people of Halifax still recall the long rebuilding process.

Attractions

❖ *The Historic Properties*

One of the more interesting places to visit in Halifax is the Historic Properties district along the waterfront. During the 1800s, it was a center for maritime trading activity. The Privateer's Warehouse, which today is a restaurant complex, was a storage place for privateers who looted ships along the New England coast during the 1700s and 1800s.

Much of the stone- and ironwork around the Historic Properties district is of great artistic value. Once threatened by developers, the district is now a protected area that continues to thrive as one of the liveliest spots in Halifax. Along the waterfront, you'll find the Maritime Museum of the Atlantic, the beautiful schooner *Bluenose II*, and many other attractions both at sea and on land.

❖ *The Maritime Museum*

With its wonderful replicas of steamships, dories, schooners and sailboats, this museum gives you an idea of the importance of Halifax as a maritime port. The museum also has a detailed film about the great Halifax Explosion of 1917. There is also a brief film about the enduring yachting traditions in and around the city. One particularly important yacht race takes place every two years between Marblehead, Massachusetts, and Halifax. The Marblehead-Halifax race is an enduring tradition that pits the talents of American yachtsmen against Canadians, ending with a huge celebration at the Royal Nova Scotia Yacht Squadron along the northwest arm.

Outside the museum, you can visit the schooner *Bluenose II*, a replica of the original *Bluenose* built by the people of Lunenburg county. The *Bluenose* is a symbol of the maritime prowess of Nova Scotians: The original vessel never lost a race in 17 years of international competition. Nearby, you can also visit the naval warship *Acadia*, a real veteran of World War II.

❖ *The Citadel*

The Citadel, sitting atop a hill overlooking all of Halifax, was built in the 1750s as a fortification against the French. Because the French had a fortification at Louisbourg on Cape Breton Island, the English had to protect their hard-won colony. So the city boasted a big network of forts, lookouts and patrols on constant alert, all part of the Halifax Defence Complex established in the 1750s. The Citadel was never attacked, although the current building was reconstructed-from 1828 to 1861. The fort is open from 9 A.M. to 8 P.M. in summer, and admission is $2. It closes at 5 P.M. from early September to mid-June.

Citadel Hill is a favorite spot for Haligonians to picnic, jog or sunbathe—the views from the top are splendid. Just below Citadel Hill, you'll see the beautifully restored Old Town Clock, built in London in 1803 at the request of the Duke of Kent, who was in command of the Citadel at that time.

❖ St. Paul's Church

Erected in 1750, this is the oldest Protestant church in Canada and the first church of British origin in North America. The remains of many distinguished men are interred here, including the first Protestant bishop of North America and Sir John Harvey, a war hero from 1812. Nearby St. John's Cemetery on Barrington Street was used for burial from 1752 to 1844. The old headstones and inscriptions are worth a look. John Connor, the first person to use a ferry to cross from Halifax to Dartmouth, is buried here. There is also a monument erected in memory of Captain Parker and Major Welsford, two Nova Scotians who were killed in the Crimean War.

Also on Barrington Street is the Dutch Church erected in 1767. Early German and Dutch settlers were buried here. At nearby Grafton Street, you'll see a plaque commemorating the first newspaper printed in Canada, which was in the year 1752. The tablet marks the sight of the printing press. Today, the paper is called the *Halifax Gazette.*

❖ Nova Scotia Museum

Located at 1747 Summer Street the Nova Scotia museum contains an excellent historical section, including an old stagecoach and a model of a sawmill from the 1800s. There are wildlife and geology exhibits as well. It is open from 9:30 A.M. to 5:30 P.M. Admission is free.

❖ Art Gallery of Nova Scotia

This modern art gallery is located in the old Post Office, a heritage building dating back to the mid-1800s. Much of the art exhibited here is by local artists. The paintings capture the changing Maritime landscape and the beauty of Nova Scotia.

❖ Halifax Public Gardens

Canadian cities always seem to have the loveliest gardens, and this one is no exception. Located on the corner of South Park Street and Spring Garden Road, this is a nice place to listen to a band concert at lunchtime during the summer, or to just come and sit anytime.

❖ Point Pleasant Park

Point Pleasant Park is a beautiful, 186-acre woodland park with trails for walking, jogging and cycling. Like the Citadel, Point Pleasant was originally designed as a fortress. The attractive Prince of Wales Martello Tower, built in 1796, commands a view of the mouth of Halifax Harbour and the northwest arm. Also within the park, close to the beach, you'll find the Point Pleasant Battery, which was built in

1762 as part of the Halifax Defense Complex. Another battery was located on McNab's Island, at the mouth of Halifax Harbour. One point of entry to this large park is via South Park Street, which is lined with beautiful Victorian homes.

❖ Dalhousie University

This university was founded in 1818 with funds collected at Castine, Maine, during the British occupation there from 1812 to 1814. Located in the west-end suburbs of Halifax on Coburg Road, it has many old stone buildings and a lovely campus. The presence of a large university in the city gives Halifax a youthful ambience, and many of the streets near Dalhousie are filled with pubs, cafes, book-stores and movie theaters.

❖ York Redoubt

The York Redoubt is a 200-year-old fort overlooking the north-west arm and the mouth of Halifax Harbour. Crumbling and barren, this old fort is a popular place for cyclists to stop for a view of the harbor while cycling along Purcell's Cove Road. The fort was part of the Halifax Defense Complex and was named after the Duke of Kent's brother, the Duke of York. It was built in 1798 and enlarged in 1877. In response to the French presence on Cape Breton, cannons were installed in 1877, and they can still be seen today. By 1906, the York Redoubt became obsolete as new guns were installed to the south and the French threat was greatly reduced. During World War I, however, it served as the temporary barracks for soldiers heading overseas. And during World War II it became a command post. If you visit the fort, it is nice to continue along Purcell's Cove Road along the northwest arm, an inland harbor that is lined with lovely homes. You'll pass the Royal Nova Scotia Yacht Squadron, which is the scene of celebrations at the finish of the famous Marblehead-Halifax race.

❖ McNab's Island

McNab's Island, at the mouth of Halifax Harbour, has long pro-tected the inner harbor from fierce Atlantic storms. Now a provincial park area, it's accessible by ferry from the Historic Properties water-front. A trip to McNab's Island is a pleasant way to spend a day. You can walk the trails to Fort McNab or hang around Hangman's Beach or Dead Man's Beach—sites (with morbid names and colorful histo-ries) that are perfect for an evening stroll.

The name Hangman's Beach originated in the 1700s when disloyal sailors and deserters of the British navy were hanged on McNab's Island. To make an example of these men, their bodies were coated with tar to slow decomposition and displayed in full view of incoming vessels. Hangman's Beach became the setting for a novel written by Thomas Raddall, a well-known Nova Scotian author, historian and philosopher.

Dead Man's Beach got its name after hundreds of French ships entered Halifax Harbour in 1746, shortly before the British claimed it for England. The French unloaded their dead near McNab's Island after the long journey across the Atlantic. When a British expedition arrived in 1749, they found hundreds of skeletons strewn along the beach and dubbed it Dead Man's Beach.

North of Hangman's Beach, there's Indian Point, named for a group of Indians who settled here after they were forced off the mainland in 1762. Indian Point overlooks the Eastern Passage, a hazardous channel for ships. The aptly named Wreck Cove at the end of the channel is where many of the ships that tried to navigate through the Eastern Passage ended up.

McNab's Island got its name in 1782, when it was sold to Peter McNab, a native of Inverness, Scotland. McNab was a shipowner and merchant who had lived in Halifax for over 30 years. At the southern end of the island, near Fort McNab, is Harrigan's Point, the 1866 burial site of some 250 cholera victims. Do I see the setting for a few more ghost stories here?

For more information on walking tours of McNab's Island, contact (if you dare) the tourist bureau on the waterfront before departure. During the summer, Parks Canada staff are available to answer any questions and give assistance. Although McNab's Island is touted as being a pleasant swimming area, many locals have doubts about the cleanliness of Halifax Harbour. At the time of this writing, some plans are underway to dump treated sewage off the northern end of McNab's Island, but this has not been confirmed.

DARTMOUTH

Dartmouth, across the harbor from Halifax, is the second largest city in Nova Scotia. It is accessible by ferry from Halifax or by bridge.

Dartmouth serves as a bedroom community for many Haligonians, who jokingly refer to it as "Darkness." Although Dartmouth was not incorporated as a city until 1961, it has long been involved with the affairs of Halifax, with a ferry link between the two cities dating back to 1752.

There are more than 20 small and large lakes within Dartmouth's borders, providing ample recreation facilities for area residents.

Attractions

❖ The Dartmouth Heritage Museum

There are two very interesting relics outside this building at 100 Wyse Road, a half mile from the Dartmouth ferry and close to St. Paul's Roman Catholic Cemetery. One is the cannon from the *Mont Blanc,* the ship that collided with the relief ship *Imo* in 1917, causing the infamous Halifax Explosion. The intensity of that explosion hurled the cannon to Albro Lake, some two and a half miles away. The other relic is a huge anchor, a symbol of Nova Scotia's Golden Age of Sail. The museum has a fine collection of artifacts, models and other displays from pre-Colonial days to the present.

❖ Historic Quaker Whaler's House

During the years 1785 to 1792, Dartmouth was the headquarters of a whaling company owned by Quaker families who had left Nantucket after the War of Independence. This prosperous company had factories and wharves where the Dartmouth shipyards are located today, and their Quaker meeting house at 57-59 Ochterloney Street is the oldest house in Dartmouth. It's open to the public during July and August.

❖ Shubie Park

Within this campground area, located off Waverly Road on Route 318, are six freshwater beaches—including Birch Cove Beach and Graham's Cove on Lake Banook. Lake Banook is the locale of international canoe and kayak competitions. Dartmouth hosted the World Junior Canoe Championships here in 1989. Windsurfing is another popular sport here. Other swimming areas are Lion's Beach on Lake Banook, Maynards Lake, Albro Lake and Penhorn Lake. With more than 20 lakes to choose from in the Dartmouth area, it is probably best to stick with the supervised beaches and campgrounds if traveling with children.

Accommodations in the Halifax/Dartmouth Area

Halifax abounds with places to stay, and the city is well-equipped to handle tour groups and families in the larger motels. However, Halifax also has many quaint bed & breakfasts and inns, as well as a large youth hostel. Accommodations are also available at the larger universities in the city. Dartmouth also has some fine hotels and bed & breakfasts and offers a slower pace for vacationers. For more information about bed & breakfasts, call the Halifax Bed & Breakfast Organization (429-7685) or talk with the friendly folks at the two tourism offices in Halifax.

Travelers on a budget can try: **Halifax Youth Hostel** (2445 Brunswick Street, 422-3863, $10 for members, $12 for nonmembers). **YMCA** (1565 South Park Street, 422-6437, $25 single, $40 double). Excellent location and inexpensive; rooms for both men and women. **YWCA** (1239 Barrington Street, 423-6162, $25 single, $40 double). For women only; weekly rates are also available.

There are three universities in Halifax that will rent rooms to tourists. At Dalhousie University, accommodation can be arranged through the **Student Union Building** (424-8840) at 6136 University Avenue.

Halifax is unique because there is pleasant bed & breakfast accommodation in close proximity to the waterfront and the shopping districts. Try **The Cat & Fiddle Inn Bed & Breakfast** (1946 Oxford Street, 422-3222, $34 single, $45 double). A nice, inexpensive bed & breakfast near Dalhousie University; 14 rooms with shared baths; complimentary breakfast and laundry facilities. **The Valhalla Bed & Breakfast** (1632 Oxford Street, 423-4604, $45 single, $55 double). Continental breakfast and cooking facilities. **Virginia Kinfolks Bed & Breakfast** (1722 Robie Street, 429-6687, $35 single, $50 double). Full breakfast plus laundry service.

Another option: **The Harbourview Tourist Accommodation** (545 Purcell's Cove Road, 477-9732, $27 for cottage with cooking facilities, $30 for room). Run by the Duggans; they have a lovely little cottage that overlooks the northwest arm. Nearby is the historic York Redoubt and the Nova Scotia Yacht Squadron.

In Dartmouth, try: **Boutilier's Bed & Breakfast** (5 Boutilliers Grove, 435-4094, $45-50 single, $50-60 double). Lakefront view with swimming, canoeing and windsurfing; full buffet breakfast and evening snack. **Brightwood Bed & Breakfast** (60 Sayter Street, 469-2109, $30 single, $40-50 double). Comfortable home behind the

Brightwood Golf Course; full breakfast served. **The Sterns Mansion Bed & Breakfast** (17 Tulip Street, 465-7414, $50-$100 single/double). Restored Victorian mansion; close to museum, restaurants and the ferry to Halifax.

❖ Inns

Two of the best inns in the Halifax/Dartmouth area are in historic Halifax: **The Halliburton House Inn** (5184 Morris Street, 420-0658) $95-105 single, $105-115 double). Built in 1809 for Sir Brenton Haliburton, this inn's restaurant is one of Nova Scotia's finest, recommended in *Where to Eat in Canada*. **The Waverly Inn** (1266 Barrington Street, 423-9346, $50-75 single, $60-80 double). This 115-year-old country inn, located in downtown Halifax, has hosted such illustrious guests as Oscar Wilde.

Other options: **The Running Lights Inn** (2060 Oxford Street, 423-9873, $35-50 single, $40-60 double). Nineteenth-century farmhouse within minutes of Dalhousie University, restaurants and shops. **The King Edward Inn** (2400 Agricola Street, 422-3266, $50 single, $80 double). Lovely Victorian inn with 44 rooms; free parking, and continental breakfast on the rooftop garden patio. **The Queen Street Inn** (1266 Queen Street, 422-9828, $45 single, $50 double). Housed in an old Halifax stone house built in 1870. **The Hilton Hall Inn** (1263 South Park Street, 423-1961, $40-65 single, $45-65 double). Elegant Victorian mansion in one of the nicest streets in downtown Halifax. There are nine rooms with antiques and collectibles; complimentary breakfast and off-street parking.

In Dartmouth, try: **The Dartmouth Inn** (9 Braemar Drive, near the Micmac Rotary, 469-0331, $45-65 single, $50-70 double). Open year-round; fully licensed dining room and lounge. **The Auberge Wandlyn Dartmouth Inn** (739 Windmill Road, 469-0810, toll free (800) 561-0006 from the United States). Licensed dining room.

❖ Hotels/Motels

One of the best hotels is **The Sheraton Halifax Hotel** (1919 Upper Water Street, 421-1700). Located across from the Privateer's Warehouse in the Historic Properties district.

Other options: **The Airport Hotel Halifax** (opposite Halifax International Airport, 873-3000, $85 single, $90 double). Licensed dining room, mini-bars, lounge and complimentary airport transfers. **The Cambridge Suites** (1583 Brunswick Street, 420-0555, toll free

(800) 565-1263, $80-90 mini-suite, $95-120 one-bedroom) **The Delta Barrington** (1875 Barrington Street, toll free (800) 887-1133, $90). Licensed dining room, room service, in-house movies and mini-bars.

In Dartmouth, try: **The Ambassador All-Suite Apartment Hotel** (356 Windmill Road, 465-1112, $50-75 single, $60-80 double). Forty-four rooms, one wheelchair unit. **The Journey's End Motel** (456 Windmill Road, six miles from downtown Dartmouth, 463-9900, $50 single, $65 double).

Campgrounds

In Dartmouth, there is a nice campground on the lake, on Route 318, two miles from Micmac Rotary at **Shubie Park**. Open from May 17 to September 29, with over 64 sites available. There are showers, a washroom, a tennis court, swimming, fishing and hiking trails. The fee is $12 per night and the telephone number is 464-2334.

Another option: **Woodhaven Park** (off Highway 102 about four miles west of Dartmouth, 835-2271, $11).

Dining

Halifax has a good variety of international cuisines, while still specializing in seafood and American-style restaurants. Some of the best places to eat are along the waterfront or in the South Park Street shopping area. The Upper, Middle and Lower Deck complex at the **Privateer's Warehouse** in the Historic Properties district has two dining rooms and a pub. **The Upper Deck** (422-1289) offers elegant dining, while **The Middle Deck** (425-1500) serves great hamburgers and fish and chips. Both restaurants have a view of Halifax Harbour. **The Lower Deck** (425-1501) is a lively place that serves traditional Maritime pub fare. There is live entertainment in the evenings.

For an unusual dining experience, try **The Ship Victory Beverage Room** (400 Windmill Road). The restaurant is located in a warship of the British Royal Navy, the *HMS Victory,* and is decorated in a style typical of the 1800s.

Also in the waterfront area, there is the **Clipper Bar and Grill** (overlooking the harbor, 429-5639). Reservations are recommended, and seafood is the specialty.

For those on a budget, try **The Bluenose Restaurant** (1824 Hollis Street, 425-5092). Portions are plentiful and wholesome, and the price is right. This is a good place to bring the kids for lunch or dinner. Try **McKelvies** (1680 Lower Water Street, 421-6161) for steamed mussels, salmon, lobster or scallops. The restaurant is across the street from the Maritime Museum.

Other options: **O'Carroll's Oyster Bar and Lounge** (1860 Upper Water Street, 423-4405). This restaurant, oyster bar and lounge is popular with the lunchtime crowd, and there is live Irish music nightly. **The Grafton Street Dinner Theater** (1741 Grafton Street, 425-1961). Live entertainment while dining; reservations required. **Cafe Scanway** (1866 Upper Water Street, 425-2133). Scandinavian cooking; near the Halifax/Dartmouth ferry terminal. **Christophers** (5218 Prince Street, 429-6954). Homemade soups and excellent sandwiches. **The Gondola** (5175 South Park Street, 423-5060). Italian food; reservations required. **Le Bistro** (1333 South Park Street, 423-8428). Featuring French and Canadian food; outdoor patio dining. **The Silver Spoon Restaurant** (1813 Granville Street, 422-1519). Seafood dining in a cozy setting.

Entertainment

Halifax is particularly enjoyable in the summertime, and this is one city where pubs and live music are synonymous. There are many pubs where traditional Irish or Scottish music can be heard, while other places feature live rock and roll or jazz. And, of course, there are symphonic and other classical music performances as well.

One of the liveliest pubs in the Historic Properties district is **The Lower Deck** (425-1501) in the **Privateer's Warehouse**. The long wooden tables are set up like an old-fashioned beer hall and the live music often gets the crowd into high spirits. There is also some stand-up comedy, featuring that dry Canadian humor. **The Middle Deck**, one flight up, also features live bands in the evening.

Other options: **The Split Crow** (1855 Granville Street, 423-5093). Very popular pub with live music. Outdoor seating in summer. Crowded on weekends. **O'Carroll's Oyster Bar and Lounge** (1860 Lower Walter Street, 423-4405). Sing along to traditional Maritime, Irish and Scottish music. **Your Father's Moustache** (5686 Spring Garden, in the area near the Halifax Public Gardens, 423-6766). Popular with young Haligonians. There are specials on draft beer, television screens for sports events and an imaginative dinner menu. **The Thirsty Duck** (5472 Spring Garden Road, 422-1548) is also good. Two other popular pubs are **Maxwell's Plum** (1600 Grafton Street, 423-8465) and **Granite Brewery** (1222 Barrington Street, 423-5660).

Shopping

Because Nova Scotians have long been famous for their crafts-manship, Halifax and neighboring Dartmouth are excellent places to look over some of the province's best work. The Historic Properties district has some excellent shops featuring handmade pewter and pottery, hand-knit sweaters and kilts—including the Nova Scotia tartan. Next to the Historic Properties shopping arcade, there is **A Pair of Trindles Bookshop** which sells Canadian and Nova Scotian literature, travel guides and glossy coffee-table books on the Maritimes. Also in the Historic Properties district is the **Brewery Center**, a granite building that houses many arts and crafts shops as well as a farmer's market every Friday and Saturday morning at 7 A.M.

Spring Garden Road, which runs parallel to the Halifax Public Gardens, has the highest pedestrian count east of Montreal and is a major shopping area. At Number 5635 is **Jennifer's of Nova Scotia**, one of the leading crafts stores in the province. Jennifer's sells everything from hand knits to artwork, including a wide selection of pottery and prints. At Number 5486, **Mills Brothers** offers some of the best clothing for men and women and is something of a Halifax institution. On Windsor Street, from 10 A.M. to 2 P.M., try the **Halifax Forum Sunday Flea Market.** The flea market features antiques, collectibles as well as fruit and vegetables.

Excursions and Organized Tours

There are plenty of opportunities in Halifax to get out on the water, and this is one of the best ways to enjoy the city. For a two-hour water tour on the *Haligonian III,* call 423-1271 at Privateer's Wharf Historic Properties. Adults are charged $10.50, children $5.25. The tour includes a live commentary about the history of Halifax. There is a licensed bar and a canteen aboard. From the Sheraton Hotel at the Historic Properties waterfront, double-decker bus tours are offered. Call (902) 420-1155 or arrange your tour through the Sheraton. There are plenty of organized tours to the scenic South Shore and the Annapolis Valley that can be arranged through the Halifax Tourism Association or directly. Some of the agencies are Ambassatours at 420-9662; Cabana Tours at 423-6066; and Calypso Tours at 429-7769.

Events

Summertime in Halifax is never dull. Events are scheduled day and night, often reflecting the Scottish influence throughout Nova Scotia, with its music, dances and clan gatherings. Many of the major clans gather around Halifax in summer, and the city also has some special parties of its own. One is a ten-day festival featuring a jazz fest, Irish festival, International Town Criers competition, big rock and roll bands and sailboat races.

The very best way to find out about the festivals in and around Halifax is through the tourism offices located at Privateer's Warehouse on the waterfront, on the corner of Bedford Row and George Street.

THE LIGHTHOUSE ROUTE

The South Shore of Nova Scotia, dubbed the Lighthouse Route by the tourist bureau, is one of the most picturesque regions in the province. Stretching from Halifax to Yarmouth along old Highway 3, the South Shore is busy on summer weekends with Haligonians who sail out of Chester or swim at Risser's Beach south of Lunenburg. For tourists, the most popular destination along the South Shore is Peggy's Cove, which boasts of having the most dramatic scenery along the Lighthouse Route. However, there are so many other attractive coastal enclaves untouched by the commercialism of Peggy's Cove that it's well worth taking a good road map and finding an off-the-beaten-path community to explore.

FROM HALIFAX TO PEGGY'S COVE

To drive along the Lighthouse Route from Halifax, begin at the Armdale Rotary at the head of the northwest arm. Take the Bay Road exit, which intersects Highway 333. Turn left here and follow the wooded road heading south towards the coastal towns of Shad Bay and Prospect.

While the Trans-Canada Highway (Route 103) provides the fastest way to reach the turn-off for Peggy's Cove, Route 333 is the most scenic. You'll reach lovely towns like Bayside, East Dover and West Dover before getting to Peggy's Cove. East and West Dover are quiet villages where the silent harbor reflects sailboats and lobster boats in still waters. It is rare to see anyone about during a weekday in summer. Just 15 minutes west of the Dovers, you'll reach Peggy's Cove. Although full of tour buses and trinket shops, there is still a charm here that, for many, is the essence of Nova Scotia.

PEGGY'S COVE

Overlooking the mouth of St. Margaret's Bay, Peggy's Cove is one of the most visited and photographed villages in Nova Scotia. Its famous lighthouse and Devonian granite draw tourists to the edge of its shores, where the Atlantic threatens those who come too close. The Devonian granite that makes Peggy's Cove so unique was formed by receding glaciers. The area around Peggy's Cove is barren, like a moonscape, and the scenery is unlike most parts of Nova Scotia. Peggy's Cove and the surrounding area are a natural preserve, and there are strict regulations about development here.

There is a myth about how Peggy's Cove got its name: A lone survivor of a shipwreck off Halibut Rock was rescued by a local family. Her name was Margaret and she ended up marrying a local bachelor. Curious people from nearby villages would come to see Peggy of the Cove, the shipwreck survivor.

Highlights

The highlights of a visit to Peggy's Cove include the lighthouse, St. John's Church and the typical Maritime architecture. One of the most attractive sights in Peggy's Cove is the monument to Canadian fishermen. Carved by William E. deGarth, who came to Canada from Finland in 1926, this 100-foot slab of Devonian granite depicts 32 fishermen hauling a dory with a single hemp rope held in the hands of each man. Their wives and children stand nearby, as well as the mythical Peggy of the Cove. The site of the sculpture is called the William E. deGarth Memorial Provincial Park. The noted sculptor, painter, author and philosopher lived in Peggy's Cove until his death in 1983. His paintings of Peggy's Cove capture the moods of this landscape. His sculpture of the fishermen of Peggy's Cove was his final project and took ten years to complete.

The lighthouse at Peggy's Cove is a prime attraction for tourists while also serving as a guide for ships. Originally, the lighthouse was a wooden structure; the first records of its existence date back to 1867. The present lighthouse, which was built in 1916, has served the community well. During World War II, it was used as a radio station for the Royal Canadian Navy. In the 1950s, the lighthouse keeper was replaced by an automatic light. Today, the lighthouse also serves as a post office, the only one of its kind in Canada. Tourists crowd around this lighthouse to take photographs and clamber over the granite slabs. Warnings have been posted around the area that tell people not to get too close to the water, for there have been instances where people have been swept away by the sea. Directly offshore, you'll see Halibut Rock where the myth of the shipwrecked schooner and Peggy of the Cove began.

St. John's Church, the lone church on the outside of town, was built in 1881. Designed in Gothic Revival style, it was built with lumber that was carried to the cove by schooner and pulled by oxen to the site. There are two deGarth murals inside the church, depicting "Storm and Turbulence" and "Calmness and Serenity."

Dining

There is one favored restaurant in Peggy's Cove, overlooking the lighthouse and St. Margaret's Bay. **The Sou'wester Restaurant** specializes in seafood and caters primarily to tourists. Because it is the only real restaurant in Peggy's Cove, it is consequently expensive and crowded in summer. Packing a lunch and picnicking on the rocks is a nice alternative to the restaurant.

Accommodations

There is no lodging in Peggy's Cove, but there are bed & breakfasts along Routes 333 and 329. And the village is only a half-hour's drive from downtown Halifax with its many hotels.

Northwest of Peggy's Cove at Indian Harbour is the **Clifty Cove Motel** (823-3178, $40-50 single/double). Other options: **Lover's Lane Cottages by the Ocean** (northwest of Peggy's Cove on Route 333, 823-2670, $35-55). Open from June to October 15. **Endomor Bed & Breakfast** (38 Moore's Road in Glen Margaret, 823-2779, $40-50 single, $45-50 double). Full breakfast available. **Oceanside Inn Bed & Breakfast** (in West Dover on Middle Village Road, 823-2765, $45-55 single/double). Full breakfast included.

FROM PEGGY'S COVE TO CHESTER

Highway 103, the Trans-Canada, is fast and efficient, but to appreciate the tranquility of the South Shore take Route 333 to 329 along the coast of St. Margaret's Bay, past towns like Hubbards, Bayswater and Deep Cove. Drive slowly and take in the beauty of this region. Hubbards is a fishing community and a suburb of Halifax. There is a yacht club here and plenty of beaches and campgrounds. Further along at Bayswater, there is a picnic area overlooking a white, sandy beach and the open ocean. The Bayswater Beach Provincial Park is located 12 miles south of Highway 103 at Exit 7, on Route 329.

Route 329 continues along beautiful Mahone Bay and before reaching the town of Chester, you pass Deep Cove and East River. East River is the site of a hardboard mill, and Deep Cove has a resort and marina.

Accommodations

The **Anchorage House and Cabins** (off Highway 103, Exit 6, 857-9402, $40 room, $60 cabin) is in a good location. Other options: **Deep Cove Resort and Marina** (at Deep Cove, 228-2200, $100 night, $500 week). Exclusive, expensive; offers deep-sea fishing and boat rentals. **East Chester Inn Bed & Breakfast** (on Route 3, one mile east of Chester, 275-3017, $35 single, $39 double). Pets are boarded next door.

Campgrounds

Hubbards Beach Campground (off Highway 103, Exit 6, one and a half miles east on Route 3, $13) offers washrooms, pay showers, a laundromat and pay phones. There is a sandy beach here, a boat launch, a play area and nearby trailer rentals. On weekends, lobster suppers are offered. **Graves Island Provincial Park** (at East River, $7.50) overlooks the ocean and has 64 usable sites.

Chester

With its architectural resemblance to New England, Chester is one of the most scenic towns along the Lighthouse Route. It dates back to 1759 when 29 men, women and children arrived from Boston by ship. The early settlers originally named the place Shoreham, and the town still reflects their New England traditions, with its Cape-Cod-style homes and clapboard churches. Chester prospered as a community of boat builders, sailors and fishermen, but since the early 1800s, the town has also been a summer resort for the wealthy. The first resort hotel was built in 1827. Today, there is a large community of wealthy Americans who reside here every summer.

Chester is an important center for yachtsmen. Chester Race Week, held each year in mid-August, is the largest sailing regatta in Atlantic Canada.

Chester is built around a peninsula surrounded by Front and Back Harbours. From the town, there is a ferry to Big Tancook Island, one of the largest of the Mahone Bay islands. Altogether, there are 365 "emerald-carpeted Isles" in the Mahone Bay area, but Big Tancook is special. This island is the birthplace of David Stevens, the famous boat builder who designed and built some of the sturdiest schooners in the world. Its boat building tradition has given Nova Scotians the famous Tancook schooners and Tancook whalers used for fishing and yachting throughout the eighteenth and nineteenth centuries. The ferry *W. G. Earnest* departs for Big and Little Tancook Islands from Chester four times daily, Monday through Thursday; six times on Fridays; and twice on Saturdays and Sundays. There are no cars permitted on the island. For more information, contact Tancook Island Transportation at 228-2340.

Chester is a small, quaint town that is easy to explore. On Water Street, there is a tourist information office. You'll find plenty of good restaurants along North and Tremont Streets. Also on Tremont Street, there's the Herring Gull Gallery selling Nova Scotian crafts. Towards the government wharf on Water Street, there's the Rope Loft and the Old Wharf Gift Shop located in a restored fish market that was built in the 1800s. Nearby is Block House, originally constructed to defend the community, with only 20 small guns in its arsenal.

South Street runs along Front Harbour to the Chester Yacht Club. The Parade Grounds are nearby with a memorial to the First World War. To the south of the Parade Grounds, there is an old canal that dates back to 1865. This canal parts the Peninsula from the mainland. The Peninsula is a wooded and quiet residential area where many of Chester's elegant homes are located.

The boatyards of Chester are located at the foot of Tremont Street along Back Harbour. Wander around the yards to get a feel for the special craft of wooden boat building and to see some of the nicest yachts in Nova Scotia.

Accommodations

Chester is a nice town to spend a day exploring or to use as a base to see other parts of the South Shore. Lodging options include: **Casa Blanca Guest House and Cabins Bed & Breakfast** (463 Duke Street, 275-3385, $40 single, $44 double). Centrally located. **Mecklenburgh Inn Bed & Breakfast** (78 Queen Street, 275-4638, $45 single, $55 double). Full breakfast; picnic lunches are also available. **Sheet Anchor House Bed & Breakfast** (Central Street, 275-2112, $60 single, $70 double). Full breakfast, open from May 15 to October 15. **The Windjammer Motel** (Exit 8 off Highway 103, 275-3567, $45 single, $50 double). Open year-round; a licensed restaurant. **Cove Bed & Breakfast** (Big Tancook Island, 228-2054, $30 single, $40 double). Transportation arranged from the ferry dock; special rates available for families and long-term guests.

Dining

The Captain's House (Water Street, 275-3501), situated on the harbor in a restored sea captain's house, is highly recommended. **The Windjammer Restaurant** (Route 3, 275-3714) specializes in seafood.

CHESTER TO MAHONE BAY VIA NEW ROSS

From Chester, there are some interesting side trips before continuing along old Highway 3 to Mahone Bay. You can explore two rural highways that cut through the center of Nova Scotia. Route 14 leads to Windsor, an agricultural town on the Minas Basin and a good starting point for the journey north to Cape Breton or south along the Evangeline Trail. The next significant rural highway is Route 12, which eventually leads to the town of Kentville in King's County. Rather than traveling all the way to Kentville, take Route 12 just 15 miles to the settlement of New Ross and the Ross Farm Museum. New Ross was settled in 1816 by Captain William Ross and a small group of soldiers. For five generations, the farm remained in the Ross family. Today, it is a living museum with a working blacksmith shop, daily demonstrations of barrel-making and a farm workshop.

There is a working team of oxen, farm animals for children to pet, and horse-drawn hayrides. At Rosebank Cottage, women carry out the tasks of making butter, spinning wool and preparing pickles, jams and jellies. The farmhands dress in traditional turn-of-the-century clothing, and much of the craftsmanship and clothing is on sale at the Pedlar's Shop on the premises. Ross Farm Museum gives a very authentic account of a settler's life in Nova Scotia. The farm is open from 9:30 A.M. to 5:30 P.M. May 15 to October 15. Admission is $2 for adults and $5 per family. While in New Ross, try the Highwayman Restaurant for its famous seafood chowder and home-cooked meals. Also try J & M's Country Kitchen for home cooking, take-out meals or coffee.

OAK ISLAND

Before reaching Mahone Bay, you'll pass Western Shore and nearby Oak Island, famous for its mysterious money pit. Back in 1795, a teenage farm boy discovered a shallow depression made by an ancient oak tree, which led him to believe that he might find buried treasure. When he began digging, the boy uncovered wooden platforms that, once removed, led to the discovery of more platforms. Well into the 1800s, miners, archeologists and the curious continued to dig for treasure, only to uncover a flat stone inscribed with a message. Translated by a cryptologist, the message read, "Forty feet below two million pounds are buried."

It is thought that the treasure was buried by the famous Captain Kidd and his band of pirates. An old shaft, built in the 1600s, is believed to hold the booty that would be worth millions of dollars today. However, the shaft flooded with seawater before treasure hunters could dig any farther. Hundreds of thousands of dollars have been spent in vain trying to stop the flooding and uncover the treasure. Four lives have been lost, but none of the fabled treasure has been found.

From the Oak Island Inn & Marina at Western Shore, you can take a boat ride out to Oak Island for a visit. The Inn, with its splendid view of Oak Island and tranquil Mahone Bay, is an excellent place to stay. There is a fully licensed restaurant, fishing charters, boat cruises, a hot tub, a swimming pool and a tennis court. Rooms run from $60 to $100 per night. For information, call 627-2600 or toll free (800) 565-5075.

By following the coast from St. Martin's River to Mahone Bay along Route 325, you will pass the quiet village of Indian Point. This was once an ancient burial ground for the Micmac Indians and their sacred meeting place. Although fishing is the traditional livelihood, there are also boat builders working here. Left alone by development, Indian Point captures the quality of the Mahone Bay region, with its ancient ties to Indians, pirates and seafarers.

MAHONE BAY

Approaching Mahone Bay along Highway 3 from Chester offers a full view of this coastal town. As the road curves, you will see three beautiful churches reflected in the bay. The harbor entrance to

Mahone Bay has a mysterious quality, thanks to a legend about a ghost ship that burns in the harbor when fog and darkness blend together on summer nights. The story goes back to the War of 1812, when an American privateer ship, the *Young Teazer*, was chased into Mahone Bay by a British warship. A young deserter from the British navy, fearing capture and certain death, lit the powder magazine in *Young Teazer's* hull, and the ship exploded. Twenty-eight crewmen were killed instantly. Over the years, plenty of locals have claimed to have seen the ghost ship, particularly around June 27, the anniversary of the night in 1813 when the *Young Teazer* burned.

Originally, Mahone Bay was settled by Micmac Indians, who referred to their encampment as Mush-a-Mush. Because of its protective islands and gentle shores, the area later became a favorite destination for French pirates and fishermen. The French word for a fast pirate craft is *mahonne*, and eventually the anglicized version of that term gave the town and the surrounding waters their name.

The town of Mahone Bay was established in 1754 by German-born Captain Ephraim Cook, who began a shipbuilding business here. The majority of the settlers were of German descent and were called "Foreign Protestants" by the British Government. They were encouraged to farm the soil of Lunenburg County and provide food for the British garrison at Halifax. Even today, the germanic element in names like Zwicker, Eisenhauer, Tanner, Heison, Weynacht (Whynot) and Kaulback attests to the ethnic background of Mahone Bay's populace.

Attractions

The Three Churches of Mahone Bay, reflected in the still waters, have been captured by photographers and artists. The symmetry of three different styles of architecture and three houses of worship along the bayside is a unique sight. The most dramatic of the three is St. James's Church at the head of the harbor. Built in 1887, this tall, English-style church was designed by William Harris, a well-known architect in Nova Scotia. Harris designed 116 buildings throughout his life; 17 of them were churches. The tall steeple is characteristic of his style and also serves as a navigational aid to incoming boats. By walking along Edgewater Street towards Indian Point, you can get a view of the Three Churches. This street also brings you to the tourist bureau on the outskirts of town.

Another attraction is the Settlers Museum and Cultural Center on Main Street. It has an exhibit of tools and household items used by the first settlers of Mahone Bay. There are period rooms, an exhibit of fine china and porcelain as well as antiques. During the summer, a guide dressed in seventeenth-century-style clothing offers insights into the lives of the early settlers. The museum is open daily from 10 A.M. to 5 P.M. from May 18 to Labor Day. Admission is free.

Mahone Bay has some architecturally interesting homes. The Mackay house, on the corner of Main and Fairmount Streets, is a good example of the New England influence on Mahone Bay's architecture. Still inhabited by Mrs. Mackay, who has lived there all her life, the house was constructed in 1835 by her great-grandfather in much the same way that the craftsmen of Mahone Bay built their ships. Two curved planks were laid horizontally, and one laid vertically. The remaining frame was filled with solid rock, covered by birch bark and then clapboarded.

Another interesting residence, called the "Gingerbread House," is on the corner of Main and Pleasant Streets. It's difficult to miss its unique porch with its curved designs and elaborate widow's walk. Many of the houses that line Main Street, overlooking the expanse of Mahone Bay, were built by the early settlers. On the corner of Fairmount and Main Streets is the Joshua Zwicker house, built in 1757 by Zwicker, who was a well-known ship builder. Two houses east is the Zwicker Inn, a very popular restaurant. Across Main Street from the Zwicker Inn is Government Wharf. This is the site of the annual Mahone Bay Wooden Boat Festival, which takes place during the last week of July and first week of August. The festival draws boat builders and craftsmen and features folk music, a dance, workshops and a schooner race. One highlight of a past year's festival was a re-enactment of the *Young Teazer's* burning in the harbor.

Dining

The Zwicker Inn (622 Main Street, 624-8045) is one of the area's best restaurants, with homemade chowder and seafood specialties. It's open year-round. Other options: **Mug and Anchor Pub** (643 Main Street, at Mader's Wharf). Good pub food overlooking the harbor. **Innlet Cafe** (Kedy's Landing at the head of the bay on the north side of town). Another good bet for seafood. **The Towne Squire Cafe, Ltd.** (525 Main Street). Inexpensive breakfasts and lunches.

Accommodations

There are quite a few bed & breakfasts in Mahone Bay, but on a busy summer weekend they tend to fill up quickly: the **Sou'Wester Inn Bed & Breakfast** (788 Main Street, 624-6326, $40 single, $50 double). Housed in a Victorian shipbuilder's home overlooking the bay. **Andrew's Bed & Breakfast** (294 Main Street, 624-8864, $35 single, $40 double). Full breakfast included; open seasonally from May to October. **Fairmont House Bed & Breakfast** (654 Main Street, 624-6173, $35 single, $50 double). Full breakfast; private baths. **Patrician Inn Bed & Breakfast** (40 Pleasant Street, 624-6383, $40 single, $45 double). Set in a Victorian home.

Around Mahone Bay: If accommodation in Mahone Bay is fully booked, try the small town of Blockhouse. **Le Couvre-Lit Bed & Breakfast** (96 Cornwall Road, 624-8192, $30 single, $45 double). **Bayview Pines Country Inn** (at Indian Point, 624-9970, $60 single, $65 double). Access to beach, walking trails and boat launch. Full breakfast served; lunch and dinner by reservation.

Shopping

Mahone Bay is a nice place to buy pottery, pewter and handicrafts. **Amos Pewterers** (589 Main St.) designs on the premises, giving buyers a unique chance to observe the craft of pewter-making. The designs are beautiful and the prices are reasonable. **The Teazer** on Edgewater Street has imported woolens, quilts and hand-knit sweaters for sale. At the **Sou'Wester Inn**, Ron Reddon's miniature sculptures of blue, fin and humpback whales are on sale. At **Mader's Wharf**, there are numerous boutiques on the ground floor that sell Nova Scotian gifts, imported clothing from South America and handicrafts.

LUNENBURG

Long considered Nova Scotia's most important seafaring port, Lunenburg is one of the most worthwhile stops along the Lighthouse Route. Although busy with tourists all summer long, the Lunenburg community still thrives: Many of the townspeople continue to make a living fishing, boat building, working in the foundry and even blacksmithing.

The township of Lunenburg was officially founded in 1753 by German, Swiss and French settlers who were brought here from

Halifax by the British. The British encouraged European settlement along the coast in hopes of increasing the colony's population as a deterrent to the French. The British promised land to the new settlers, and their surveyors drew up lots for homes and businesses, giving the town the crowded, unique character it has today. Initially ordered to farm the land and provide food for the British garrisons in Halifax, the new settlers soon saw that the soil was not as rich as the fishing grounds. So they turned to the sea for a living.

Descendants of these "Foreign Protestants," the original settlers, began to prosper in both domestic and international trading. They fished the rich Grand Banks off Newfoundland in well-built vessels and began the lucrative trade of exporting salt cod to the West Indies. Their shipbuilding and seagoing prowess created the need for sail-makers, caulkers, block-makers and blacksmiths. A foundry was established to make stoves for heating and cooking on board the ships. Outfitters were needed to supply provisions for the men going to sea, who were often away for months at a time.

By 1860, Lunenburg was a prosperous town, and many of the homes received fancy additions with the Victorian-style Lunenburg "bump," scrolled doorways and stained-glass windows. The Lunenburg "bump" is the protruding decorative window that was a common addition to homes in the late 1800s and is said to have come from the five-sided Scottish dormer.

One of the most famous shipyards in Lunenburg was the Smith and Rhuland, Ltd., shipyard, which built over 270 commercial vessels and 100 yachts in its hundred years of existence. The *Bluenose*, the famous schooner, was built in the Smith and Rhuland yard and launched on March 26, 1921. As the salt cod trade with the West Indies declined, schooners continued to sail for the Grand Banks where the men of Lunenburg would leave the mother ship and head off in their dories (rowboats) to hook and net fish. Lunenburgers designed a special double-ended dory that is still built today and can be seen along Montague Street. It was a dangerous way to make a living—and, of course, some men never returned.

The *Bluenose* was used for this type of schooner/dory fishing, but its fame comes from being a fine racing vessel. During the 1920s and 1930s, under the leadership of Captain Angus Walters, the *Bluenose* became the champion of the North Atlantic fishing fleet and four-time winner of the International Schooner Races against American schooners out of Gloucester, Massachusetts. She never lost a race in 17 years of competition and became a symbol of a maritime heritage recognized around the world. During World War II, despite her Captain's efforts to keep her in Lunenburg, the *Bluenose* was sold to a West Indian company and finally vanished off the reefs of Haiti in 1946. The image of the original *Bluenose* appears on the reverse side of the Canadian dime to this day. There is a memorial plaque to the *Bluenose* on the corner of Falkland and Victoria Streets in Lunenburg, and the memory of this great schooner prompted the building of the *Bluenose II* in 1963.

During the 1930s, when the sale of alcohol was prohibited in the United States, Lunenburg's citizens gained notoriety for building vessels for rum runners and for doing a bit of smuggling themselves. They built the famous *I'm Alone* as well as the *Schgatawake,* the *Mudathalapadu,* the *Corticella* and the *Atacama.*

Competition from Europe in the salt cod trade with the Caribbean eventually brought about a decline in the shipbuilding trade. In the 1950s, a way of life among the dory fishermen and schooner sailors of Lunenburg came to an end. The *Theresa E. Connor,* the last of the salt-bank schooners, is tied up to the dock in Lunenburg. Locals recall the day the era ended—when there weren't enough men willing to make a trip on the *Theresa E. Connor* to fish the Grand Banks; they had all opted for the steel-hulled trawlers that were far safer than dories. What is left of the grand days of shipbuilding and fishing in Lunenburg is captured at the Fisheries Museum of the Atlantic on the western end of Montague Street.

However, before the Smith and Rhuland shipyard shut down in the 1970s, three famous replicas were built there by the men of Lunenburg. The square-rigged British *Bounty* was built in 1960 to be used in the film *Mutiny on the Bounty,* starring Marlon Brando. The *Bounty* is now in St. Petersburg, Florida. The *Bluenose II,* built in 1963, still sails out of Halifax, and a replica of Admiral Nelson's flagship, the *HMS Rose,* which was built in 1970, is moored in Newport, Rhode Island. There are plans afoot to build the *Bluenose III,* with funding by the Canadian government. Most Lunenburgers expect to see it built where the legacy still lives, at the old boatyards along Montague Street.

Although Lunenburg today is a far quieter town, and her harbor seems empty after the prosperous days at the turn of the century, the fine craftsmanship passed through the generations is still evident. There is an active blacksmith shop along Montague Street, the

Lunenburg Foundry still makes excellent stoves, and parts for ships, dories and wooden yachts continue to be built. On many old farms around Lunenburg County, men like David Stevens and his family retain a legacy for fine craftsmanship. Stevens built some of the best small schooners in the world, and craftsmen came from as far away as Australia to watch him work. His offspring are still hard at work, mastering the craft.

The time to see Lunenburgers revel in their former glory is during the Nova Scotia Fisheries Exhibition and Reunion, the Folk Harbour Festival and the Lunenburg Craft Festival, all held in August. The Fishermen's Reunion features a traditional dory race against the men of Gloucester, Massachusetts. The Folk Harbour Festival is a time for music and folk songs. At other times, however, one can still wander the attractive streets, talk with craftsmen—whether they be builders of boat models or artists—and learn about the Lunenburg that they remember.

Attractions

Drive or walk along Lincoln Street to the top of Blockhouse Hill Road, at the eastern end of town, to get a full view of Lunenburg Harbour and Back Harbour. Here, you'll find the tourist bureau located in a small lighthouse. Blockhouse Hill serves as a campsite and makes an excellent place to stay cheaply, take in the sunsets and talk with the locals.

Blockhouse Hill is quite removed from town, but it makes a nice place to park in order to wander about on foot. Two interesting booklets available here are "A Walk Through Old Lunenburg" and "Understanding the Architecture of Lunenburg." There are guided tours of St. John's Anglican Church, the first of its kind in Lunenburg. You may also notice the golf course on the other side of Lunenburg Harbour: This is a nine-hole course and is open to the public.

❖ *The Fisheries Museum of the Atlantic*

This excellent museum along the waterfront at the western end of town captivates most visitors, even if they formerly had little interest in the legacy of a leading Maritime community. The museum has a live aquarium, a favorite with children, featuring marine life of the Atlantic. The second and third floors cover the history of Lunenburg as a seafaring port, with photos and stories about individuals and events that formed its history. You can also view an excellent film called *Sea Got in Your Blood,* narrated by a young man who took the *Peking,* one of the last big sailing ships, around Cape Horn. Photos of the *Bluenose* and the men who competed in the International Schooner Races capture the excitement of those days. There is also a restaurant and gift shop here. Outside the building, you can board the *Theresa E. Connor,* the last salt-bank schooner, and the *Cape Sable,* a steel-hulled trawler. The museum is open daily from 9:30 A.M. to 5:30 P.M. from May 15 to October 15. Admission is $3.

❖ St. John's Anglican Church

This lovely church, located off Cumberland Street, is the site of the first church services in Lunenburg, held on the church lawn in 1753 in three languages: English, German and French. A memorial in the yard marks the event. The church was built in 1758 with materials shipped from Boston. Wander around the interior to see the arched ceiling, resembling the inside of a schooner. There are memorials here to many of the original families of Lunenburg. The exterior of the church looks gothic, but its clapboarded simplicity makes it a very appealing building. Because of the Puritan influence here, a stove was not installed to heat the building until the 1800s. In 1902, the Vestry Clerk E. C. Kaulback gave the church its beautiful bells. The bells are still rung by a hand pump and every day at 2 P.M., retired shoemaker Edward Tanner plays a few songs. It is well worth going up to the second floor to watch him ring ten bells to the tune of "Danny Boy" or "Amazing Grace." The talented Tanner is also an expert builder of boat models.

❖ The Lunenburg Academy

The Lunenburg Academy, high on Gallows Hill, was opened in 1895 after the original school was destroyed by fire. Its unusual style and fine views of the surrounding county make it worthwhile to visit. When originally built, the Academy was way ahead of its time. With a science lab and library, it was thought to be the finest school building in the Maritime province. From 1896 to 1966, the young people of Lunenburg were educated here until the age of 17 or 18. Now, the school is for the town's students from kindergarten to grade 4.

❖ Private Homes

There are numerous private homes in Lunenburg that are of architectural interest. Wander around town to your heart's content to get a feel for the unchanging quality of the place. Of particular interest is the Zwicker house on King's Street, which is now the Compass Rose Bed & Breakfast. The Zwicker house was a fine example of Georgian architecture when it was built in 1825, but the distinctive Lunenburg "bump" changed its style in 1875. The Boscawen Manor on Lincoln Street is the biggest mansion in town. It was built as a wedding gift in the 1880s. Another beautiful home, with its elegant exterior, is the Morris Wilson house on 315 Lincoln Street.

Many of the homes have the typical Lunenburg "bump," while in others the "bump" has been removed to return the homes to their simple Georgian- or New-England-style architecture.

❖ Lunenburg Art Gallery

This small art gallery at 19 Pelham Street is housed in the same building as the public library. There is a special emphasis here on local artists. The gallery is open in July and August only.

❖ The Lunenburg Foundry and Walter's Blacksmith Shop

The Lunenburg Foundry and Walter's Blacksmith Shop are not tourist attractions but working places for Lunenburgers. However, the foundry and the blacksmith shop are of interest to those who want to see old ways of producing beautiful work. The technology is somewhat outdated, but seeing the workmanship of Walter at his forge or the huge furnace at the foundry gives one an idea of the way things were before technology gave the edge to machines over men. The blacksmith shop is on the corner of Montague and Kemp Streets and the Lunenburg Foundry is on Linden Avenue at the western end of town. If the foundry is not too busy, visitors are invited to have a look at work areas. If you happen to drop in when the foundry is open for viewing, definitely seize the opportunity.

Accommodations

There are quite a few inns and bed & breakfasts in Lunenburg, oftentimes with fully licensed restaurants serving excellent food: **The Boscawen Inn** (150 Cumberland Street, 634-3325, $35-50 single, $60-80 double). One of the finest inns around Lunenburg. Common sitting room; dining room overlooks the harbor. **The Bluenose Lodge** (Falkland Avenue and Dufferin Street, 634-8851, $60 single, $70 double). Restored Victorian mansion, popular with summer visitors; breakfast, lunch and dinner available. **The Lunenburg Inn** (26 Dufferin Street, 634-3963, $55 single, $80 double). Fully licensed dining room with outdoor seating. **The Rum Runners Inn** (66 Montague Street, 634-9200, $56-125 single/double). Fully licensed dining room overlooking the waterfront. **The Kaulback House Historic Inn** (75 Pelham Street, 634-8818, $45 single/double). Registered heritage property built in the 1800s. **Snug Harbour Bed & Breakfast** (9 King Street, 634-9146, $40 single, $50 double, $15 for first-floor youth hostel). Well-run bed & breakfast that accommodates budget travelers with kitchen facilities. **Compass Rose Inn and Bed & Breakfast** (15 King Street, 634-8509, $35 single, $50-60 double). Excellent restaurant; nice, spacious rooms.

Dining

There are plenty of eateries in Lunenburg and the selection is diverse: **The Knot Pub** (corner of Lincoln and Starr Streets). A lesser-known spot that serves great food. Try the Caesar salad. Good place to meet local people. **The Magnolia Grill** (128 Montague Street). Excellent homemade soups, sandwiches, quiches and fresh pies. Beer and wine is also served. Fun atmosphere and a good spot for people-watching. **Big Reds Family Restaurant** (Montague Street overlooking the Fisheries Museum). Cheap, good meals. **Brigantine Inn and Bistro** (82 Montague Street). Great seafood. **Capt'n Angus Seafood Restaurant** (within the Fisheries Museum, 634-4794). Fully licensed dining room; popular with tour groups. **Lunenburg Dinner Theatre** (116 Montague Street, 643-4814). Harbor cruise serving a full dinner; presents *The Run for Rum*—an adaptation of the famous rum-running days. In summer, the boat embarks at 6:45 P.M. Tuesday through Sunday.

Shopping

There are plenty of crafts people in Lunenburg, and some well-known artists too. Try **Black Duck Handcrafts Co-op** (8 Pelham Street) for a selection of Nova Scotia's craftsmanship. The adjoining art gallery features local artists. **Lincoln Reef Craft Shop and Gallery** (218 Lincoln Street) has an excellent variety of crafts in a turn-of-the-century shop. For pottery, try **Lunenburg Pottery** (corner of Montague and King Streets) for some beautiful earthenware bowls, dishes and mugs with lovely designs. At 110 Montague Street, the **Houston North Gallery** specializes in Nova Scotia folk art and Innuit (Eskimo) art that originates in Labrador and parts of Newfoundland.

LUNENBURG TO LIVERPOOL

Following the backroads is particularly rewarding from Lunenburg to Liverpool. Because of the milder climate along the South Shore, this area is particularly peaceful, with farms and fishing towns dotting the gentle landscape.

Five miles southeast of Lunenburg, there's the small fishing village of Blue Rocks with its dramatic ledges and fishing shanties on the edge of the sea. Blue Rocks is a favorite place for photographers and artists, who capture the quiet beauty here.

THE OVENS NATURAL PARK

From Blue Rocks, it is possible to drive south along Route 324 to the Ovens Natural Park near the town of Riverport. This unique park was the scene of a gold rush in 1861, when gold was discovered amidst the caves and along the shore here. Lots were sold quickly for up to $4,800, and a town with a tavern sprang up overnight. In a few short years, the gold became scarce and the rush ended. The area is still known to have some gold deposits, and the park management offers a metal panning dish to those who want to try their luck. The Ovens is an ideal camping area; the grounds overlook the ocean and sit above some spectacular caves. Paths carved by miners to reach the gold are used today to get a look at these magnificent caves that line the shore like so many large bread ovens. The anticlinal or oven-like shape of these caves is a common feature of Nova Scotia's gold-bearing regions. The park is open from May 20 to September 10 from 7 A.M. to 11 P.M. Entrance fee and camping fee total $6. There is a small museum, a cafeteria, changing rooms, showers and toilets. Highly recommended for campers and cyclists or as a place to spend the afternoon.

BRIDGEWATER

While many tourists prefer to take the Lighthouse Route along the scenic South Shore, others detour inland along Route 3 to the town of Bridgewater. Built along La Have River, Bridgewater was first settled in the early 1800s. It is the home of the Des Brisay Museum, one of the oldest in Nova Scotia. Bridgewater has the feel of an old river town. Removed from the sea, it has a rural, inland character that distinguishes it from Lunenburg, its long-standing rival. Bridgewater has all the available services, with its large shopping mall, liquor store and movie theater. However, it lacks the charm of other South Shore communities and is not on my list of must-see places.

For diversion, browse through Sagor's Bookstore at 686 King Street. This store has the best selection of books outside of Halifax along the South Shore. A visit to the Des Brisay Museum on Jubilee Street is worthwhile if time permits. It has changing exhibits plus a permanent collection of Micmac artifacts. There are numerous publications about the region on sale and the museum staff is extremely helpful. The area around the museum is full of pines and is a peaceful spot to take a break. The tourist office is across the main bridge on the north side of La Have river.

One of the most important events in Bridgewater is the South Shore Exhibition, which is held each year at the end of July. This is a real country-style event featuring the International Ox and Horse Pull Championship between Canadians and Americans. A highlight of a previous year's event came when a local Lunenburg man lifted two yoked oxen off the ground. The combined weight was over a ton, giving him the distinction of being one of the strongest men in the world.

THE LIGHTHOUSE ROUTE TO LIVERPOOL

Follow Route 332 along the Lighthouse Route towards the small community of East La Have. From East La Have, take a cable-drawn car ferry across the river to La Have. The five-minute crossing gives you an opportunity to take in the lovely scenery.

Just outside of La Have, at Dublin Shore, visit the Fort Point Museum in the home of the former lighthouse keeper. This is the site of the first landing of the Acadians who came here under the guidance of Isaac de Razilly in 1632. Although the Acadians did not stay, La Have and the surrounding area prospered as an important town at the mouth of a busy waterway. Many of the fine homes one sees along the river belonged to wealthy merchants and sea captains. From La Have, continue along Route 332 to Crescent Beach and the popular Risser's Beach with its sand dunes and surf. Crescent Beach, at low tide, extends for three miles and one can walk out to La Have Islands. By turning left at Crescent Beach, you'll reach the road to

Bell Island where the Marine Museum is located. This small museum is housed in the La Have Islands United Church and has exhibits on local history.

The next stop is Risser's Beach, a provincial camping area and popular weekend destination for Nova Scotians. From the boardwalks extending one and a half miles along the Salt Marsh Trail, it is common to sight herons and egrets. The boardwalks were set up so that the delicate marram grass and sand dunes would not be disturbed. If there has been a storm or high winds, the beaches in this area are covered with Irish Moss, a type of lacy, red seaweed. Irish Moss is used by Nova Scotians for thickening foods and as a fertilizer for gardens. Dried Irish Moss is on sale in many of the small stores around Lunenburg County. During my visit to a relative at Broad Cove, we made a delicious blueberry pie, using Irish Moss to make it thick. Clam digging is another popular pastime in this area.

The next town on this route is Petite Rivière. Originally founded by the Acadians in 1632, it is one of the first settlements in North America. The Acadians eventually left the area long before the Germans and Scots arrived. Petite Rivière is also the home of painter Joan Dewar, whose work is featured in many Nova Scotian galleries.

By turning right at Petite Rivière you reach Green Bay, an excellent beach with cottage accommodations and a small canteen. There is an unpaved road running past the canteen. This is an old post road that was used to round a small point to reach the town of Broad Cove. The two-hour walk to Broad Cove along the old road passes marsh ponds with herons and egrets, and unspoiled views of pine trees above the rocky shore. As I walked this post road, I noticed that much of the land is for sale and slated for development. It's a shame, because this is an absolutely pristine place. Broad Cove is a very quiet town, with a few fishing sheds lining the shore.

Farther south, the town of Cherry Hill sits on a spit of land overlooking Medway Harbour. Cherry Hill is a nice place to gather driftwood. Rounding the point, Route 331 passes Volger's Cove, named after an early German settler.

Route 331 then intersects the Trans-Canada Highway at East Medway, where one has a choice to take a detour to Greenfield, 15 miles inland. Greenfield was founded in 1830 by Samuel Hunt, and his original home is fully restored and open to the public. Greenfield is popular with trout and salmon fishermen, canoeing enthusiasts and walkers. The Medway River is a well-known salmon river with a famous lakepool. The area is surrounded by campsites along scenic Lake Panhook and Lake Molega. Except for some logging, the Greenfield area is like an unspoiled sanctuary.

Back on the Lighthouse Route for the homestretch to Liverpool, the road passes Port Medway overlooking Coffin Island and its lighthouse. Continue on to West Berlin and Beach Meadows for more scenic vistas. The route then passes through Brooklyn, just outside of Liverpool. Brooklyn, once called Herring Cove, is best known for its paper mill and hydroelectric plant.

After Brooklyn, the Lighthouse Route passes through Liverpool, an old Loyalist settlement and jumping off point for trips to Greenfield or Kejimkujik National Park.

LIVERPOOL

Liverpool Harbour was one of the first places French explorers Sieur de Monts and Samuel de Champlain dropped anchor in North America in 1604. The explorers did not stay long, and the town was not officially settled until 1760. During the 1770s, Loyalists fleeing the newly formed United States began to settle here. Many of the Loyalist homes around Liverpool reflect the New England style of architecture.

The historic area of Liverpool is centered around its harbor, where much of the development of this shipbuilding town began. During the American Revolution and the War of 1812, many a privateer sailed out of this harbor to roam the New England coast. Their efforts against the Americans are marked at Old Fort Point on the south side of the harbor where a plaque heralds them as courageous men who "upheld the best tradition of the British navy."

While many turned to the sea for their livelihood, one Liverpool man, William Burke, traveled inland through the area that is now the Kejimkujik National Park. Burke found plentiful game and rich soil here. He and his brothers settled vast tracks of land that stretched as far west as Annapolis Royal. Route 8 to Caledonia and Kejimkujik National Park passes by much of the land that was originally settled by Burke.

Another one of Liverpool's illustrious citizens is Thomas Raddall, one of Canada's leading authors and historians. His stories of the settlement of North America make fascinating reading.

Attractions

The architecture of old Liverpool is very interesting, distinguished by the "widow's walk" features on many of the homes. The widow's walk is a small deck on the roof of a house, traditionally a place for women to scan the horizon for the homecoming ships of their husbands or sons. The fact that many men were lost at sea gave these sad vantage points their name.

Perkins house on Main Street has an interesting history. It was built in 1766 for Simeon Perkins, a store owner, shipbuilder and trader in fish and lumber. Perkins also maintained an excellent diary of Liverpool's early history from 1766 to 1812, writing with some knowledge of clandestine trading and smuggling activities, as well as the dubious activities of the Royal Navy press gangs who forced young men to a life at sea serving the Crown. Adjacent to Perkins house is the Queens County Museum. The museum was once the warehouse of Simeon Perkins' business. There is a Thomas Raddall reading room here featuring much of that author's published work.

❖ Fort Point

Fort Point, overlooking the mouth of Liverpool Harbour, was built in the early 1800s by Martin McNutt. There is a cairn here commemorating the first landing of de Monts and Champlain at Liverpool in 1604. Another nearby cairn mentions the brave work of the gallant privateers during the early 1800s. Privateering between Nova Scotia and the American states was very common in those days, but these Liverpool men were also after French ships. A privateer could capture any ship flying an enemy flag and take the booty that was on board. The most famous privateer in Liverpool was Captain Joseph Barss, Jr., in charge of the schooner *Liverpool Packet*. Fort Point offers an excellent view of Liverpool Harbour with its all-important lighthouse.

❖ The Old Settler's Cemetery

This cemetery, located on Main Street, has headstones that date back to 1761. Take a few minutes to scan the surnames. Many tourists from the New England states find that their ancestors originated in Liverpool and other Loyalist settlements along the South Shore. Also of interest is the oldest church in town, the Trinity Anglican Church built in 1822. The county courthouse nearby was built in 1854 and is still used today.

At the tip of the entrance to Liverpool Harbour, a ten-mile drive from town, is Western Head. The road goes to the end of the land, to Western Head lighthouse.

TO KEJIMKUJIK NATIONAL PARK

From Liverpool, this wooded 382-square-mile park is accessible by Route 8. The drive takes you into the interior of the Nova Scotia peninsula, the land that early settler William Burke found so abundant with wildlife and rich soil. The route is sparsely settled and unique—an alpine region with a network of waterways that are excellent for canoeing. The rounded hills characteristic of this region, called drumlins, were formed by retreating glaciers during the last Ice Age.

On the road to the park, you'll pass through the towns of Brookfield and Caledonia, which bustled with activity during the 1800s when gold was discovered here. Mines were in operation for several years, but soon the gold was depleted and the mines closed.

The Kejimkujik Park System and the adjacent Tobeatic Wildlife Management Area remain a favorite retreat for nature-loving Nova Scotians. Those with campers and recreational vehicles can stay at Jeremy's Bay Campground within Kejimkujik Park. Located off Route 8 on Kejimkujik Lake near Maitland Bridge, the campground has 329 sites and an information center. There is a boat launch area, swimming, fishing, as well as canoe, bicycle and boat rentals. You'll also find hiking trails, and a number of nature programs are offered. During winter, there is cross-country skiing and winter camping.

Throughout the vast park area are rough campsites for pitching a tent. Be sure to get a complete map of the area, available at the information center at the entrance to the park.

Accommodations

Accommodations in the area from Lunenburg to Liverpool range from inns and hotels to bed & breakfasts. Registered youth hostels are in Liverpool and La Have as well.

In Bridgewater, try: **The Mariner Inn** (324 Aberdeen Road, 543-5545, $48 single, $55 double). **The Flying Dutchman Motel** (35 High Street, 543-2407, $35-40 single, $50 double).

Bridgewater to Broad Cove: **The South Shore Country Inn** (Route 331, 677-2042). Highly recommended. Four rooms with sitting room and library. Licensed dining room and full breakfast. The Inn is in close proximity to the beach. **MacLeod Cottages** (in Petite Rivière, 688-2866, $20 for cottage or $250 weekly). Cottages have fireplaces in living rooms and overlook the ocean. **Tannery Hollow Lodge Bed & Breakfast** (on Route 331, 15 miles from Bridgewater, 688-2186, $30 single, $40 double). Full breakfast is available. **Oceanus Housekeeping Cottages** (six and a third miles from Bridgewater, 688-2186). Full breakfast served.

Towards Kejimkujik National Park: **The Wood Whims Bed & Breakfast** (in Caledonia off Route 8, 682-2223, $35 single, $40 double). There are three rooms; full breakfast is served. **The Whitman Inn** (off Route 8, two and a half miles south of the park, 682-2226). Highly recommended. Ten rooms with weekly and monthly rates available. Licensed dining room, pool, sauna and jacuzzi. Cycling and canoeing packages can be arranged.

In Liverpool, try: **Lanes Privateer Bed & Breakfast** (33 Bristol Avenue, 354-3456, $38-40 single, $45 double). Continental breakfast, plus fully licensed dining room. **Lanes Privateer Motor Inn** (27 Bristol Avenue, along the Mersey River, 354-3456, $50 single, $55 double). **Hopkins House Bed & Breakfast** (120 Main Street, 354-5484, $30 single, $40 double). Former home of a Loyalist family; children and cyclists are welcome. **Pat's Overnight Guests** (388 Main Street, 354-4071, $25 single, $35 double). Full breakfast served. **Motel Transcotia** (four miles east of Liverpool in Brooklyn, 354-3494, $40 single, $45 double). Licensed dining room.

Youth Hostels

There are two youth hostels between Lunenburg and Liverpool that are very popular with travelers and international hostelers. **La Have Marine Hostel** is about 15 minutes' drive from Bridgewater on Route 331. Eight beds are available, with kitchen and laundry facilities. The fee is $8. Write to La Have Marine Hostel, P.O. Box 92, La Have, Nova Scotia, Canada BOR 1CO (688-2908). **Liverpool Hostel** is located on Main Street in Liverpool. The entrance is at the rear of Trinity Church Parish Hall. This summer hostel has 15 beds with showers and a small kitchenette. The mailing address is Liverpool Hostel, P.O. Box 219, Liverpool, Nova Scotia, Canada BOT 1KO (345-3533). The fee for members is $5.00, $6.00 for nonmembers.

Campgrounds

Oakhill Pines Campground (Exit 12 off Highway 103 into Bridgewater, 543-2885, $10 per night). Open from May 15 to October 1. Hiking trails and swimming pool. **La Have River Campground** (Exit 11 from Highway 103, 644-2654, $10 per night). **Shore Boat View Camping** (off Route 332 in Bayport, 766-4873, $10 per night). Hiking trails and a swimming pool. In Riverport, the **Ovens Natural Park** is an excellent place to stay. (See description on page 50.)

Dining

Many of the inns throughout the Lighthouse Route have licensed dining rooms: **The Tops' Beverage Room and Grill** (777 King Street, Bridgewater, 543-8070). Reasonable prices. **Big Red's** (705 King Street, Bridgewater, 543-8777). Pizza and seafood to eat in or take out. **Lane's Privateer Inn and Bed & Breakfast** (in Liverpool off Highway 103, Exit 19, 354-3456). Recommended by the tourism authority's guide *Taste of Nova Scotia* for its fresh seafood, steak and pasta dishes. **The Fin n' Feather** (Waterfront Plaza in Liverpool, 354-4994). Specialties include pizza, fried chicken and chowder. **The Hilltop Restaurant and Chowder House** (off Highway 103 on Exit 14 between Bridgewater and Liverpool, 543-7055). Specialties are seafood and chowder.

On summer evenings, local churches will often have chowder suppers available to the public. Just look for signs outside the various churches along the Lighthouse Route. Suppers usually include homemade chowder, corn bread and baked desserts and coffee. The cost is little more than $4. This is an enjoyable way to meet local people and well worth trying. I attended one chowder supper, chatted with locals and was lucky enough to receive an invitation to go sailing the next day.

LIVERPOOL TO YARMOUTH

The southern half of the Lighthouse Route involves plenty of detours to private harbors and historic towns, most notably Shelburne and Yarmouth. The latter is the terminus of the Bar Harbor and Portland, Maine, ferries. If you have the time, there is ample reason to mosey. The first stop out of Liverpool is White Point with is popular seaside resort. The White Point Beach Lodge is situated on the beach, adjacent to the Liverpool Golf Club. Nearby Hunt's Point has oceanfront cottages and a fine view of the "Head Rocks" directly offshore.

Continue to Port Mouton, a spot discovered by de Monts in 1604. (According to the story, the name *Mouton* [French for "mutton"] stems from a mishap on the French explorer's ship that resulted in valuable sheep falling overboard.) On the left side of the road, there is a cairn that commemorates Tarleton's Legion, who arrived in 1783. British soldiers were stationed here for a few years, but a fire swept through the settlement and the garrison moved to Guysborough County. Near the town of Port Joli, one passes the location of the seaside adjunct of Kejimkujik National Park. The park protects one of the last tracts of undisturbed Atlantic coastline left in North America, and is a favorite nesting ground of the endangered Piping Plover. There are walking trails that lead to St. Catherine's River Beach, although sections are closed from late April to late July to allow the Piping Plover to nest. Port Joli (French for "beautiful port") is a favorite resting place for wild Canada geese.

Drive on to Sable River at the junction of Highway 103 and Route 3. There is a footbridge here that crosses Sable River. This bridge has connected the village with the church and school for over 100 years.

By continuing along the Lighthouse Route, you reach the town of Lockeport, founded in 1761 by a small group of New England Loyalists led by Jonathan Locke. Like other towns along the South Shore, Lockeport was involved in the lucrative West Indies trade during the Golden Age of Sail. The Locke Family Streetscape, the five lovely homes along South Street, are fine examples of the architectural tastes of the affluent sea captains and merchants of the 1800s. Lockeport has some shops, a take-out restaurant and a tourist information center that is open during the summer months.

Continue along the Lighthouse Route next to Jordan Bay. The road leads around the Bay to Sandy Point, location of the Canadian Forces Military Base. Jordan Falls is at the junction of Highway 103 and the Lighthouse Route and the birthplace of Donald McKay, who built clipper ships in Boston. A memorial to McKay stands near the Jordan River.

SHELBURNE

Shelburne is a popular destination along the Lighthouse Route. With its colorful history and attractive homes, it's a fine place to stop and rest. Shelburne's history dates back to 1785, when 30 ships and 3,000 United Empire Loyalists arrived from New York City. The

Loyalists maintained an allegiance to the British Crown and settled in Nova Scotia after the American Revolution. Thanks to the influx of manpower and money, as well as its setting on one of the best natural harbors in the world, Shelburne grew and prospered throughout the 1700s. By 1786, there were 16,000 people living in Shelburne, making it the fourth largest settlement in North America. But then settlers began to disperse and move on to new towns throughout Nova Scotia. Soon Shelburne was a far quieter town. The remaining residents focused on fishing and shipbuilding, two trades that Shelburne is still famous for.

Influenced by the Loyalists, the residents of Shelburne built many attractive homes. You can check them out with the aid of a walking tour brochure available from the local tourist bureau. The Ross-Thompson house, built by Loyalists in 1784, is a provincial museum and the only example of an eighteenth-century store in Nova Scotia. Its shelves are stacked with the items used by the early settlers.

The David Nairn house, built in 1787, has been restored as the Shelburne County Museum. The museum features information about Shelburne's shipbuilding past and Loyalist heritage.

Also of interest is the Dory house on Dock Street along the waterfront. This three-story dory factory had been in operation from 1880 to 1970. It was ceremoniously reopened in 1983 by the Prince and Princess of Wales. Today, visitors can see demonstrations of how the Shelburne dory is built.

Accommodations/Dining

The Loyalist Inn (160 Water Street, 875-2343, $45 single, $50 double). Licensed dining room open year-round from 7 A.M. to 10 P.M. **Mill Stones Country Inn** (2 Falls Lane, 875-3958, $45 single, $70 double). Licensed dining room and full breakfast. **The Ox Bow Motel** (off Highway 103, Exit 25, 875-3000, $50 single, $60 double). Licensed dining room and 47 units. **Cooper's Inn and Restaurant** (36 Dock Street, 875-3411, $55-65 single/double). Inn built in 1785; licensed dining room, complimentary breakfast and luncheon.

Campgrounds

In Shelburne, try the **Islands Provincial Park Campground** (off Route 3, 875-4304, $7.50). Open May through October. Another option: **Pine Hills Campground** (off Highway 103 at Sable River, 656- 3400, $6). Ten campsites available.

SHELBURNE TO YARMOUTH

The drive south from Shelburne along Route 3 involves many twists and, turns with stops in places like Northeast Harbour and Cape Negro. One of the first towns after Shelburne is Birchtown, named in honor of General Birch, the New York commandant who protected blacks who gave support to the British cause during the Revolutionary War. The original settlement was made up of 1,000 blacks who came to Shelburne with the Loyalists in 1783. At that time, Birchtown had the largest free black settlement in North America.

At Birchtown, Highway 103 intersects with the Lighthouse Route and if you have the time, the scenic route is certainly worth taking. The road passes Round Bay and Northeast Harbour, continuing to Port Clyde and the Clyde River. The river enters Negro Harbour, so named for the early settlement of blacks along these shores. There is a two-mile canal here that was used to cross the isthmus between Negro and Port La Tour harbors. The canal is just large enough for a Cape Island fishing boat to pass through.

At scenic Port La Tour there are the remains of Fort Saint Louis, built in 1627 by Charles Saint-Etienne de la Tour. La Tour's father Claude arrived at the sight in 1630 with an Anglo-Scottish expedition. He tried in vain to persuade his son to surrender this last foothold of France left in Acadia (Nova Scotia). Ironically, a few years later, Claude de la Tour was driven out of Port Royal and took refuge with his son at Fort Saint Louis. At Port La Tour, there is a cairn and grave-yard near the remains of the fort. Although the fort is a designated National Historic Site, the property is private and closed to the public.

BARRINGTON

The Lighthouse Route rounds Barrington Bay and reaches the town of Barrington—originally called La Passage by the French. In 1755, La Passage was a thriving Acadian settlement with a stone church and grist mill. But all was destroyed when the British arrived to drive the Acadians out of Nova Scotia. Cattle were slaughtered, crops were burned and the Acadians were shipped off to Boston. Then in 1761, Barrington was settled by New England fishermen who came from Cape Cod, Plymouth and Nantucket, Massachusetts. The new arrivals did not know the whereabouts of the fishing grounds so they recruited two Acadians to help them. In return, the Acadians were allowed to stay on Cape Sable for the winter and were given a fishing boat, muskets, ammunition and trapping gear. Imagine the Acadians, as original settlers, reduced to outcasts and refugees!

Barrington was named after William Wildman, the second Viscount Barrington from England. The original Barrington Meeting House with its New-England-style meeting house structure, still stands. The nearby graveyard, where the early arrivals were buried, features headstones and epitaphs done in a unique style commonly found in old New England cemeteries. Also of interest is the Barrington Woolen Mill, built in 1884. The mill offers demonstrations using original machinery including carders, spinning jennies and looms. It's open from June 15 to September 30 from 9:30 A.M. to 5:30 P.M. While in Barrington, you can also visit the Seal Island Lighthouse, a replica of an original, which guided ships for hundreds of years. The Cape Sable Historical Society also has local exhibits and archives detailing the colorful history of this region of the South Shore.

CLARK'S HARBOUR AND CAPE SABLE

A 4,000-foot causeway, built in 1949, links Barrington passage to northeast point on Cape Sable. A few miles farther south is Clark's Harbour, a classic Nova Scotian fishing village with one of the best ocean fishing fleets in the province. It was founded by Loyalists from Nantucket and Cape Cod in 1760, although Acadians had been living there until the British drove them out in 1758. The town got its name because the only local man who was literate enough to do clerk's work lived in the community. (The British pronounce clerk as clark.) Clark's Harbour is the most southerly point of Nova Scotia.

The island of Cape Sable is famous for the Cape Island boat, originally designed by Ephraim Atkinson at Clark's Harbour in 1907. Now considered the standard for all small lobster boats from Newfoundland to Rhode Island, Cape Islanders are noted for their stability and efficiency. These boats are an integral part of any Maritime seascape and have been captured by many photographers and artists. Cape Sable has always been treacherous to passing ships and there have been many shipwrecks here. At Newellton, visit the Archelaus Smith Museum, which details the wrecks, the lives of the sea captains and the history of the Cape Islander boat.

SHAG HARBOUR TO YARMOUTH

Shag Harbour is a scenic town on Route 3 that overlooks Seal Island. The Chapel Hill Museum, located on a hill in the center of town, houses a collection of artifacts left by the early settlers. The museum, formerly a church, has a belfry that serves as an observation tower. The sweeping views of the outlying islands and the rocky coast are lovely to behold on a clear day.

From Shag Harbour, the Lighthouse Route continues north through the seven Pubnicos: Pubnico Beach, Lower West Pubnico, Middle Pubnico, West Pubnico, Middle West Pubnico, East Pubnico and finally, Pubnico. The seven Pubnicos were settled in 1653 by the Acadians, making them the oldest French villages in Nova Scotia. In Lower West Pubnico, there is a memorial to the baron Phillippe Mius d'Entremont, the only baron to ever settle in ancient Acadia. With the exception of Pubnico and East Pubnico, the region is still French-speaking. The villages rely on fishing for their livelihood and retain their Acadian traditions. West Pubnico's Musée Acadien is located opposite the fire station. Built in 1864, this converted museum has Acadian memorabilia, as well as the original land grants of the area dating back to the 1700's. It's open in summer and admission is free. The name *Pubnico*, incidentally, is from the Micmac Indian word for "cleared land."

On the approach to Yarmouth, one passes through Ste. Anne du Ruisseau, an Acadian town dating back to 1767. Ste. Anne's Church is notable; it's the first Roman Catholic chapel in Nova Scotia, established in 1784 by Abbé Sigogne. Two miles east of Yarmouth, at the head of the Chebogue River, lies the town of Arcadia, named after the Brig *Arcadia* and built in 1817. Here, an interesting light-green house called the House of Four Peoples was built on an ancient Micmac dwelling. Part of the house was constructed by French settlers, then expanded by both English and Dutch dwellers.

A quick detour off Route 3 will take you to Chebogue Point and Rockville. *Chebogue* is a Micmac Indian name for "great still water." Records show that in March 1774, the Boston privateer vessel *Cabot* was forced ashore by British naval vessels. The villagers of Chebogue gave shelter to the Bostonians and the crew of 140 men and officers hid there until the British had gone. The crew was then provided with safe passage back to Boston. This feeling of comradeship between Nova Scotians and New Englanders still seems to thrive today. Perhaps the common roots, cultural heritage and migration between the two regions has helped maintain this special bond.

Accommodations

Along this section of the Lighthouse Route between Shelburne and Yarmouth, you'll find: **Lighthouse Walk Bed & Breakfast** (in Barrington on Route 3, 637-3409, $35-45 single/double). **Cape Island Bed & Breakfast** (at Clark's Harbour, 745-1356, $35-40) Open year-round. **La Baronnie Motel** (in West Pubnico, 762-3388, $30-40 single/double). **Red Cap Motel** (in West Pubnico, 762-2112, $40-50 single/double). Licensed restaurant features Acadian cooking.

Campgrounds

There is a campground in Barrington called **Bayberry Campground** (one mile off Route 3, 637-2181, $10 water site, $7 wooded site). **Derrydown Campground** (Lower East Pubnico on Forbes Point Road, 723-2939, $9) is near Woods Harbour, with fishing, wooded trails to the ocean and fireplace sites.

Dining

For meals, the **Old School House Restaurant** (Barrington Passage, 637-3770) serves wholesome food and home-baked goods. **Geneva's Restaurant** (Clark's Harbour, 745-2659) serves seafood and chowders and is open seven days a week. In Lower Woods Harbour, try the **Captain's Landing** (723-2249), a licensed restaurant open seven nights a week.

YARMOUTH

Yarmouth, an important town on the southwestern tip of Nova Scotia, is the terminus for the Bar Harbor and Portland, Maine, ferries. For those arriving by ferry, tours of the Fundy Shore or the Lighthouse Route begin here, and the large, very informative tourist office at the ferry terminus should be the first stop before setting out to see Nova Scotia.

Yarmouth was settled primarily by New England Loyalists from Massachusetts. It is recorded that five families arrived from the area of Plymouth, Cape Cod and Nantucket, Massachusetts, in June 1761, and eight more families arrived in late summer. The story goes that the first winter was so cold that 27 cattle died of starvation and the settlers were so hungry they boiled hides for soup. But the group survived and by 1764, they had built and launched their first sailing vessel. Yarmouth, like other Nova Scotian communities, became a leading shipbuilding and fisheries center and was one of the most important ports in North America during the 1800s.

Also in the 1800s, Yarmouth had become a popular destination for Canadians and Americans who lived inland or in colder climes and liked to vacation on the coast. The temperate summers and proximity to the sea began a tradition for vacationers that continues today. Yarmouth's charm may be a bit faded today; its commercialism is not really representative of Nova Scotia. Yarmouth County offers plenty of diversion, however, and the real beauty of Yarmouth is its harbor, lighthouse, fishing fleet and proud history.

Attractions

❖ Yarmouth County Museum and Archives

Located at 22 Collins Street (742-5539), this award-winning museum features Yarmouth's history with an emphasis on its seafaring past. There are period rooms, a blacksmith's shop, ship models and a china collection. Of special interest is the Runic Stone, a strange, carved rock that may indicate the presence of Norsemen or Vikings in the Yarmouth area over 1,000 years ago.

Because of Yarmouth's shipbuilding heritage, the Canadian government erected a memorial to Nova Scotian shipbuilders on the corner of Main and Marshall streets. The plaque recalls the Golden Age of Sail when Nova Scotia was the fourth largest ship-owning area in the world.

❖ The Firefighter's Museum

At 451 Main Street you can visit Nova Scotia's only Firefighter's Museum (742-5525) with apparatuses that date back to the early days of fire fighting. There is also a collection of beautiful fire engines dating back to the 1930s. The museum is open from 9 A.M. to 9 P.M. Monday through Saturday, and from 9 A.M. to 5 P.M. on Sundays.

❖ Cape Forchu and Yarmouth Light

Right on the outskirts of Yarmouth is Cape Forchu, named by Samuel de Champlain in 1604 while on his way to settling Annapolis Royal. Here in the mouth of this vast harbor, a lighthouse was built in

1840 to guide ships. It was replaced by a modern, electrically run lighthouse in the 1960s. There is a plaque describing the history of the lighthouse, and a nearby picnic area—the Leif Ericksson Picnic Park. Perhaps, 1,000 years ago, the Viking Leif Ericksson and his mob stood at this very site, taking in the view of their new world, light-years removed from the picnic tables and station wagons that now crowd this spot.

Accommodations

Yarmouth is a good jumping off point but offers little for the visitor to do for days at a stretch. It is a good place to get acclimated to Nova Scotia, but there is a great deal more to do and see farther north. Lodging options include: **MidTown Motel** (13 Parade Street, 742-5333, $50-60, special rate of $14 for backpackers/cylists). Five minutes from the ferry terminal. **Lakelawn Motel** (641 Main Street, 742-8427, $35 single, $50 double). Good location. **Clementine's Bed & Breakfast** (21 Clements Street, 742-0079, $35 single, $50 double). Gourmet breakfast included.

For more upscale accommodation, try: **Best Western Mermaid Motel** (545 Main Street, 742-2966, $75-90 single/double). Open year-round; heated pool; English-style pub. **Murray Manor Guest House Bed & Breakfast** (17 Forest Street, 742-9625, $35 single, $45 double). Eight rooms and kitchen facilities. On the outskirts of Yarmouth, try the highly recommended **Manor Inn** (Route 1, five miles northeast of Yarmouth, 742-2487, $75-80 standard room, $80-90 superior and $120-125 deluxe). Facilities include a coachhouse, a rose garden and lakeside rooms (with whirlpool baths and fireplaces), a licensed dining room, fishing, boating, a pool, and tennis courts.

Dining

There are some very good restaurants in Yarmouth and plenty of average ones. For typical Nova Scotian fare, try **Captain Kelley's Restaurant and Lounge** (577 Main Street, 742-7820). Nearby is a **McDonald's** and a **Kentucky Fried Chicken. Five Corners Restaurant** (626 Main Street, 742-6061), located next to the famous "Horse Fountain" on Main Street, is best known for its seafood chowder. Pasta, salads and specialty pizzas are also available. One of the finer dining rooms in the Yarmouth area is at the **Manor Inn** (minutes from Cape Forchu Lighthouse, 742-2487) where specialties include Digby scallops, Atlantic salmon and fresh-baked breads. **China Court** (67 Starr's Road, 742-9128) is a fully licensed restaurant that's a good deal for budget-conscious travelers.

Shopping

Because Yarmouth is a major exit point for American travelers who board the ferries for Maine, there is a slew of tourist shops along Main Street. One quality shop is the **Yarmouth Wool Shoppe, Ltd.** (352 Main Street, 742-2255). Here, you can buy Hudson Bay coats and blankets, English woolens and Scottish tartans. These goods are somewhat more difficult to find in other parts of Nova Scotia. For souvenirs, try **R. H. Davis & Co.** at 361 Main Street. The store features maps, logos, handcrafted gifts and tartan clothing of Nova Scotia.

Ferry Crossings

From Yarmouth, there are two choices. The Canadian-owned Marine Atlantic ferry runs from Yarmouth to Bar Harbor, Maine. This is the best trip for the price because it is shorter and less expensive than the Portland run. However, it involves more driving for motorists from Boston, New York or other more southern regions of the country. Ferries depart from Yarmouth for Bar Harbor every day at 4:30 P.M. and the trip takes 6 hours. Departures from Bar Harbor to Yarmouth are scheduled at 8:30 A.M. daily. The fare is $74.00 one way for a car and $40 for each passenger. The Prince of Fundy Cruises company runs a ferry service from Yarmouth to Portland, Maine, departing once a day at 9:30 A.M. The fare is $200 for a car and $85 for individuals. The ship is a floating casino, and most passengers spend their time with the slot machines or rolling dice. The trip takes 11 hours. The trip from Portland to Yarmouth leaves in the evening. Many travelers rent a cabin and sleep throughout the trip.

Buses

For those without a car, there are two bus companies that depart from Yarmouth. Acadian Lines (742-5131) has a twice-daily bus service to Digby for $18 and two direct buses a day to Halifax for $35. The depot is a part of the VIA Rail Station at the far southern end of town. MacKenzie Lines also goes to Halifax along the South Shore with stops in Liverpool, Bridgewater and Chester. This is a somewhat longer route, but if you are interested in seeing the South Shore, this is the bus to take. Departure time is 9:15 a.m. daily except Sundays and holidays. The price is $26 from Yarmouth to Halifax.

There is a train leaving from Yarmouth to Halifax once a day with a stop in Kentville along the Annapolis Valley. The trip takes almost six hours and costs $35 one way. The train is accessible next to the Acadian bus depot.

THE EVANGELINE TRAIL

T he route from Yarmouth to Windsor spans an interesting, diverse area that once evolved around the historic settlement and subsequent expulsion of the Acadian people. Commonly referred to as the Evangeline Trail, the route is named after the fictional heroine in Longfellow's epic poem "Evangeline," which chronicles the sad history of the Acadian expulsion from Nova Scotia and resettlement in the swamplands of Louisiana.

Heading northward out of Yarmouth, the Evangeline Trail takes in the length and breadth of St. Mary's Bay and the French Shore before sweeping through the rich farmlands of the historic Annapolis Valley, whose shores overlook the Bay of Fundy and the Minas Basin. One of the fascinating things about the Bay of Fundy is its dramatic tides, rising and dropping to levels not often seen elsewhere in the world. Also of great interest to visitors are the humpback, minke and fin whales that feed in the rich waters off Brier Island, the Land's End of the Bay of Fundy. Internationally, there has been such a keen interest in whales and their natural habitat that remote Brier Island has become a very popular destination for both North American and overseas visitors who come a long way to watch the whales feed and play.

THE FRENCH SHORE

The Evangeline Trail out of Yarmouth follows the old Route 1 that runs parallel to Highway 101 towards Digby. The trail first passes through Hebron's "Lupine Trail," named for the wild herbs growing along the roadside. In June, the countryside is covered with blue, white and pink lupine, so lush and colorful that the scene resembles a French impressionist painting. Just north of Hebron, on Route 340, an inland road passes through evergreen forests that were once harvested for lumber to build ships and homes. Close to South Ohio and Deerfield, towns along this inland route, you'll find the Chebogue Meadows nature trail near Lake George.

Next, the Evangeline Trail passes through Port Maitland, a fishing village and center of Yarmouth County's dairy farm region. Rough terrain made oxen the chosen beast for plowing this land, and they are still commonly seen along this route. By turning left towards the breakwater here, you'll reach Sandy Beach Provincial Park, which is a nice spot for a picnic.

Shortly after leaving Port Maitland, you enter the Municipality of Clare, where the French Shore begins. This district was settled by the Acadians who returned to this region after being expelled by the British in 1755. Because this land was undesirable to British settlers, the Acadians were allowed to live here. It is believed that 335 Acadian families walked from Boston to this region in the summer of 1768. Look for the tricolor Acadian flag with its single star flying in front of the homes. The flag symbolizes water, earth and sky. Its guiding star, Stella Maris, represents the strength of the Acadians in times of persecution. If you do not see the Acadian flag flying in front of a home, another way to determine if a French-speaking family lives there is to read the occupants' names. Thibodeau, Poiret and Entremont, for example, are sure signs of the heritage of those living within. The Acadians still speak a dialect that both French Canadians of Québec and Parisians find quite different from their own language. They have managed to preserve both their language and customs, which are centered around their Catholic churches, the community and family. Long before the Acadians settled the Municipality of Clare, the Micmac Indians lived and fished along St. Mary's Bay. Evidence of their presence here is found in the names of towns like Meteghan and Sissiboo.

For an interesting side trip before reaching Meteghan, take the road to North Bear Cove and South Bear Cove, where dramatic cliffs meet the ocean. From here, you'll reach Smuggler's Cove near the provincial Picnic Park in Meteghan. During Prohibition days, this cove was used quite extensively by smugglers or rum runners. They kept the rum in a cave here until it was smuggled to places like Eastport, Maine, for distribution in the States. The cave is 15 feet high and runs a distance of 60 feet inland. There was plenty of rum-running all along this coast, and locals still tell of wild stories about the money made and lost during the heyday of prohibition.

Meteghan, a small town settled by the Acadians in 1785, is now the French Shore's busiest port. The harbor is full of scallop draggers, trawlers, herring seiners and lobster boats, all part of the Acadian fishing fleet. Because the land along the French Shore was poor and difficult to farm, the Acadians were obliged to turn to the sea for their livelihood and became excellent fishermen. The oldest home in Meteghan, La Vielle Maison, is a museum detailing nineteenth-century Acadian life. At Meteghan River, there is a shipyard, drydock and waterfront buildings that were used to build some of the largest wooden ships in the Atlantic Provinces. In 1966, the boat builders of Meteghan gained international acclaim for building a 165-foot replica of the renowned American clipper ship *Flying Cloud*.

The nearby village of Comeauville is where the popular Acadian dish *pâté à la rapure* (rappie pie) was first recognized internationally. A bit like shepherd's pie, it's made with meat and grated potatoes covered with a light crust. This hot dish is available in many of the restaurants along the French Shore. Many Nova Scotians agree that the best food in the province can be found here, so take your time and stop for lunch along this unusual stretch of ancient land.

Church Point is a tiny village with the tallest and largest wooden church in all of North America. It is located on the campus of Université Ste. Anne, the province's only French language university. Founded in 1891 by Eudis priests from France, this degree-granting university is popular with Acadians and more recently, with other Nova Scotians who want to learn the country's second official language. The vast church, its spire reaching 185 feet, was built from 1903 to 1905. Because strong winds off St. Mary's Bay threaten to topple the spire, 40 tons of rock have been lodged in the steeple to act as ballast. The church is open for tours from May to October.

Church Point is also the site of one of the oldest Acadian festivals in Atlantic Canada. The Festival Acadien de Clare, held during the second week of July, features traditional Acadian dancing performed by la Baie en Joie, a dance troupe based in Church Point. The festival also features concert bands, arts and crafts and Acadian cuisine— including traditional rappie pie.

Of interest further along Route 1 is Grosses Coques (the town's name means "large clams" in French). It's said that clams here along the eastern shore of St. Mary's Bay were once so plentiful that the settlers lived solely on them for a whole winter. At Grosses Coques is the first Acadian cemetery to be established after the expulsion of 1755 and subsequent return of the Acadians. A cairn and small chapel mark the spot. Continuing north, Belliveau Cove with a well-protected harbor, features some of the highest tides in the world. The town was once known as a lumbering community, and its citizens are still known for their wood-carving skills.

At St. Bernard, a huge, granite, gothic church looms over the small village. Although the village population stands at 322, this church can seat 1,000 people. About a half mile beyond the church, to the left, a road leads to the coast and New Edinburgh. Three Scottish Loyalists traced the layout of a township here in 1783, which was named but never built. Traces of the survey still remain. After passing New Edinburgh, the Acadian presence starts to dwindle.

One of the first Loyalist settlements along the French Shore, Weymouth was settled in 1783 and named after the town of Weymouth, Massachusetts. Situated on St. Mary's Bay at the mouth of the Sissiboo River, the village prospered during the schooner building days. Because of the Fundy tides, schooners could be launched from the riverbanks when the tides were high. Waterfront shops were built on logs to allow the river to flow underneath, although on occasion, the first floors of the shops took on water.

A museum and cultural center housed in the restored St. Thomas Anglican Church, opposite the Royal Bank, is open to the public during summer months. Afternoon teas are held every Thursday from 3 P.M. to 5 P.M.

Although the stretch from Weymouth to Digby is lumber country, the route passes coastal settlements like Weymouth North, known for its deep-sea fishing and yachting facilities. Gilbert Cove has a restored lighthouse, with picnic tables and a tea room.

Marshalltown, five miles south of Digby, is the home of Maud Lewis, an artist who painted primitively yet won international acclaim. Her tiny house has been moved to Halifax, where it is under restoration by the Art Gallery of Nova Scotia.

Just to the right, off Route 101 at the entrance to Digby, the town of Acaciaville offers fine views of the Bay of Fundy and Digby Neck.

Accommodations and Dining along the French Shore

There are plenty of bed & breakfasts and other accommodations along the French Shore, including: **Cape View Motel and Cottages** (north of Yarmouth on Route 1, 645-2258, $40-50 motel, $75 cottages). Offers whale-watching and deep-sea fishing. **Chez Benoit Stuart Band** (Church Point, 769-2715, $25 single, $30 double). **Gilbert's Cove Farm Bed & Breakfast** (in Weymouth off Highway 101, 837-4505, $30 single, $35 double). Full breakfast is available.

In Saulnierville, **Pizza Delight** (769-0820, located off Highway 1 in the center of town) has pizza and other Italian dishes.

DIGBY

Digby is a great town with a very active scallop fleet. It may strike the visitor as being a quiet place; but once the scallop fleet comes in or the ferry from Saint John, New Brunswick, arrives, Digby really bustles.

The town was named after Robert Digby, a British admiral who brought the *HMS Atlanta* to these shores after the American Revolution. The vessel carried 1,500 Loyalists from New England, and many of them settled in Digby or farther inland along the Annapolis Valley.

Digby overlooks the Annapolis Basin and the Digby Gut, which opens out to the Bay of Fundy. Its location is ideal for those who make their living from the sea, as the Bay of Fundy and St. Mary's Bay have given this town its world famous Digby scallops. For all its notoriety as a fishing center, it is still difficult to find a good seafood restaurant in downtown Digby. Chinese food, yes, but succulent scallops in a rustic, seaside restaurant—no.

Highlights

One of the highlights of visiting Digby is a visit to the famous Pines Resort Motel operated by the Department of Tourism and Culture. At the Pines dining room, you can have seafood ranging from scallops to salmon. The best bet is to go there for lunch.

Digby is also the jumping off point for trips down Digby Neck to Long and Brier Islands, choice places for whale and bird watching, including hawk migrations in the fall. Digby is also the terminus of the Princess of Acadia ferry that sails daily from Saint John, New Brunswick.

One of the best times to be in Digby is during the Digby Scallop Days held in August each year. Chosen as one of the top 100 attractions in North America, Scallop Days feature the Queen's Ball, a street parade, scallop shucking and gear knitting competitions and a fireworks display above a parade of Digby's scallop fleet.

While in town, be sure to walk down to the waterfront where the scallop boats are tied up. The evening I arrived in Digby, the fleet of over 50 large vessels was heading out for a night of scallop fishing. By the next morning, at least 40 tractor-trailer rigs were pulling into town to pick up the evening's catch for delivery throughout Canada and the United States. Perhaps this explains why it's hard to get scallops at restaurants in Digby: The Mack trucks get them first!

Also stroll along Admiral's Walk overlooking Digby Harbour. This seaside promenade passes the cannons from Admiral Digby's ship, the *Atlanta*. The stroll continues to the Fisherman's Wharf with its bandstand and summer concerts. The small Loyalist Park here marks the original landing sight of the settlers. At the end of Admiral's Walk, you'll reach the tourist bureau on Water Street, which is very informative, particularly for those continuing along the Evangeline Trail. An important historic sight is the Admiral Digby Museum at 91 Montague Row. The museum has a collection of old furnishings, a marine room, old photographs of Digby and models of early wooden ships. Admission is free and the museum is open from July to September.

Also of interest is the Annapolis Basin Lookoff along Route 303 towards the ferry wharf and opposite the information center. The splendid view takes in Digby Gut and the Annapolis Basin.

Accommodations

There are bed & breakfasts here that are very nice, with fine views of the harbor and within close proximity to the center of town. However, for a really elegant Maritime experience, why not stay at **The Pines Resort Motel** (245-2511) along Shore Road in Digby? Originally operated by the Canadian Pacific Railway, this elegant resort has been a favorite for summertime guests for over 100 years. There are cottages with fireplaces, an excellent dining room and a licensed lounge with entertainment. During dinner, a dress code is in effect. The Pines also has a swimming pool, tennis courts, hiking trails and movies. Rates are $95-100 single and $110-240 double.

Other options include: the **Admiral Digby Inn** (on Shore Road on the way to the Saint John ferry, 245-2531, $65 single, $89 with a fridge. Cottages are $115 single/double). Licensed dining room and a lounge. There are deluxe cottages, 44 motel units and an indoor swimming pool. **The Mountain Gap Inn and Resort** (off Highway 101, Exit 24/25 east of Digby, 245-5841, $67-85 single, $80-100 double). Swimming pool, tennis court, whale-watching and deep-sea fishing arranged. **The Thistle Down Inn Bed & Breakfast** (98 Montague Row, 245-4490, $35-45 single, $40-55 double; includes full breakfast). Open May 15 to October 13. **The Admiral's Landing Bed & Breakfast** (115 Montague Row, 245-2247, $45-50 single, $55-60 double). Popular with cyclists and young couples. **The Westway House Bed & Breakfast** (6 Carleton Street, 245-5071, $29 single, $40 double). Spartan rooms, but clean.

Dining

There are some pretty good restaurants in Digby, but, as mentioned previously, they're not as good as one would hope with the rich Bay of Fundy so close by. **The Pines Resort Motel** (245-2511) has an excellent dining room specializing in those elusive Digby scallops. **The Fundy Restaurant** (34 Water Street, 245-4950) is a licensed restaurant serving lunch and dinner. The House of Wong (110 Water Street, 245-4125) has mediocre Chinese food. **The Admiral Digby Inn** (245-2531) near the Saint John Ferry has a good menu at their licensed restaurant.

The Saint John Ferry

The Saint John, New Brunswick/Digby, Nova Scotia ferry plies the waters of the Bay of Fundy. Sightings of porpoises and even whales are common on this pleasant 2 1/2-hour trip that is an excellent way to get to or from Nova Scotia. Many East Coast Americans heading back home take the expensive 11-hour ferry from Yarmouth to Portland, Maine, but then they miss seeing the Bay of Fundy and the wonderful towns and islands of New Brunswick. If you take the ferry from Digby to Saint John, there is the opportunity to see places in New Brunswick like Grand Manan Island, the city of Saint Andrew's and Fundy National Park. The Trans-Canada Highway connects to the Maine Turnpike, making the journey back to the United States quite easy.

The ferry departs from Digby three times a day in summer at 5 A.M., 1 P.M. and 8:15 P.M. Monday through Saturday, and at 1 P.M. and 8:15 P.M. on Sundays. The fee is $16 for individuals and $48.75 for an automobile. Cabins with shower facilities are $15.

Digby Neck and the Islands

Beyond Digby, jutting out into the Bay of Fundy is a "spinal column" called Digby Neck and the Islands. This route takes you all the way to Brier Island, Nova Scotia's Land's End in the Bay of Fundy. Whale-watching has become a very popular attraction here, and both native Nova Scotians and visitors from all over the world make the trip along Digby Neck to Tiverton on Long Island or Westport on Brier Island to join an organized whale watch.

Route 217 down Digby Neck first passes Gulliver's Cove where, legend has it, the pirate Gulliver buried his treasure. There have been plenty of hunts for this buried treasure, but at best folks have found only semi-precious stones and agate.

Sandy Cove is a lovely town with a population of only 173. Some of the attractive homes here are bed & breakfasts. With its twin beaches and scenic views, Sandy Cove is a quiet alternative to spending a night in Digby. There's a mysterious story about a man named Jerome who was found on the beach here in 1854. When the townspeople spotted him, he was dressed in fine clothes with a can of water and a tin of biscuits beside him. Both his legs were missing above the knee. He was unable to speak and could tell no one where he came from, but the locals at Sandy Cove cared for him for 58 years. He is buried at Meteghan Cemetery.

The first ferry ride you'll encounter on the way down Digby Neck is at East Ferry. The ferry, which runs year-round, leaves for Tiverton, Long Island, hourly on the half hour and costs $1 per car. Try to get there well ahead of time; otherwise, you could wind up at the end of a long ferry line and be obliged to wait another hour. The town of Tiverton is one of the places where you can join a whale-watching tour. Contact Pirates Cove Whale Cruises, Tiverton, Nova Scotia, Canada B0V 1G0, (902) 839-2242.

Tiverton, settled in 1785, was originally called Petite Passage. In 1842 it took its present name from a borough in Devon, England. Tiverton continues to be an important fishing port and the Tiverton Islands Museum just west of the village has some interesting information about the town's maritime history. From Tiverton, it's a short drive to the southern tip of Long Island, at Freeport. From Freeport, there is a year-round ferry service on *The Spray,* which leaves for Westport, Brier Island, every half hour.

BRIER ISLAND

Happily isolated from tourism until the general public began taking such a great interest in whale-watching, Brier Island is a very special place. Whale-watching cruises run twice a day in summer from Westport, so at least during July and August, quiet Brier Island bustles with activity. There are guaranteed spottings here as great numbers of humpback, minke, as well as fin whales and porpoises feed in the plankton-rich waters of St. Mary's Bay and the Bay of Fundy. During my day of whale-watching, our boat had visitors from England,

Germany, Australia, the States and Canada, and we happily watched a trio of humpback whales perform for us all afternoon. We also spotted the fast-swimming fin whale and many more humpbacks.

The town of Westport was initially a fishing station used by David Welch and his family in 1769. There was a sudden jump in the population in 1783, when eleven Loyalist families arrived. The descendants of these original families still live on the island, and one of them, Philip Shea, has written a definitive guide on Brier Island and the people who made it so special.

One of the island's most illustrious residents was Joshua Slocum, who was born on the mainland but spent most of his formative years on Brier Island. Slocum was the first man to sail alone around the world, and his epic journey on the 36-foot sloop *Spray* took from 1895 to 1898. He recorded his adventures in the Maritime classic *Sailing Alone Around the World*, which he partially wrote at Westport. When Slocum began his epic journey he sailed out of Gloucester, Massachusetts, but Brier Island was his first port of call and his last stop before crossing the Atlantic. There is a memorial plaque to Captain Slocum at the southern end of Brier Island, overlooking the Green Head, the basalt rock formations unique to Brier Island.

Slocum made a final journey with his aged vessel in 1909 at the age of 65. Bound for South America, he hoped to navigate up the Orinoco River and find the headwaters of the Amazon. He and the *Spray* were never heard from again, and it is presumed that he was lost at sea.

When wandering around Westport, you'll notice that the homes have lovely stained-glass windows. Most of these were brought home by sea captains and sailors returning from long journeys abroad.

Westport was greatly changed when a sudden, violent storm in February 1976 destroyed a great deal of property along the waterfront. Many of the long-standing shops and shanties along the harbor were destroyed. All told, there was millions of dollars of damage. Luckily, the shoe shop where Joshua Slocum once worked with his father was saved and is now an attraction for tourists. At the eastern and western points of the island there are two lighthouses that still serve as a guide to ships. The waters off Brier Island have always been difficult to navigate, with shoals and reefs snagging many ships.

Stories of the people of Brier Island are always intriguing, including the one about the islanders' fondness for drinking vanilla extract on Saturday nights. If ever the townspeople got too rowdy, the Canadian Mounties were called from Digby. Two ferry crossings later, the troublemakers had long since settled down after being informed by other islanders that the Mounties were on their way.

Accommodations and Dining
on Digby Neck and the Islands

There are some nice inns along Digby Neck and the Islands that also have fully licensed restaurants. The best places to stay and eat are at Sandy Cove and Westport. **Olde Village Inn** (Sandy Cove, 834-2202, $55-75 single, $60-75 double), built in 1890, has six rooms and three cottages with a licensed dining room and ocean views. **Sandy Cove Bed & Breakfast** (Route 217, 834-2675, $30 single, $40 double) is open from June to November; breakfast, lunch and dinner are available. On Brier Island, all the available accommodation is in the village of Westport. One of the nicest spots to stay is the **Brier Island Lodge and Restaurant** (839-2300, $55 single, $70 double), which sits above the village with spectacular dining-room views. The nearby **Westport Inn** (839-2675, $35 single, $45 double) serves lunch and dinner and provides box lunches for whale-watching trips.

In the height of summer, accommodation is difficult to find on Brier Island. If you want to spend a day whale-watching and then decide to stay on the island, you may find everything fully booked. Try to phone early in the morning or a day in advance to secure lodging.

DIGBY TO WINDSOR

This section of the Evangeline Trail is of great historical interest, passing through both Annapolis Royal (settled by the French in 1604) and Grand Pré National Historic Park (location of the statue of Evangeline and memorial to the Acadian people).

The Annapolis Valley is ancient, formed two million years ago by metamorphic rocks and volcanic basalts of two mountain ranges. The valley was originally settled by Micmacs. The Acadians came next, but once they were ousted, New England planters established themselves here.

The Evangeline Trail from Digby to Windsor lacks the sea breezes and oceanfront activity that characterized the Lighthouse Route, but those attractions are replaced by rolling hills, apple orchards, meadows and marshland.

From Digby, before heading inland away from the Bay of Fundy, the Trail passes Smith Cove and Bear River, two very scenic and popular places to stop. Smith Cove is a summer activities center, with excellent facilities for swimming, sailing and tennis. There are views of the Annapolis Basin and Digby Gut. Farther upriver from Smith Cove is Bear River, settled by Loyalists in the eighteenth century. These settlers were not all English; many were Hessian mercenary soldiers conscripted to fight for the British during the American Revolution. Bear River's shipping and lumbering industries prospered particularly from 1870 to 1930. Bear River is known for its incredibly high tides, rising more than 20 feet. In the past, schooners were able to navigate from Bear River all the way to the Bay of Fundy when the tide was high.

The next point of interest along this route is Clementsport, founded by United Empire Loyalists in 1784. This is the beginning of Annapolis County, which is Nova Scotia's produce-growing region. The Annapolis River runs along this valley, bordered by 20 miles of fertile, diked marshland. The Acadians were the first to dike this marshy land and plant crops here. Near Clementsport and 5 miles west of Annapolis Royal on Route 1 is Upper Clements Park. Both a wildlife and theme park, the site overlooks the scenic Annapolis Basin. Admission is free. There are some clever rides here including the Sissiboo Sizzler and Flume Ride, a water ride in a large log that seats four. There is also a Company of Good Cheer Dinner Theater that serves traditional foods and offers old-fashioned entertainment.

ANNAPOLIS ROYAL

Annapolis Royal is the oldest settlement in Canada, founded in 1605 by French explorers Samuel de Champlain and Sieur de Monts. The original settlement, called Port Royal by the French, is located five miles downriver at the Port Royal National Historic Park. Port Royal marks the scene of the first bloodshed in Canada, as a bitter, century-long struggle ensued between the French and English over possession of Port Royal and Acadia (or Nova Scotia). Port Royal also marks the beginning of commerce in Canada: It was here that the first vessels built in North America were launched and used for fishing and trading.

Highlights

Fort Anne National Historic Park is located in the center of Annapolis Royal. Originally built in 1635, the fort has been attacked over the centuries by the English, the French, New Englanders, Acadians, Indians and even pirates. The battles for Port Royal clearly represent the power struggles of seventeenth- and eighteenth-century North America. In one instance in 1690, New Englanders sailed into Port Royal and attacked the Acadians, killing livestock and burning homes.

A decisive battle was carried out in the winter of 1709, when men from Massachusetts, under the leadership of Colonel Francis Nicholson, were finally able to capture the fort. The French flag was lowered and Port Royal was renamed Annapolis Royal after Queen Anne. The victors carried the key to the fort all the way to Boston; it's now housed in the museum here. Much of the fort has retained its original look: The headquarters of the Duke of Kent, father of Queen Victoria, is intact as are the barracks for the soldiers.

The Port Royal National Historic Park, five miles south of Annapolis Royal, is a replica of the small village of Port Royal, which was once the oldest permanent white settlement in North America north of Florida. Here there are replicas of buildings erected by explorers Samuel de Champlain and Sieur de Monts, and a mention of the founding of the Order of Good Cheer, the first social club in North America. The club originally had a charter membership of 15 Frenchmen including Champlain and de Monts, who ended each gathering (and most likely began it) with a ceremonial drink from a cup of wine.

Within the town of Annapolis Royal, there are many fine homes built after the arrival of the United Empire Loyalists in the 1780s. Lower St. George Street, the oldest town street in Canada, is particularly interesting with many elegant homes. The O'Dell Inn Museum (circa 1869) and the Robertson-McNamara house (circa 1785) are both open to the public during the summer months. Admission is free. Lower St. George Street turns into Upper St. George Street, which leads to a military cemetery and historic gardens. Back on Lower St. George Street, the road leads to the waterfront and wharf. This overlooks the village of Granville Ferry, which is one of the most popular spots for photographers to capture the drama of the rising and falling Fundy tides.

At 441 Lower St. George Street, visit the beautiful Annapolis Royal Historic Gardens, with its ten acres of gardens and bird sanctuary.

The range of flowers is impressive. The grounds overlook the Allains River and salt marshes. The site is believed to be the spot where the Acadians first began to dike the marshes and then installed one of North America's first grist mills on the continent's first wheatfield. As a New Englander, I was struck by the similarities between Annapolis Royal and numerous towns throughout Massachusetts. The clapboard homes with their generous porches facing the sea, the expansive lawns and well-tended gardens, the quiet streets and sailboats in the harbor seemed very similar to towns around Boston.

Accommodations

Among the many options for lodging: **The Auberge Wandlyn Royal Anne Motel** (west of town on Route 1, (800) 561-0000 in the Maritimes, $60-80 single/double). Handicapped facilities, nonsmoking rooms, honeymoon suites and regular units. **Sandy Bottom Lake Hostel** (20 minutes south of Annapolis Royal off Route 8, 532-2497, $8 night). Youth hostel with cooking facilities. **Bread and Roses Country Inn** (82 Victoria Street, 532-5727, $50-60). Restored Victorian mansion; breakfast and afternoon tea served. **The Garrison House Inn** (350 St. George Street, 532-5750, $45-55 single, $48-70 double). Licensed dining room. **The Queen Anne Inn** (494 Upper Street, 532-7850, $75-80 single/double). Registered heritage property. **The Auberge Sieur de Monts** at Port Royal (532-7883, $30-50 single/double). Named after the early French explorer. Open from May to October. Licensed dining room.

Campgrounds

At Annapolis Royal, the **Dunromin Campsite and Trailer Court** (near Granville Ferry, 532-2808, $11) has open and wooded campsites; swimming and fishing offered. **Fundy Trail Campground** (532-7711) at Port Williams overlooks the Bay of Fundy at Delaps Cove. Rates are $9 per night.

Dining

Restaurants in this area are usually part of an inn or motel. Noted for its food is the **Garrison House Inn** (350 St. George Street, 532-5750). Licensed dining room serves lunch and dinner. **Charlie's Place Restaurant** (Highway 1, 532-2111) in Annapolis Royal serves

Chinese-Canadian food. Near Fort Anne, **Tom's Pizzeria** (532-5207) serves pizza and basic Canadian food.

Festivals

Annapolis Royal is the site of some of Canada's more colorful festivals. Of particular note is the celebration of Canada Day in Canada's Oldest Settlement from June 29 to 30. There's also the King's Theatre Festival from July 1 to August 31, the Natal Days from August 2 to 5 and the Landing of the Scots at Port Royal on August 24.

ANNAPOLIS ROYAL TO WOLFVILLE

The drive north from Annapolis Royal along the Evangeline Trail follows an inland route that eventually reaches the Minas Basin and the Grand Pré National Historic Park. It is difficult to take a coastal drive here because of the low-lying marshlands, so the route takes on a countrified quality. You'll pass apple orchards, farms and vegetable stands. Some of the best apples in the Maritimes can be bought here, and chatting with the local farmers over produce is a good way to get to know the people of this region. This is one of the few places in Nova Scotia that feels landlocked, as if the sea were hundreds of miles away instead of a mere ten. A highlight of this drive is a visit to Cape Blomidon, the Grand Pré Memorial Church and the Statue of Evangeline.

Starting from Annapolis Royal, the Evangeline Trail passes through Bridgetown on Route 1. This town has some lovely homes and a particularly interesting gallery. The Tolmie Gallery, in a private home at Carleton Corner, displays the work of Kenneth Tolmie, an internationally renowned artist. Situated at the head of the Annapolis River, Bridgetown was an important shipbuilding center during the Golden Age of Sail. I found it to be a friendly, quiet town, where I was even invited to a home for some seafood chowder. From Bridgetown, the road leads to Middleton, the heart of the apple-growing region of the Annapolis Valley. Middleton holds an annual summer festival, called the Heart of the Valley Days, on the third Saturday in July.

At Middleton, the Trail intersects Route 10, a cross-province rural route that ends in Lunenburg on the South Shore. It's a real off-the-beaten-track road passing through lumber and farming country. Near the town of Springfield, Nova Scotians like to canoe and fish on Springfield Lake.

Back on the Evangeline Trail, the road continues to Kingston, another farming town specializing in dairy and fruit, particularly apples. Nearby is Clairmont Provincial Park, a picnic area and former residence of Nova Scotia's first Anglican bishop, Loyalist Dr. Charles Inglis. Nearby Auburn, with a population of only 402, is surrounded by cranberry bogs. Once an Acadian area, the rich farmlands were resettled by Loyalists in the 1790s.

From Auburn, off Route 1, a road leads to the Bay of Fundy and the town of Morden. Settled by James Morden in 1783, the town was originally called French Cross because of the large cross erected here in memory of the Acadian expulsion. Many Acadian refugees died here during the winter of 1756, where they were hiding from the British. The inscription on the cross, written in French, reads "On this site the Acadians from Belle Isle wintered in 1755 to 1756." In the spring of 1756, Pierre Melanson, with an Indian boy, crossed the bay for aid. On the return trip, Melanson died. The original cross was erected by the Acadians.

Off Routes 1 and 101, look for the town of Berwick, a bustling rural community with a bakery, fruit-packing warehouses and restaurants. Close to Berwick is the birthplace of Alfred C. Fuller, founder of the internationally known Fuller Brush Company. Born in 1885, Fuller came from modest roots but became a billionaire with his brush company. His home is a private residence with a huge, gothic-looking barn that houses crafts and antiques. (Fuller's rise to fame is particularly ironic for this author because one of my Nova Scotian relatives was a neighbor of Fuller's and they dated when they were young. However, when stern elders told my relative that Fuller would never amount to anything, she broke off the romance.)

Kentville, a fairly large community along the Evangeline Trail, was originally settled by New England Loyalists after the Acadian expulsion. The area was named for the Duke of Kent, Queen Victoria's father. The annual Annapolis Valley Apple Blossom Festival is held here every spring. Kentville is a four-corners kind of town, with highways intersecting both Route 12, which leads to the South Shore, and Route 359, which heads north to beautiful Cape Blomidon.

TO CAPE BLOMIDON

Route 359 crosses the Cornwallis River—known for its brown trout—and heads to Upper Dyke. The route then enters Centreville, an apple-growing region, and Halls Harbour, a former hiding place for privateers. Route 358 out of Centreville passes Port Williams, the Lookoff, Canning and Scots Bay. This area once belonged to the Micmac Indians. The area was then settled by the Acadians until their expulsion. Finally, the New England Planters took over and prospered on this minerally rich land. The drive out to Cape Blomidon is beautiful. Vast marshes and farms overlook the Minas Basin with its dramatic high and low tides. Cape Blomidon and Blomidon Provincial Park are excellent areas for swimming and picnicking. Both Cape Split and Cape Blomidon offer dramatic views of blood red cliffs dropping to the sea.

Cape Blomidon's past is tied to a Micmac legend about the mythical warrior Glooscap who lived here and protected the "children of light" (the Micmacs). One legend of Glooscap claims that he was a giant immortal who used the Minas Basin as a huge beaver pond, thus creating the numerous islands here. A more plausible legend speaks of him as a great warrior who tricked the Mohawks by leading them up the Minas Basin and attacking them from all sides. Because Cape Blomidon is well known for its semiprecious gemstones including agate, jasper and amethyst, the legend claims that Glooscap wore a necklace of amethysts. It is recorded that as early as 1400 A.D., bands of Micmacs were living here and making agate arrowheads. The legend says that Glooscap canoed to Newfoundland and met a strange but friendly tribe (the Vikings) and gave a woman with blue eyes and golden hair his necklace. He later found the necklace on an Indian brave who told of the death of the Viking tribe on the shores of the Northumberland Strait.

From Cape Blomidon (named by mariners who called it Blow Me Down Cape), you can see the distant Glooscap Trail along the Minas Channel and Cobequid Bay.

WOLFVILLE

This beautiful college town, with its unique architecture and energetic student population, is a fun place for a traveler to rest and get to know the community. Originally founded by New England Planters, Wolfville is the location of Acadia University, founded in 1838 by the Baptists of Nova Scotia. The town was originally called Mud Creek, but that was changed by two nieces of Postmaster Lisha DeWolfe, Jr., in 1830. They persuaded the government to allow them to change the name to Wolfville. With their affluent reserve, one can't really picture the residents here hailing from a place called Mud Creek!

Wolfville is the kind of town where walking is a pleasure—the architecture of homes and university buildings is reminiscent of Harvard Yard in Cambridge, Massachusetts. In the center of town, Willow Park is a vast area for walking and cycling. It's also the location of the tourist information office. The Wolfville Historical Museum at 171 Main Street has a vast collection of furniture and other artifacts from the eighteenth and nineteenth centuries. Also of interest is the Beveridge Arts Centre on the corner of Highland and Main Streets (on the Acadia University campus). The internationally renowned artist Alex Colville lives in Wolfville and some of his work is on permanent display at the museum.

Accommodations

In Wolfville, try: **The Birchcliff Bed & Breakfast** (84 Main Street, 542-3391, $35 single, $40 double, $50 includes full breakfast). Splendid views, open May 15 to August 31. **Tattingstone Inn** (434 Main Street, 542-7696, $78-98 main house, $70-85 carriage house, $125 per cottage). Heated swimming pool, licensed dining room, tennis court and music room. **Victoria's Historic Inn and Motel** (416 Main Street, 542-5744, $49 single, $59 double). Licensed dining room and close to town center. **Blomidon Inn** (127 Main Street, $39-80 single, $49-90 suites). Fireplace; honeymoon suite. Pricey. **Roselawn Cottages and Motel** (32 Main Street, 542-3420, $40-80 single, $50-90 double). Wheelchair accessible; full bath/shower; outdoor pool.

South of Wolfville, try: **The Farmhouse Inn Bed & Breakfast** (Exit 11 to Route 1 to Route 358 in Canning, 582-7900, $50 single, $52 double). Afternoon tea; library and lawn games; full country breakfast. **Country Squire Bed & Breakfast** (990 Main Street in Port Williams, 542-9125). Full breakfast; library and outdoor pool. **Fundy Trail Farms Bed & Breakfast** (on Route 360 in Berwick, 538-9481, $30 single, $35 double). Open year-round; full breakfast; family farm. **The Coach Stop Bed & Breakfast** (133 Granville Street, Bridgetown, 665-2869, $30 single, $40 double). Full country breakfast; shared bath/shower.

Campgrounds

Annapolis River Campground (56 Queen Street in Bridgetown, 665-4232, $8 night). Open May 15 to October 15. Ten units; camping on river; boat launch area. **Sherwood Forest Camping Park** (four miles west of Coldbrook). **Blomidon Provincial Park** (on Cobequid Bay north of Canning off Route 358, 678-9086, $8.50 night). Scenic view; campsites with kitchen shelter and fire grills; hiking trail. **Look-off Campground** (on North Mountain in Canning off Route 358, 582-3373, $9-12 night). Scenic views of Cape Split and Cape Blomidon; swimming pool, gift shop and canteen.

Dining

In Wolfville, try: **Tattingstone Inn** (434 Main Street, 542-7696). Licensed dining room featuring home cooking. **Blomidon Inn** (127 Main Street, 542-2291). Elegant dining; excellent reputation. **The Wolf's Lair Pub** on Main Street offers pub food, beer and wine. Popular with the university crowd, this is a friendly place with a lively atmosphere. **Chez La Vigne** (Main Street, 542-5077). French cuisine, fresh seafood and complete wine selection. Recommended.

South of Wolfville, try: **The K Kafe** (1065 Central Avenue, in Greenwood Mall, Greenwood, 765-2232). Good, inexpensive family restaurant. **Michael's Licensed Family Restaurant** (also in Greenwood Mall, 765-2600). Specializes in pizza, steaks and pasta. **Freddy's** (8772 Commercial Street, New Minas, 681-1454). Specialties are pizza and steak. **The White Spot Restaurant and Motel** (9060 Commercial Street, New Minas, 681-3244). Air-conditioned, licensed restaurant. **Gardner's Family Restaurant** (on Route 358, 582-3243). Light lunches to full home-cooked meals.

GRAND PRÉ NATIONAL HISTORIC PARK

Grand Pré or "Great Meadows" is an area that stretches east from the Acadian dikes to the shores of the Minas Basin. This encompasses Grand Pré National Historic Park, where Acadian settlers established homes in the 1600s. Because their ancestors had farmed the marsh-lands of Saintonge, Poitou and Aunis in France, these new settlers were attracted to the wet terrain and constructed 28,455 feet of dikes with logs and clay. Much of the land was reclaimed from the sea.

The Acadian farmers were very productive, and the lush dike-lands were perfect for wheat, rye, oats and peas. As in France, the landscape was bordered by willow trees. While some willows still remain on the lands around Grand Pré, there are no original buildings left: They were all destroyed during the Acadian expulsion in 1755. The Acadians might have lived on peacefully and prospered on these lands, but Britain and France were continually at war, forcing the Acadians to sign unfavorable treaties and choose alliances. Their reluctance to choose sides resulted in a large-scale deportation from their lands, causing great suffering and deprivation.

The expulsion of the Acadians from Nova Scotia is a tragic event in Canadian history, and the impact of the deportation is deeply felt at the Grand Pré National Historic Park. Here, the Acadian people have established a monument to record the deportation, as well as list the names of those families who were forced to leave. But the event could have been almost forgotten in history if the poignancy of the Acadian's plight had not been immortalized by the poet Henry Wadsworth Longfellow. Longfellow wrote of a woman, Evangeline, who lost her lover during the confusion of the deportations.

There is a bronze statue of Evangeline on the premises that was sculpted in Paris by Philippe Hebert, a noted Acadian sculptor. The statue must be circled clockwise to appreciate the effect of this work of art. Initially, you see a young woman's face, happy and strong. As you round the statue, she turns into a tired, old woman. The gaze is piercing as the tragic woman looks for Gabriel, lost to her somewhere in the swamplands of Louisiana. This statue overlooks the Memorial Chapel, which records the history of the Acadian expulsion.

My relatives grew up around Grand Pré, and I often recall seeing smudged black-and-white photos from the 1920s of my father's family picnicking around Grand Pré, all standing in front of Evangeline, smiling for the family portrait. I was doubly saddened when I first saw this beautiful statue, because Evangeline's people are lost forever and, for the most part, my Nova Scotian great uncles and grandparents are long gone as well.

The Memorial Chapel was built in 1922 on the site of the original Acadian Church of St. Charles. The steep roof and Romanesque windows reflect mid-eighteenth-century French architecture. The arched window has a stained glass piece installed in 1984 by Acadian artist Terry Smith-Lamothe. The glass piece depicts the expulsion, as Acadians were loaded onto dories and ships, leaving others behind on shore to never be seen again. Inside the chapel are oil paintings that chronicle the events leading to the expulsion. There is also a marble stone with an engraved list of the surnames of the deported families. The day I visited the memorial, a man found his family name on the list of the deported and was greatly moved by the discovery. Meanwhile, a group of girls sat quietly singing Acadian songs in clear voices. The entire area is a very contemplative place with a certain silent dignity.

The town of Grand Pré itself is very small but serves as the center of a wine-growing region. Grand Pré Wines, in business since 1970, offers tours daily. The winery is on the estate of an original Georgian Planter. Call 542-1470 for more information.

HORTONVILLE AND HANTSPORT

The fairly nondescript village of Hortonville was the landing spot for the first New Englanders to arrive at the Minas Basin. They came by ship in 1760 and took over the empty farmlands of the Acadians. The settlement of the Acadian lands was highly successful and the New Englanders prospered. A plaque in Hortonville mentions that "by 1780, Edmund Burke described the province as 'formed by the overflowings of the exuberant population of New England.'"

Nearby Hantsport is a quiet town, rich in history from the days of shipbuilding. Wooden ships were built on the banks of the Avon River, and were subsequently used to ship cargo all over the globe. At the public wharf at the end of Williams Street, you can view the high tides of the Minas Basin and wander around the natural dry docks to the former site of Churchill & Sons Shipyard. Hantsport is also noteworthy because it was the home of the Fullertons, the ancestors of yours truly.

The Churchill house in Hantsport was built in 1860 by the powerful Senator Ezra Churchill. Owner of the Churchill Shipyard, the house now contains a great deal of memorabilia from the Golden Age of Sail. The Marine Room has many details from the shipping industry of the late nineteenth century.

Hantsport is also the birthplace of William Hall, the first Canadian and the first black man to ever win the Victorian Cross. Hall's memorial is on the lawn of the Hantsport United Baptist Church.

WINDSOR

Windsor is called the "Gateway in and out of the Annapolis Valley" and, to top that, it is also exactly midway between the

Equator and the North Pole. Originally settled by Acadians in the early 1700s, the town became their temporary prison in 1755 as they awaited deportation by ships to faraway lands. After the expulsion, New England planters settled the area. Windsor is best known for its tidal bore and the exciting rafting trips available here. A tidal bore is the leading edge of an incoming tide, and it is quite a sight as it gushes up the Meander River. The point of the tidal bore rafting is to set out and ride the incoming tide for almost 18 miles upriver. It's a bit like surfing, but the presence of whirlpools makes it a real adventure. The most turbulent runs are during the high tides near the full moon. The trip costs $55 per person and reservations must be made in advance. You are on the water for about three hours. For more information contact Tidal Bore Rafting, Ltd., P.O. Box 893, Stellarton, Nova Scotia, Canada, (902) 755-5560 or 752-0899.

Historically, Windsor's past is tied to the settlement of the area by the Loyalists, after the Acadians were forced out. Fort Edward, built in 1750, served as an early defense for the English. Judge Thomas Haliburton, a native of Windsor, was the creator of Yankee pedlar Sam Slick, a fictional character who traveled the province and tried to swindle Nova Scotians. Slick's axioms have become commonplace phrases like "raining cats and dogs," "truth is stranger than fiction" and "quick as a wink." Windsor also has the distinction of being the center of the World Pumpkin Festival held annually on Thanksgiving Day (Canadian Thanksgiving).

Windsor sits at the crossroads with Route 14, which passes through Mount Martock, a winter ski resort, on its way to Chester on the South Shore. The Glooscap Trail begins nearby, on Route 14, heading north towards Brooklyn. The remainder of the Evangeline Trail continues to Three Mile Plain, Mount Uniacke and on to Bedford.

Accommodations

In Grand Pré, try: **Inn the Vineyard Bed & Breakfast** (off Exit 10, right on Grand Pré Road, 542-9554, $30-50 single, $45-55 double). Restored eighteenth-century heritage home. **The Clockmakers Inn Bed & Breakfast** (1399 King Street, Curry's Corner, 798-5265, $35 single, $40 double). Full breakfast; furnished with antiques. **The Meander Inn Bed & Breakfast** (153 Albert Street, Windsor, 798-2325, $35 single, $50 double). Full breakfast; fireplace in lounge.

Campgrounds

The Land of Evangeline Family Camping (Hantsport, Exit 10 on Highway 101, 542-5309, $13.50 night). Laundromat, fireplaces, hayrides and swimming pool. **Hants County Exhibition Trailer Park** (Wentworth Road, on Exhibition Grounds, 798-2011).

Dining

Horton Landing and Cafe (Exit 10 off Highway 101). Home-made food and nearby farm market. **Crimson and Clover** (Main Street, Hantsport, 684-3683). Tea Room and desserts. **Downeast Motel and Restaurant** (Exit 5 off Highway 101, in Windsor, 798-2522). Fully licensed restaurant; Canadian and Chinese cuisine.

THE GLOOSCAP TRAIL

T he Noel Shore, which runs from Windsor to Shubenacadie, is rarely visited by tourists, but it is along this coast that the highest tides in the world have been recorded. This is a region of Nova Scotia where rivers, basins and bays all converge with the incoming Fundy Tides, creating a dramatic rise and fall in water levels. The Noel Shore is also part of the Glooscap Trail, named after the legendary Indian who supposedly traded beads with the Vikings.

WINDSOR TO TRURO

Before following the coastal roads of the Minas Basin, the route from Windsor first crosses the Avon River, where a tidal estuary teems with marine life. This area is also full of gypsum, a relative of the chalk that makes up the white cliffs of Dover in England. Used to make plaster, the gypsum was once quarried by the local people and hauled by horses to the nearest port. Now the quarrying is done by two large mining corporations. After crossing the Kennycook River into Brooklyn, the route enters a rural area characterized by stone houses reminiscent of the farmhouses of rural England.

The coastal road of the Noel Shore was once populated by relatively isolated farmers and fishermen, but it is now more common for the residents to be commuters to Halifax. A highlight of this drive is a stop at Noel Head and Burntcoat Head, two headlands that take the brunt of the incoming Fundy tides. Each year, more and more of these red cliffs erode due to the powerful persistence of the water. By looking at a map of the Minas Basin, you can assess the power of the tides. Twice a day, 115 billion tons of water come tearing through the Minas Channel, which is less than 4 miles wide. The onrushing torrent fills the Minas Basin like a swimming pool, traveling at 15 miles an hour and heading straight for Burntcoat Head. The tide normally rises some 30 to 40 feet, although the record stands at 59 feet— set in the 1870s when the tide, moon and sea were aligned for danger.

The Noel Shore turns inland along the Shubenacadie River, passing the town of Maitland. Here is the home of William D. Lawrence, who in 1874 built the 80-foot-long *Great Ship,* one of the largest wooden ships built in Canada up to that time. Because of the tidal bore, the ship could be launched in the river, travel down the Minas Basin to the Bay of Fundy and beyond. The day when it was launched, neighbors gathered around to watch it sink, not believing that a ship so big could float. The Great Ship did float, however, and Lawrence used her until 1883, finally selling her to Norwegian interests. Incidentally, the ships along the Minas Basin had to be built strong, because when the tide was out they sat on their keels in the mud, a precarious place for any wooden vessel. At this point, the Glooscap Trail passes through the city of Truro.

TRURO

Called the "Hub of Nova Scotia," Truro has been a railroad town since 1858. The area around Truro is some of the oldest settled land in Canada—other Indian tribes lived here even before the arrival of the Micmacs. Truro was called *Cobequid* by the Micmacs and went on to become a large Acadian settlement, until the expulsion in 1755. Truro was eventually populated by a community of Northern Irish settlers and New Hampshire Loyalists—the latter came here in 1759. Today, Truro is a busy town, with a charming downtown area. A major attraction is beautiful Victoria Park, with a natural brook, streams, hiking trails, cycling routes and two waterfalls that reach some 50 feet. There is also a steep 200-step climb to Jacob's Ladder, which overlooks a gorge and the Salmon River in the distance.

Truro is also the place to get involved with tidal bore rafting. The Salmon River runs right through the center of town, and you can join a group and ride a wave of water in a Zodiac rubber boat moving upstream against an outgoing current. If you just want to witness the tidal bore phenomenon, call 426-5494 in Truro (DIAL-A-TIDE) so that you'll know the correct time to watch.

Accommodations/Dining

In Truro, **Tidal Bore Inn** (RR 1, 895-9241, $40-50 single, $50-55 double) has a licensed dining room and patio deck. **The Blue House Inn Bed & Breakfast** (43 Dominion Street, 895-4150, $30 single, $40 double) offers full breakfast and complimentary refreshments. **The Stonehouse Motel and Restaurant** (165 Willow Street, 893-9413,

$40 single, $50 double) has a licensed restaurant, units for handicapped and a senior's discount. In Maitland, **Foley House Inn Bed & Breakfast** (Highway 102, Exit 10 to Route 215, 261-2844, $40 single, $50 double) has a licensed dining room and full breakfast. For an all-you-can-eat lobster buffet, try **Rainbow Motel** (341 Prince Street, 893-9438). For quiet dining, **Stonehouse Inn** (165 Willow Street, (800) 561-7666) has home-cooked food and a coffee shop.

Campgrounds

In Shubenacadie, **Green Acres Camping** (Route 102, north on Route 215, 758-2177, $12) has washrooms, fishing, tidal-bore tours and hayrides. **Shubenacadie Provincial Wildlife Park** (off Highway 102 at Exit 11) is suited for day-use picnics, with its natural woodlands and wildlife display. **Shubenacadie Tidal Bore Park** (Highway 102, Exit 10 on Route 215, 758-2177) is a day-use park with tidal-bore and river-rapids boat tours. **Maitland Recreational Park** (Exit 10 to Route 215, 261-2704, $7) is an open campground with canteen.

Tidal Bore Rafting

To join a rafting trip, contact the tourism office in Truro or **Tidal Bore and Upriver Rafting** (RR 4, Shubenacadie, 758-2177 or 758-4066). Also try **Tidal Bore Rafting, Ltd.** (755-5560 or 752-0899). The latter is the organization that I went with and it was fun. You travel up the Shubenacadie River, charging over tides and getting close to whirlpools. The ride takes about three hours. It's exciting: Bring warm clothes and be prepared to get wet. The cost is $55 per person, lunch included.

FROM TRURO TO AMHERST—
THE PARRSBORO SHORE

The drive from Truro to Amherst along the coast is part of the Glooscap Trail, but locals most often call it the Parrsboro Shore or the Cobequid Shore. They take pride in living along one of Nova Scotia's least hospitable shores with its dramatic tides, infertile soil and remoteness from larger towns and cities. The locals, mostly from Scottish and Irish descent, refer to anyone who does not live on this shore as an "inlander."

The Parrsboro Shore from Truro passes towns that were well known for shipbuilding, such as Great Village, which was an important port of call from 1817 to 1891. Towns in this area like Londonderry (the earliest Nova Scotia boomtown) and Glenholme were once mining centers for iron ore.

When passing the town of Economy (the name is derived from the Micmac word *Kenomee,* meaning "long point jutting into the sea"), try the clams—they're claimed to be the "world's best." The conditions of the Minas Basin are perfect for clam digging. Farther west, you pass Five Islands, a popular tourist destination with campgrounds and beaches. There are five small islands called Moose, Diamond, Long, Egg and Pinnacle. Legend refers to the giant Glooscap throwing handfuls of sod at a large beaver who had mocked his powers, thus forming the small islands. Moose Island is of particular interest to adventurers, as there is said to be a pirate's treasure here. You can walk to Moose Island at low tide.

PARRSBORO

Parrsboro, the largest town on the Minas Basin, has all the amenities for tourists. This was once a boomtown for the shipping industry. Fish, timber and coal were the town's main exports. Today, Parrsboro is a quiet town frequented by visiting "rockhounds" who come to look for zeolites (semiprecious stones of agate and amethyst) found along the shores here. There is a Geological Mineral and Gem Museum in Parrsboro featuring a collection of semiprecious stones and a collection of dinosaur fossils. Nearby stands the giant statue of Glooscap who, legend has it, created the Fundy tides and scattered his grandmother's jewelry (the semiprecious stones) along the Minas shore.

A road north of Parrsboro leads to the 85-square-mile Chignecto Game Sanctuary, which is on the River Herbert watershed. If you have time, bypass Route 2 and follow Route 209 around the remote region near Cape d'Or and Cape Chignecto. This far-flung bit of Nova Scotia is a good place to watch the Fundy Tides. It's also excellent for digging clams and finding dulse, an edible seaweed that grows in cold water. Advocate Harbour, at the southwestern tip, was spotted by Samuel de Champlain in 1607. During the Expulsion of the Acadians in 1755, the French at Belleisle (near Annapolis Royal), with help from the Micmacs, sailed across the Minas Channel and settled in Refugee Cove, near Cape d'Or Lighthouse. There is still a lighthouse keeper here who welcomes visitors and will give a tour of his lighthouse.

Route 209 turns into a dirt road north of Sand River but becomes highway again at Joggins. From Joggins, it is a fairly quick drive to Amherst. Before reaching Amherst, you may want to detour through Springhill, a former mining town and the hometown of internationally known pop singer Anne Murray, of "Snowbird" fame. She was a school teacher in Nova Scotia before embarking on her singing career. Springhill is a rather sad place, with seemingly more monuments than people. The town was the site of large-scale coal mining that began in 1872. There was a 4,000-foot mine here that was the deepest in Canada. The monuments around Springhill are not only for the war dead, but commemorate three major mining disasters that are detailed at the Springhill Miner's Museum. The first disaster occurred in 1891, when 125 miners were lost. The next two occurred in 1956, when an explosion killed 39, and in 1958 when a massive earth disturbance killed 76.

AMHERST

Amherst is a junction town, bordering New Brunswick and sitting astride several possible routes towards the center of Nova Scotia: Highway 104 and Routes 2, 4 and 6. Amherst has that red brick look of a former bustling mill town of the 1800s. The town has at least one unusual claim to fame—it was the location of a prisoner of war camp where Leon Trotsky was jailed briefly in 1917. The town was named after Baron Jeffrey Amherst (1717-1797), who led a successful Louisbourg expedition in 1758 and received the surrender of Montreal to the English in 1760. Amherst, Massachusetts, site of Amherst College, was named after the same man. Just west of Amherst is Fort Lawrence, Nova Scotia's inland gateway where a stoic bagpiper dressed in his clan's tartan greets incoming visitors via New Brunswick.

Accommodations

In Amherst, **National Bed & Breakfast Keilor Homestead** (RR 6, Exit 3, 667-5513, $35 single, $40 double) offers full breakfast and evening snack. Other options include: **Auberge Wandlyn Inn** (Exit Highway 104 at Victoria Street, 667-0475, $55-95) open year-round;

---

licensed dining room. **Chignecto Motel** (Exit 2 off Highway 104, 667-3386, $32 single, $35 double). Licensed dining room; home-style cooking. In Springhill, **The Rollways Motel** (9 Church Street, 597-3713 $35 single, $45 double) is open year-round. Parrsboro has the **Glooscap Motel** (north on Route 2, 254-3135, $45 single, $50 double) with fishing, hiking and lake swimming. **The Maple Inn Bed & Breakfast** (17 Western Avenue, 254-3735, single $40, double $50) is open year-round; serves full breakfast.

Campgrounds

Sand Point Campground (Five Islands, 254-2755, $10) has ocean views, boating, swimming, clam digging and a seafood restaurant. **Glooscap Park Campground** (Parrsboro, 254-2529, $10) is an open and wooded campground. **Loch Lomond Tent and Trailer Park** (Highway 104, Exit 4, 667-3890, $10) has a swimming pool, boat rental and pay showers.

Dining

In Amherst, because the choices are slim, your best bet is to try a hotel dining room. For home cooking, try the **Chignecto Dining Room** (LaPlanche Street, 667-3331) or the licensed dining room at the **Wandyln Inn** (Victoria Street, 667-3331). In Springhill, you'll find that special (and bland) combination called Canadian-Chinese food at **Jade Palace Restaurant** (2 Fir Street, 597-3009), which has a licensed dining room and take-out service. In Parrsboro, **Stowaway Inn and Restaurant** (254-3371) specializes in seafood.

THE SUNRISE TRAIL

T he Northumberland Shore, called the Sunrise Trail by the tourist authority, runs east along the Northumberland Strait. As you drive, the towns gradually take on a Scottish flavor, for the Scots first settled along the Northumberland Shore when they arrived in the 1700s. Towns like New Glasgow, Gairloch, Glengarry, and McGregor have a clear Scottish ring to their names. You could spend your entire vacation poking along the Northumberland Shore, with its 40 or more beaches and warm water for swimming. Water temperatures along this coast average 70 degrees in summer—vastly warmer than the frigid waters of the Bay of Fundy or the Atlantic on the South Shore. From this shore, you can look out over the Northumberland Strait and see Prince Edward Island and New Brunswick in the distance.

AMHERST TO NEW GLASGOW

Many visitors travel directly from Amherst towards Cape Breton on the Trans-Canada Highway, perhaps stopping only in Antigonish before crossing the Canso Causeway. By taking the shore route, though, you can stop in places like *Tidnish* (the word means "paddle" in Micmac) and *Lorneville* (named for the Marquis of Lorne). The town of *Pugwash* (Micmac for "shallow water") is also worth stopping at, with its beautiful harbor at the mouth of the Pugwash River.

Pugwash was once an active shipping, fishing and mining community. It was also formerly the site of the world-famous Thinker's Conference, organized by Cyrus W. Eaton, one of America's leading financiers. Folks still flock to Pugwash for the Gathering of the Clans and the July 1 celebration of the town's Scottish heritage. On that day, all street signs are displayed in Gaelic.

This beautiful route leads next to Tatamagouche, a farming and fishing town at the mouth of the French and Waugh rivers, which empty into Tatamagouche Bay. (In Micmac, the word *Tatamagouche* means "a meeting place of the waters.")

The Sunrise Trail continues into Pictou County, a traditionally Scottish area and location of the first Scottish settlement. If you are traveling the Trans-Canada, at the Colchester-Pictou County border you will pass Mount Thom—a kind of ethnic dividing line in Nova Scotia. To the west of Mount Thom, most of the early settlers were New Englanders, English and Irish. But to the east, the early pioneers were Scottish. From here on, the people are different, the landscape is different, and the climate is rougher. In 1801, 700 Scottish Highlanders sailed to Nova Scotia on the *Sarah,* and those who survived settled around Mount Thom. The very first Scots to arrive in Nova Scotia, however, sailed into Pictou Harbour on September 15, 1773, aboard the *Hector.* There were 33 families in all and 25 unmarried men. The Scots were escaping the oppression of the highland clearances after they and their Bonnie Prince Charlie lost their war against the English.

The Scots in Scotland had been forbidden to play their bagpipes or wear their tartans. But with the advent of Scottish immigration to Nova Scotia and their subsequent freedom, the Scots resumed celebrating their traditional festivals and language. The preservation of these rituals makes Nova Scotia more Scottish than Scotland at times. In 1923, Pictou County celebrated its 150th anniversary of the landing of the *Hector* by erecting a monument (still standing) to those pioneers in Pictou's Market Square.

Nearby Caribou on the coast is the terminus of the Caribou/ Wood Island year-round ferry service to Prince Edward Island. If you have a chance, this is a beautiful crossing and a great way to get to "P.E.I.," as it is commonly called by all Maritimers. If you are taking the ferry from Caribou, try to arrive early in the morning. The ferry is small and holds relatively few cars. However, the tourist traffic at peak season is phenomenal, with everyone lined up to cross over to Prince Edward Island. It can be a real hassle, but it's well worth making the trip. Just arrive early.

New Glasgow was originally settled by Scottish highlanders in the 1700s, and grew in importance along with coal mining, steel making and shipbuilding. The first Nova-Scotian-built steamship, the *Richard Smith,* was launched here. This is also the site of the Festival of the Tartans that is held in mid-July every year with traditional highland music and Scottish games—which are not for the weak! Just south of New Glasgow is the town of Stellarton, Canada's pioneer coal-mining center and railroad town. Coal was discovered here in 1798. The first steam engine was operated here in 1827, and the first iron rails in North America were cast here a year later.

BETWEEN NEW GLASGOW AND ANTIGONISH

For an interesting coastal drive, follow the Sunrise Trail from New Glasgow around Cape George towards Antigonish. This route, called the "Mini Cabot Trail," follows St. Georges Bay with its excellent beaches and splendid views. You'll pass through *Merigomish*, which is a Micmac word for "place of merrymaking." (The Micmacs once gathered at Merigomish to compete in summer sports of running, leaping and wrestling. Later, around 1784, Merigomish was settled by Loyalists.) You'll then pass Malignant Cove, which got its ominous name from the British warship *HMS Malignant,* which was wrecked here during the American Revolution. As you round Cape George, you will see Ballantynes Cove and the lighthouse, which was first built in 1895. From the lighthouse you get a splendid view of Cape Breton and Prince Edward Island. Continue south past Cribbens Point until you reach the lovely town of Antigonish.

ANTIGONISH

As a seven year old, I was made aware of my Scottish heritage when my family arrived in Antigonish in our station wagon in 1967 during the town's annual Highland Games celebration. I was mesmerized by a Scottish sword dance at the local high school, and I remember watching in awe my first parade led by men in kilts playing bagpipes. My sisters and I got our tartan kilts and our Scottish berets in Antigonish, and we wore them proudly around town to the obvious approval of the locals.

Antigonish is a Micmac word meaning "the place where branches were broken off" (by bears gathering beechnuts). The town is the site of St. Francis Xavier University, which offers courses in Gaelic and Celtic studies. The highlight of the year in Antigonish is the above-mentioned annual Antigonish Highland Games held in early July. The games have been held annually since 1861. The festival offers the very best in Scottish music, dance and sports. Among the most popular events is the ancient Scottish sport called the caber toss, in which competitors hurl heavy tree trunks. There is nothing fabricated about this Scottish celebration; these games are very true to the people's hearts. Don't be surprised if you find the spirit infectious and end up marching around town in a kilt like everybody else.

Antigonish is the home of the Clan Thompson Pipe Band and the Scotia Highland Dancers. Both groups perform throughout Canada and in Scotland but are always present for the games.

FROM ANTIGONISH TO CANSO CAUSEWAY

The Sunrise Trail meets the Trans-Canada Highway after leaving Antigonish, but there are still plenty of worthwhile detours to the beaches and coastal enclaves of St. Georges Bay. The small village of Tracadie on the coast was originally mentioned by Samuel de Champlain in 1631, who called it Tregate.

Monastery is an interesting place. Named by Trappist monks in 1825, the monastery they established here now belongs to the Augustinian Order, who took it over in 1938. The chapel is open to the public. The town of Havre Boucher is next, named for Captain Francis Boucher though he spent no more than a winter here in 1759. The last stop before the Canso Causeway is Auld Cove. Before the Canso Causeway was built, a ferry operated across the Strait of Canso between Auld Cove and Balache Point.

There is plenty of sports fishing in this area. St. Georges Bay is rich in large fish like bluefin tuna, which congregate north of the Causeway and feed on mackerel. In fact, a native Prince Edward Islander caught a world-record giant bluefin tuna here.

Accommodations

In Antigonish, if you plan to visit during the Highland Games, you most likely will have difficulty getting a room unless you've made reservations in advance. However, Antigonish has more accommodations for tourists than most towns in this area. **Auberge Wandlyn Inn** (158 Main Street, (800) 561-0000, $55 single, $80 double) is open year-round with a licensed lounge and dining room, lawn games and a swimming pool. **Best Western Claymore Inn** (Church Street, (800) 528-1234, $70 single, $85 double) has a swimming pool, sauna, hot tub, Scottish gift shop and piano bar.

Other options: **Chateau Motel** (112 Post Road, 863-4842, $50 single, $55 double). Cottages and cabins; rustic setting. **Days Inn** (41 James Street, 863-4212, $50 single, $55 double). **MacIsaac Bed & Breakfast** (18 Hillcrest Street, 863-2947, $30 single, $40 double). Full breakfast; 3 rooms; shared baths. **Whidden's Motel Apartments H** (11 Hawthorne Street, 863-3736, $55 single, $65 double). Full bath/shower; open June to August.

In New Glasgow, **Heather Motor Hotel** (Stellarton, Exit 24, Highway 104, 752-8401) has a licensed dining room, lounge and room service. **Journey's End Motel** (740 Westville Road, 755-6450, $50 single, $60 double) is open year-round with 62 rooms. Also try the **Tara Motel** (917 East River Road, 752-8458, $60 single, $70 double). Licensed restaurant, open year-round. In nearby Merigomish, **Country Inn** (RR 1, Route 245, $30 single, $40 double) is open year-round; fully licensed restaurant. Also near New Glasgow, **Harbourside Inn Bed & Breakfast** (Exit 1A towards Trenton, 755-2080, $37 single, $42 double) is worth trying.

In Pictou, **Braeside Inn** (80 Front Street, 485-4288, $60 single, $70 double) has rooms overlooking the harbor; summer deck dining. **Pictou Lodge** (on Braeshore Road, east of Pictou, two and one-quarter miles from the ferry, 485-4322, $75-150, rates available for one-bedroom units) has a licensed dining room, units with fireplace and kitchenette, ocean swimming, canoes and rowboats. **Munro's Bed & Breakfast** (66 High Street, 485-8382, $25 single, $32 double) offers full breakfast and three rooms with shared bath. In Pugwash, **Blue Heron Inn Bed & Breakfast** (Durham Street, 243-2516, $40 single, $50 double) has five rooms with shared bath; continental breakfast.

Campgrounds

In Antigonish, there's **A. E. Whidden Trailer Court** (Highway 104, Exit 31, 32, or 34 to Route 245, 863-3736, $14) with wooded campgrounds on the river, fireplaces and a swimming pool. **Brierly Brook** (near Antigonish, at Brierly Brook, 863-4141, $10) is both an open and wooded campground with monthly and weekly rates. **Cranberry Campground** (on Merigomish Harbour, 926-2222, $9) has ocean swimming, hiking trails and bird-watching.

Near New Glasgow, **King's Head Campground** (on ocean at Little Harbour on Route 289, 752-3631, $13) is located on the beach with swimming and clam digging available. **Harbour Light Trailer Court and Family Camping Grounds** (in Pictou, three miles east of town, 485-5733, $11) overlooks the ocean.

Dining

In Antigonish, many hotels have licensed restaurants, but there are only a few independent restaurants. **Farmer Brown's Family Restaurant** (23 East Main Street) features fish and chips, clams and good breakfasts. **Moonlight Restaurant** (Main Street, 863-3667) has Canadian-Chinese fare, everything from spring rolls to french fries. **China Cup Tea Room** (95 College Street) features seafood and large portions. It's expensive. In New Glasgow, **MacDonald's Family Restaurant** (700 East River Road, 755-4742) has home-cooked meals, homemade biscuits and jam. **Smitty's Family Restaurant** (980 East River, 752-0300) and **Sam's Restaurant and Lounge** (255 Ford Street, 752-5655) offer basic food and good prices. In Pictou, **Homestead Restaurant** (Central West River, 952-2433) has basic home-cooked meals. **Braeside Inn** (80 Front Street, 485-5046) has a nice view, a comfortable dining room and a famous Sunday brunch. **Braeside Inn** was recommended in *Where to Eat in Canada*. **Fougère's** (on the way to the Prince Edward Island ferry, 485-6984) is something of a gourmet restaurant with fresh seafood, lobster and a licensed dining room overlooking the Northumberland Strait.

CAPE BRETON ISLAND

I have travelled around the globe. I have seen the Canadian and American Rockies, the Alps and the Highlands of Scotland, butfor simple beauty Cape Breton outrivals them all," said Alexander Graham Bell.

And the immense popularity of Cape Breton Island among tourists confirms that modern travelers agree. The traffic jams along the Cabot Trail and the mob at the lookout points can be frustrating, yet the vast network of hiking trails, campsites and beaches makes it fairly easy to avoid the crowds and simply enjoy those steep, dramatic highlands.

One of North America's most scenic regions, Cape Breton was settled by Scottish highlanders in the early 1800s. It is one of the few-places outside of the British Isles and Ireland where Gaelic is still spoken and where livelihoods are made in traditional ways, despite the changes ushered in by twentieth-century life. Cape Breton is made up of four counties that border upon the Bras d'Or Lake, an inland sea that is 50 miles long and 20 miles wide. The Bras d'Or Lake is a favorite of intrepid yachtsmen who sail north from Halifax in summer to cruise along the calm waters of this vast waterway. The region supports a vast array of wildlife—most notably, the bald eagle, this region being their main breeding ground on the east coast.

Cape Breton was originally inhabited by Micmac Indians, who took advantage of the abundant fishing and hunting around the Bras d'Or Lake region. Today, there are four large Micmac reservations here at Whycocomagh, Eskasoni (the largest reserve in Nova Scotia), Wagmatcook and Chapel Island. Acadians settled in Cape Breton in the early 1700s, and a large community at Cheticamp still retains the language and customs so unique to these people. But the background of the majority of Cape Bretoners is Scottish—primarily highland Scots who settled these lands after fleeing the repressions of landlords and highland clearances in their native Scotland. The land of Cape Breton appealed to these rugged people, who raised sheep, mined and fished the waters, retaining their Gaelic language and customs. Once you cross the Canso Causeway into Cape Breton, the inhabitants no longer refer to themselves as Nova Scotians; they are Cape Bretoners, fiercely loyal to their scattered islands.

Three quarters of Cape Bretoners live in "the Sydneys," seven or eight towns that make up the backbone of industrial Cape Breton. The area around Sydney and Glace Bay in northeastern Cape Breton once thrived, but as the mining and steel industries declined, so too did the fortunes of many Cape Bretoners. Work, or lack of it, is a constant topic of conversation among Cape Bretoners. Sadly, most of them are forced to go to Toronto or farther west to find employment. Like Newfoundlanders, Cape Bretoners working in distant Canadian or American cities will seek each other out and talk of home and the good times they had there.

For the convenience of tourists, Cape Breton's roads are divided into four "trails," the Ceilidh Trail, the Cabot Trail, the Marconi Trail and the Fleur-de-lis Trail. The most popular drive is the Cabot Trail, named after the explorer John Cabot who landed at Cape Breton on June 23, 1497. Once ashore, Cabot unfurled a royal banner and claimed the entire area for England. At the time, Cabot believed that he had discovered the northeastern coast of Asia. Getting to China from here is a bit of a trek—but the Cabot Trail does pass through the Cape Breton Highlands National Park, a beautiful, windswept wilderness with fantastic views of the cliffs and the sea.

Undoubtedly, the most dramatic scenery along the Cabot Trail is on the western side from Cheticamp to Pleasant Bay, after which the trail turns inland and crosses to the eastern side of Cape Breton, which possesses a gentler beauty. Traveling west to east along the Cabot Trail is the most logical itinerary because along the steep cliffs climbing towards Pleasant Bay you'll be hugging the inside of the road, which is somewhat safer. A major attraction along the Cabot Trail is the town of Baddeck, nestled by Great Bras d'Or Lake. This was the summer home of Alexander Graham Bell, a Scotsman, whose inventions—including the telephone and hearing devices for the deaf—are world-renowned. Bell experimented with hydrofoils, kites and aircraft at his summer home in Baddeck, and locals were often involved in assisting him with his numerous experiments. His house is still occupied by his descendants, who continue to summer here each year.

THE CEILIDH TRAIL

Beginning in Port Hastings, the Ceilidh Trail (pronouced kay-lee) is the first of many scenic drives in Cape Breton.

You travel the Ceilidh Trail to reach Margaree Harbour, where the dramatic cliffs and scenery of the Cabot Trail begin. While many tourists take the Trans-Canada Highway to Baddeck and the Cabot Trail, the Ceilidh Trail, passing through Inverness County, offers a better introduction to the rugged character of Cape Breton. For along this route you will meet more locals, hear more Gaelic and encounter less traffic. Because the Inverness shoreline runs along the Northumberland Strait, the water is warm and there are some 17 long, sandy beaches to enjoy, plus two freshwater beaches along Lake Ainslie.

The area north of Long Point is called the district of Judique, and includes Judique South, Judique, Judique North, Judique Intervale and Little Judique. Judique (or Shoodique as some locals call it) was first settled and named by Acadians, but Highland Scots took over the land when four families from the Hebrides Islands arrived in 1776. In mid-July, there is a Scottish heritage celebration with Judique-on-the-Floor Days. In this European-style dance, a caller shouts "Judique on the floor! Who'll pull him off?" as the participants spin around with an intricate step and plenty of laughter.

Port Hood, the county seat of Inverness, is best known for its warm water and sandy beaches. Nearby Port Hood Island was quarried by the French in the 1700s for stone to build the famous Fortress of Louisbourg. Route 19 continues to Mabou, another Scottish community where the Gaelic language is still taught in schools. Mabou is the home of Coisir an Eilean (an Island Chorus), who perform Gaelic songs and stories around Cape Breton. On Canada Day, July 1, a Mabou Ceilidh and Scottish picnic features traditional music and dance. At nearby Glenville, you'll find the Elenora Distillery, North America's only distillery of single-malt Scotch whiskey. There is an inn and restaurant near the "still," which stands by a peaceful brook.

Heading towards the town of Inverness on Route 19, look for an interesting detour down a dirt road to Sight Point. From here, there is an open, windswept trail to McDonald Glen. The hike is rugged, but it gives you a chance to peer over the vast cliffs of Cape Breton, down to the distant sea. The walk takes about three hours round-trip, and you need to be accustomed to good, long hikes if you plan to tackle it.

Inverness, named after lovely Inverness in Scotland, is the largest town on the Ceilidh Trail. There is an excellent beach here as well as restaurants and accommodations. Inverness was once a mining town, and some of the coal company houses still stand. There is a Miners

Museum with exhibits that provide insight into the struggles of the miners against the demands of the large companies who owned the mines.

From Inverness, you can drive on to Dunvegan, named after Dunvegan on the Isle of Skye in Scotland. Near Dunvegan is the small community of St. Rose, birthplace of the Honorable Angus L. MacDonald, premier of Nova Scotia until his death in 1954. As with clans of the Scottish highlanders, the surnames of Cape Bretoners tend to be associated with particular regions. During my visit, I met three different men with the name Angus MacDonald, and they were probably a part of the original MacDonald clan from St. Rose. In some areas, you meet many MacLeods; in others, the names MacKenzie or MacInnis are ever present. Whatever their surnames, all Cape Bretoners seem to be united in their friendliness and their belief that they would rather be from Cape Breton than anywhere else in the world.

After Dunvegan and St. Rose, the Ceilidh Trail reaches Margaree Harbour and Route 19 ends. At this point, the Cabot Trail begins.

Accommodations

Port Hastings is the first stop after crossing the Canso Causeway. Although most tourists prefer to travel onward towards the Cabot Trail, you may want to stop here at the popular **Mackenzie Inn** (junction of Highway 105 and Route 4, 625-2283, $55 single, $60 double), which has a swimming pool, covered sundeck, coffee shop and recreational area. **Keddy's Inn** (junction of Highways 104, 105, and Route 19, 625-0460, $65 single, $75 double) is also a convenient overnight stop. In Port Hood, **Haus Treuburg Guest House, Restaurant and Cottages** (Central Avenue, Port Hood, 787-2116, $55 single, $70 double) is recommended with its French and Italian restaurant, cottages with views of the sea and full breakfast. Or try **Lighthouse Cottages** (Route 19 near Judique, south of Port Hood, 787-2787, $55 single, $60 double). There is ocean swimming at a splendid beach in front of the cottages. Slightly farther north, you can stay right near the only single malt distillery in Canada at the **Glenora Distillery** (5 miles north of Mabou on Route 19, 258-2662, $75 single, $85 double). You can tour the distillery, eat in the licensed dining room or visit the pub. In Mabou, **Ceilidh Cottages** (West Mabou Road, 945-2486, $65 daily, $350 weekly) has tennis courts and a heated pool.

At Inverness, the popular **Inverness Lodge Hotel and Motel** (Central Avenue, 258-2193, $50 single, $55 double) offers a licensed dining room, ocean swimming and proximity to town. The **Inverness Beach Village** (two miles north on Route 19, 258-2653, $55-70 single/double) has deep-sea fishing, ocean swimming, tennis and windsurfing.

Campgrounds

At Port Hood, **Island View Campground** (open campground on beach, 787-2803, $12) and **Ceilidh Trailer Park** (West Mabou Road in Mabou, 945-2486, $14) feature swimming, tennis and a canteen. In Inverness, **Inverness Beach Village** (on Route 19 along the beach, 258-2653, $10) has beachfront camping sites, windsurfing rentals and tennis courts.

Dining

Besides the dining rooms listed in the accommodations section, try the **Inverness Chowder House** (Route 19, Inverness, 258-2545) for chowders, English fish and chips and other seafood. Nearby, try **Kayla's Restaurant** (258-2784) with a licensed dining room and a full menu with fish and lobster.

THE CABOT TRAIL

The Cabot Trail is one of North America's most scenic drives. Dangerous in winter, exhilarating on a crystal-clear summer day, this coastal road with precipitous curves dropping hundreds of feet to the restless Atlantic is a highlight of any visit to Nova Scotia. The trail begins for many in Baddeck. People often drive northeast towards Ingonish and Neil's Harbour, rounding the highlands from east to west. But I prefer to head northwest towards Margaree Harbour and Cheticamp.

BADDECK

Baddeck, a beautiful town situated on the Cabot Trail and the Bras d'Or Lake, is easily reached along the Trans-Canada Highway. Baddeck's simple beauty attracted the great inventor Alexander Graham Bell, who came here in the summer of 1885 en route to a summer holiday in Newfoundland. Traveling by steamer through the

Bras d'Or Lake with his wife Mabel, Bell was captivated by the region. "The Bras d'Or is the most beautiful saltwater lake I have ever seen," he observed. The Bells cut short their trip to Newfoundland and settled in at Baddeck, where they continued to summer for the rest of their lives. Mabel said, "We would be content to stay here many weeks just enjoying the lights and shades on all the hills and isles and lakes." Baddeck is still as beautiful as it was when the Bells saw it more than 100 years ago. Though far more touristy than in the days of steamers and railroads, the Bras d'Or Lake region seems to have escaped development, and Baddeck, with its lighthouse, wooden boats at anchor and still waters, is absolutely captivating.

Although closed to the public, Alexander Graham Bell's home—a sprawling mansion on a high peninsula called Red Head—is within view from the public docks at Baddeck. He named his home Beinn Bhreagh (pronounced ben bray-ah) which is Gaelic for "beautiful mountain." On this property he carried out numerous experiments. With a hydrofoil, he broke the world water-speed record. Here, Bell also designed and built the *Silver Dart*, the first aircraft to fly in Canada or anywhere else in the British Empire. The Silver Dart took off over the ice of the Bras d'Or Lake on February 23, 1909. Bell's impact on the community was far-reaching, for he brought some fascinating people to his home in Baddeck. As he said during his aviation experiments from 1907 to 1909, "So, there we were, living in my house—myself, an elderly man, surrounded by brilliant young men, each an expert in his own field."

The Bell Museum on the northern end of town is well worth a look, for it chronicles the inventor's life. Adults often spend quite a long time at the museum, which can get a little dull for children (but intrigues the rest of us). One of the last photos of Bell shows him as an old man, on the boat pier beneath his beloved Beinn Bhreagh, looking at the sky, perhaps contemplating a future that he would not be part of. Alexander Graham Bell died at Beinn Bhreagh on August 2, 1922, and was buried on the top of the mountain above his Baddeck home.

The government wharf in Baddeck is the center of much of the town's activity—particularly in summer when yachts from all over the Atlantic coast tie up and gather supplies for their cruises throughout the Bras d'Or Lake. There is a free shuttle boat that ferries people to Kidston Beach, a small island across the harbor where a lighthouse is located.

In July, the Bras d'Or Yacht Club holds its annual racing regatta, an event that has taken place since 1904.

Accommodations

Baddeck has plenty of rooms for tourists, some in simple bed & breakfasts, others in full-blown resorts. The well-known **Inverary Inn Resort** (Exit 8 to Route 205 and Shore Road, 295-2674, $60-120 single/double) is very popular. I stayed at the Inverary Inn as a seven year old, and its cottages and comfortable dining room overlooking the misty Bras d'Or Lake seemed greatly changed when I viewed them again as an adult. Where there was once a grassy field, there is now a tennis court, a new hotel complex, two licensed restaurants and a huge parking lot.

In the center of Baddeck, try the **Telegraph House** (Chebucto Street, 295-9988, $50-70 single, $50-80 double). Run by a friendly family, the Telegraph House has a library and lounge, and a dining room serving breakfast, lunch and dinner. Also try **Silver Dart Lodge** (Shore Road, 295-2340, $55-80 single, $60-90 double) with live Scottish entertainment, a licensed dining room and lakeside views. **Sealladh Aluinn Bed & Breakfast** (Route 205, Shore Road, 295-2807, $30 single, $35 double) is also good.

Campgrounds

Baddeck Cabot Trail K.O.A. Campground (five miles west of Baddeck on Highway 105, 295-2288, $14) is a wooded area on a river, with fishing, children's programs, trail and riverboat tours. **Bras d'Or Lake Campground** (three miles west of Baddeck, 295-2329, $12) has organized tours, a swimming pool and a recreation hall. **Silver Spruce Resort** (five miles west of Baddeck, 295-3036, $12) has a boat launch, free showers and a heated swimming pool.

Dining

Try the **Bell Buoy Restaurant** (on the waterfront near government wharf, Chebucto Street, 295-2581). They have fresh seafood, home-baked bread and homemade ice cream. For a bit more local color, try **Yellow Cello Cafe** (Chebucto Street, across the street from Bell Buoy) for take-out pizza, sandwiches and breakfasts. A special place for lobster lovers is the **Baddeck Lobster Suppers** (center of town in the former Canadian Legion Hall, 295-3307) with specials on lobster and chowder. With red-checked tablecloths, this licensed dining room is a great place for dinner and is popular with both locals and tourists.

FROM BADDECK TO CHETICAMP

This is a beautiful drive, from Baddeck through the Margaree Valley towards the coast. On reaching Margaree Harbour, on the west coast of Cape Breton, look for the old schooner, the *Marion Elizabeth*, docked in the harbor here. It was built by the famous Smith and Rhuland Shipyards of Lunenburg, the same company that built the *Bluenose*. The *Marion Elizabeth*, built in 1918, is now a public museum and restaurant. The Cabot Trail intersects the Ceilidh Trail here, crossing the Margaree River into Belle Côte and continuing north to Cap Lemoine. From here you'll see the distant highlands and will most likely not hear any English spoken until you get past Cheticamp. The route is exciting, and the windswept hills overlooking the Northumberland Strait and Gulf of St. Lawrence are beautiful and remote. The approach to Cheticamp is a series of turns and twists. Once you pull into this bustling community, you will hear Acadian French and feel like you're in a coastal village in Normandy.

CHETICAMP

Cheticamp is an Acadian fishing town on the Gulf of St. Lawrence, where an active fleet plies the rich waters of the Gulf during the summer months. The Acadians here are ancestors of the original settlers who were expelled from the Annapolis valley. When you wander around Cheticamp, listen to and observe the locals. Their appearance is as Nova Scotian as the rest, but the rugged burr of Acadian French is heard instead of English. Shopkeepers, bank tellers and just about everybody else in Cheticamp is French-speaking. (The employees at the tourist information office do speak English, however.)

Cheticamp is in a beautiful setting at the foot of the Cape Breton highlands and nestled by an inland harbor that is protected from the fierce Gulf of St. Lawrence weather by Cheticamp Island. At Cheticamp, you can join a whale-watching cruise to where minke, fin and humpback whale have been sighted. On Main Street, visit the Acadian Museum, which offers a small display of Acadian artifacts and demonstrations in wool carding, spinning, weaving and rug hooking. There is Acadian food available here, which is prepared on the spot. Before entering the town of Cheticamp, you'll pass a home with a series of tall, scarecrowlike dolls standing in formation on the front lawn. A native of Cheticamp makes these dolls for fun and profit, and they are meant to be caricatures of his Cheticamp neighbors. The house is on the right-hand side of the road driving in from Margaree Harbour.

Accommodations

In Margaree Harbour, there's **Duck Cove Inn** (junction of Ceilidh and Cabot Trails, 235-2658, $55 single, $65 double), offering ocean swimming and whale-watching cruises. The inn has good access for the handicapped to the dining room and rooms. Another favorite is the **Whale Cove Summer Village** (two miles south of Margaree Harbour on Route 219, 235-2202, $60-65 one-bedroom cottage, $70-85 two-bedroom cottage). There's a sandy beach nearby, hiking trails and ocean swimming.

In Cheticamp, try **Laurie's Motel** (Main Street, 224-2400, $70-80 single, $75-85 double). Laurie's is a charming place with a licensed dining room, cocktail area and outdoor patio. Other options: **Ocean View Motel, Ltd.** (Main Street, 224-2313, $50 single, $60 double). Bilingual; six motel units; barbecue pits. **Acadian Motel** (Main Street, 224-2640, $50 single, $60 double). Sixteen units with full bath. In nearby Pleasant Bay, **Beachside Motel** (224-2467), on the road to Cape Breton Highlands National Park, has a licensed dining room and weekly rates.

Campgrounds

Within the national park, there are two campgrounds: **Cheticamp Campground** (just north of Cheticamp, 224-2310, daily and weekly rates) and **Robert Brook Group Campground** (north of Cheticamp, 224-2310, $1 night, reservations required). At Pleasant Bay, also within the national park, there's **MacIntosh Brook Campground** (224-2306, daily and weekly rates, pay at the Visitors Center) with hiking trails nearby and shelters with wood stoves.

Dining

In Cheticamp, there's the **Acadian Restaurant** (774 Main Street, 224-2170) with its delicious Acadian cuisine and its famous butterscotch pie. Attached to the restaurant is a museum and Acadian craft shop. **Harbour Restaurant** (Main Street, 224-2042) is a fully licensed restaurant specializing in seafood and steaks. A favorite of local

Acadians, **Evangeline Restaurant** (Main Street, 224-2044) has home-made soups and pies. On the way to the Cabot Trail, try **The Black Whale** (Pleasant Bay, 224-2185). With its splendid views of the ocean and rustic atmosphere, this restaurant has earned international acclaim. In the Margaree Valley, a real must is the **Normaway Inn** (Egypt Road, 248-2987), best known for its fresh vegetables from the garden, Atlantic salmon, Cape Breton lamb and homemade pies.

Whale-Watching

Besides Brier Island on the Bay of Fundy, Cheticamp is another popular place to go whale-watching, although many experts agree that the autumn is a better time to sight whales off Cheticamp. To join a tour here, contact Captain Bill Crawford, c/o Whale Cruisers, Ltd., P.O. Box 10, Grand Étang, Nova Scotia, Canada BOE 1LO, 224-3376.

CAPE BRETON HIGHLANDS NATIONAL PARK

At Petit Étang, just north of Cheticamp, you enter the Cape Breton Highlands National Park. The road from here to Pleasant Bay is the dramatic drive in the highlands. Around Presqu'Île, Cap Rouge and MacKenzie Point, you can look north or south and witness the road's precarious claim on the side of the mountains, which drop unabashedly into the sea. This is the kind of drive you don't want to make in bad weather, but on a clear, summer day the scenery is inspiring.

Cape Breton Highlands National Park is approximately 370 square miles in area and borders both the Gulf of St. Lawrence and the Atlantic Ocean. While it is part of a great tableland, which makes its interior quite flat, the altitude and steep drops to the sea should not be underestimated. In some places the distance between the sheer cliffs and sea level is 1,750 feet. The park—the oldest in eastern Canada—protects the habitats of the bald eagle, moose, coyote, bear and bobcat. There is camping, hiking, canoeing and swimming available within the park, but the real draw here is the dramatic scenery.

From Pleasant Bay, the road turns inland towards the eastern side of the park. There is a road at Pleasant Bay that continues on north to Red River. The scenery doesn't get any better than this, and the pastoral, unfettered quality of a town like Pleasant Bay or Red River is unbeatable. Pleasant Bay was inaccessible by road until 1927. Before that time, visitors had to take a narrow footpath over the mountains and cross three rivers—the MacKenzie, Pond and Red—in order to reach it. The people here have always made their living from the sea, and unlike Cheticamp, the conversation around the picturesque waterfront will be in English or Gaelic. Today Pleasant Bay has accommodations and a village store and a new phenomenon in their neighborhood—a Tibetan monastery. On the cliffs near Red River, a group of Tibetan Buddhists from Colorado established a monastery on a deserted hillside. The building is simple, and the residents go about their business at a quiet pace. I visited the monastery and enjoyed the splendid isolation of the place and the fine views of Pollett Cove and High Capes. On summer nights around Pleasant Bay watch for the northern lights, or *aurora borealis*, streaking the sky with rays of sparkly light.

PLEASANT BAY TO MEAT COVE

The Cabot Trail swings eastward, climbing in elevation to 1,460 feet, near the top of North Mountain. The road then descends across the gorges and valleys along the Aspy River. It passes Cape North, the most northerly point on the Trail. There is a variety store, a motel and a restaurant here. You have the option of leaving the Cabot Trail and heading north to the very tip of Cape Breton at Bay St. Lawrence or Meat Cove. This little adventure may not appeal to parents with children, but if you have the time, try to reach these isolated, individualistic communities that are a stronghold of Gaelic culture and language.

On this most northern road, there is an historic site near the town of Sugar Loaf, which marks the sight where John Cabot and his son Sebastian landed in 1497. Each year, on June 24, the landing ceremony is re-enacted on the beach. Northeast of Cape North is the village of Dingwall, where you can swim and go clam digging.

Meat Cove, the most remote town on the route, can be reached by dirt road from Capstick. Its homes are built along the rugged cliffs that drop 1,000 feet to the sea. The lore of Meat Cove is built around the automobiles found smashed at the bottom of the cliffs. Ask some locals about this and you'll probably get as many versions of the story as I did. As I understand it, the government sold subsidized cars to the people of Meat Cove and then reneged on their agreement. When the government decided to reclaim the cars, the folks of Meat Cove decided that the government could retrieve them at the bottom of the cliffs.

There is a genuinely remote quality to Meat Cove. It's not unusual to sight bald eagles, moose or brown bears. There is summer hiking and camping available in the area around Meat Cove, as well as whale-watching in Bay St. Lawrence and clam digging at Cabot Beach.

CAPE NORTH TO NEIL'S HARBOUR

From Cape North past Effies Brook, the Cabot Trail re-enters the national park. It continues through pine forests to Neil's Harbour, settled by men from Newfoundland. The simple homes, built on the rims of rocks leading to the sea, are typical of Newfoundland-style architecture. Neil's Harbour and scenic Neil Head mark the beginning of the eastern shores of the national park, with less rugged terrain but plenty of beaches, brooks and rivers. Black Brook near South Point is a great place to stop to have a picnic. I remember swimming at Black Brook as a girl and convincing myself that it was bottomless—I'd never seen such black yet clear water.

INGONISH

My approach to the bays and islands of Ingonish brought back memories of staying at the famous Keltic Lodge as a child, and spending days swimming in the fine, chilly waters along Ingonish Beach. This is a marvelous vacation spot with its cottages along the beach, swimming, hiking and views of nearby Cape Smokey and Middle Head. Ingonish has retained its charm and is a very worthwhile place to stop for a day or more. The Ingonish area is divided by Middle Head peninsula, site of the Keltic Lodge.

This is one of the oldest settled areas in North America—Portuguese fishermen used to summer here as far back as 1521. The French, who took over the area in the 1740s, had a large fishing fleet moored in the protective harbors. When the English seized Louisbourg in 1758, they destroyed the French settlement here, and the French moved on to St. Ann's. The English finally settled here around 1810.

At Ingonish Beach, you'll find the administrative headquarters of Cape Breton Highlands National Park. You'll also find that if the ocean is too cold for swimming, nearby Freshwater Lake is just right and less salty. The Keltic Lodge is in view of the beach, and this resort hotel hasn't changed much since I saw it in 1967. It still provides one of the best locations for a relaxing vacation, honeymoon or retirement trip. Nearby is Highlands Links, a world-class, 18-hole golf course designed in the Scottish style. You can take a ferry at Ingonish Ferry over to Cape Smokey, which reaches 1,200 feet. There is a well-traveled hiking trail to the top of Cape Smokey, but only attempt it if you're in good shape and get a proper map from the tourist authority before heading out.

Accommodations

At Ingonish Beach, the **Keltic Lodge** (285-2880, $170-180 single, $235-240 double) is Nova Scotia's finest. Operated by the provincial government, the Lodge offers private cottages or luxurious rooms, excellent cuisine in a classic dining room, flower gardens, spectacular views of the coastline and ample room for children to wander. Located at the entrance to the national park, **Sea Breeze Cottages and Motel** (Ingonish, 285-2879, $55 single, $65 double) has cottages overlooking the ocean, with full bath and sundeck. Along Freshwater Lake, there's the **Cape Breton Highlands Bungalows** (Ingonish Beach, 285-2743, $55 single, $60 double), which offers lake swimming, canoe rentals and 25 cottages. The **Glenghorn Resort** (Ingonish Center, 285-2049 $70 single, $80 double) has a licensed dining room, cottages, ocean swimming and 22 acres with oceanfront property. At Cape North, en route to the eastern side of the national park, try **MacDonald's Motel and Cabins** (RR 1, Dingwall, 383-2054) $45 single, $50 double), which features 12 units with full bath.

Campgrounds

Within the national park near Ingonish, **Broad Cove Campground** (Ingonish, 285-2524, daily and weekly rates) and **Marrach Group Campground** (Ingonish Beach, 285-2691, $1) are both near the beach and close to Freshwater Lake. Also at Ingonish Beach, **Ingonish Campground** (285-2329, daily and weekly rates) has beach swimming, tennis nearby and a playground.

At Cape North, try **Big Intervale Campground** (in the national park, 224-2306) with hiking trails, shelters with woodstoves and coastal views.

Dining

At Ingonish Beach, **Sherwood Restaurant and Lounge** (285-2777) specializes in seafood, steak and chops. Also try the licensed dining room at **Glenghorn Resort** and the beautiful restaurant at the **Keltic**

Lodge, both mentioned in the accommodations section on page 114.

At Dingwall, beyond Cape North, try **Morrison's Pioneer Restaurant** (383-2051) for local seafood and home baking.

SOUTH OF INGONISH

The road from Ingonish heading south gradually descends out of the highlands, and some of the drama begins to fade a bit. To liven it up, take the road to Jersey Cove and board a small cable ferry to Englishtown. The scenery around St. Ann's Bay and St. Ann's Harbour is spectacular, and after the ferry crossing, you're on the Trans-Canada Highway 105 for the drive to Sydney and the Fortress of Louisbourg. At Englishtown, you'll see signs indicating the burial site of Angus MacAskill, a giant man who weighed 425 pounds. He was an internationally acclaimed strongman with the P. T. Barnum Circus in the nineteenth century, but he injured his back when he tried to lift a heavy anchor at a New York pier in a moment of bravado. He died at St. Ann's at the age of 38. Englishtown is also the site of a Jesuit mission.

The road from Englishtown to South Gut St. Ann's is very pretty, with rugged hills in the distance and water all around. South Gut St. Ann's, settled by highland Scots, is the site of the Nova Scotia Gaelic College of Celtic Arts and Culture. This is the only Gaelic college in North America, and it offers six-week summer courses in highland arts and crafts, the Gaelic language, bagpipe playing, highland dancing and weaving of clan and family tartans. Be sure to visit the Great Hall of the Clans, which depicts the history of the Great Migration from the highlands to Cape Breton, an event that gives the island such a special character today. For more information about summer courses, write to the Nova Scotia Gaelic College of Celtic Arts and Crafts, P.O. Box 9, Baddeck, Nova Scotia, Canada BOE 1BO, (902) 295-3411.

From St. Ann's, you can take Highway 105 either south to Baddeck or north to Sydney, Glace Bay and Louisbourg.

Accommodations

At Indian Brook, there's **Piper's Guest House** (929-2067, $30 single, $35 double) with five rooms. At South Gut St. Ann's, **St. Ann's Motel** (Highway 105, Exit 11, 295-2876) has eight units with full bath/shower. Also, **Scott's Tourist Haven** (St. Ann's Bay, 929-2833, $25 single, $30 double) has three rooms.

Campgrounds

At Englishtown, try **St. Ann's Bay Campark** (929-2582, $8) north of the Englishtown ferry. Also try **Pipers Trailer Court** (Indian Brook, between Ingonish and Baddeck, 929-2233, $8) with a licensed restaurant, heated pool and fishing.

SOUTHERN CAPE BRETON

Southern Cape Breton offers opportunities for many different side trips. But while the St. Andrew's Channel, Boularderie Island and the area of West Bay and St. Peter's Inlet all have their unique appeal, you'll find the vast majority of visitors taking the Trans-Canada to Sydney, then following Route 22 to the Fortress of Louisbourg, a National Historic Site and extremely popular tourist destination.

After finishing the Cabot Trail, many tourists end up in Baddeck or nearby, from where they begin the trip to Louisbourg. This involves taking Trans-Canada Highway 105 from Baddeck to New Harris Forks where the highway crosses a magnificent suspension bridge over the Great Bras d'Or to Boularderie Island. Named after Chevalier de la Boularderie, an early French colonialist who was granted land here in 1719, the island has very fertile land for farming. By leaving Highway 105, you can follow a scenic route to the town of Big Bras d'Or and Black Rock Lighthouse. From here you'll see the famous Bird Islands, a few miles offshore. There are two islands: The inner one is called Hertford and the outer island is Ciboux. The Bird Islands are nesting areas for the Atlantic puffins that come here from mid-May to mid-August. The puffin is an unusual bird with a rainbowlike curved beak and white chest. Guaranteed spottings of puffins, as well as razorbills, petrels and terns, are promised by operators of tours to the islands. For more information while in Big Bras d'Or, call Bird Islands Boat Tour, at 674-2384.

For still another side trip, take Route 162 north from Highway 105 to Groves Point Provincial Park and Point Aconi, on the northern tip of Boularderie Island. Point Aconi is the site of Prince Coal Mine, which extends far beneath the ocean floor. Highway 105 continues to North Sydney, terminus of the Newfoundland ferries from Port aux Basques and Argentia, Newfoundland. If you take a slight detour before North Sydney, along Route 305 from Bras d'Or, you'll reach the community of Sydney Mines, where coal mining began in 1766. The entire area of "the Sydneys" became a very important coal-mining region. It was dangerous work, and miners were often poorly paid. Mining communities like Sydney Mines, Glace Bay, and Port Morien have many residents who remember the mining days, the hardships and the good times. North Sydney is a small, picturesque town situated on the northwest arm of Sydney Harbour. From here, the highway circles the northwest arm and brings you to the city of Sydney.

SYDNEY AND GLACE BAY

Sydney was settled by Loyalists from New York State in 1785 who were later joined by immigrants from Scotland in the early 1800s. At the turn of this century, the Dominion Steel and Coal Company was founded in Sydney and became the largest self-contained steel plant in North America. Sydney is often referred to as "The Steel City," but residents have paid a price for such heavy industry. The Canadian government is now involved in a huge toxic waste clean-up—the largest in Canada—at the tar ponds near the steel mills. The toxic tar has been linked to illnesses among Sydney residents. I got a sense of how the locals feel about the tar ponds when a Sydney cab driver said to me, "Enjoy your stay in Sydney. Just don't breathe!"

Sydney lies due south of its rival town of Glace Bay, once an important mining center. According to an old Sydney resident, an annual hockey match between Sydney and Glace Bay fueled rivalries between the steel workers of Sydney and the miners of Glace Bay. But it didn't stop the fellows from visiting one another's towns to seek out the pretty girls, added the old-timer with a smile.

THE MARCONI TRAIL

Towns like Dominion and Glace Bay are on Route 28, part of the Marconi Trail. Glace Bay is noted for its extensive coal mines. If you're in the area, be sure to visit the Miner's Museum at Quarry Point. This fascinating museum is well worth a stop: You'll find the facts behind the old photographs of the miners to be very sobering. Conditions in the deep, dangerous mines were treacherous, and as hard as the miners fought for good pay and other amenities, the big mining monopolies fought harder to prevent change and improvements. There is a film at the museum that documents some of the hardships these miners and their families faced. There is also a tour of Ocean Deeps Colliery, a 45-minute trip beneath the ocean floor to the mines of Glace Bay. The tour is conducted by a former miner and long-term resident of Glace Bay.

Accommodations

In Sydney Mines, try the highly recommended **Gowrie House Bed & Breakfast** (139 Shore Road, 544-1050, $50-60 single/double) or **Annandale Bed & Breakfast** (157 Shore Road, 544-1052, $35 single, $45 double).

Sydney has abundant accommodations, ranging from large hotels to bed & breakfasts. Try the **Best Western Cape Bretoner Motel** (560 Kings Road, (800) 528-1234, $65 single, $75 double) complete with pool, exercise room and licensed dining room. **Cambridge Suites Hotel** (380 Esplanade, 562-6500, $70 single, $80 double) has a licensed restaurant, rooftop spa, sundeck, mini-bars.

Other options: **Holiday Inn Sydney** (480 Kings Road, 539-6750, $90 single, $100 double). Licensed restaurant and lounge; room service. **Journey's End Motel** (368 Kings Road, 562-0200, $50 single, $60 double). Complimentary coffee and newspaper. **Vista Motel** (140 Kings Road, 539-6550, $55 single, $60 double). At Glace Bay, **Will-Bridg House Bed & Breakfast** (322 King Edward Street, 727-2800, $30 single, $35 double) offers full breakfast; home-cooked meals on request.

Campgrounds

Near Dominion, north of Sydney, there's **River Ryan Campground** (RR 1, River Ryan, 862-8367, $10) with eight campsites, boat and canoe rental, saltwater swimming. Also try **Mira River Provincial Park** (Albert Bridge, 564-8088, $8) south of Sydney en route to Louisbourg, with freshwater beach and boat ramp.

Dining

In North Sydney, **Rollies Wharf** (411 Purves Street close to the ferry terminal, 794-7774) features lobster, steaks and seafood. At Sydney Mines, try the **Gowrie House County Inn** (139 Shore Road, 544-1050) with a fine dining room. Be sure to make dinner reservations in advance—there is one seating at 7:30 P.M. On the grounds of the Miner's Museum in Glace Bay, try the **Miner's Village** (Quarry Point, 849-1788) for traditional Cape Breton meals like Cape Breton Lamb, Poor Man's Pudding and Coal Dust Pie. In Sydney, **Peking Restaurant** (five minutes from Sydney center, 539-7775) serves Cantonese and Szechuan dishes, as well as Canadian cooking. **Soupy's** (350 Charlotte Street, 564-4496) has fresh salads and seafood chowders.

SOUTH OF SYDNEY—
THE MARCONI TRAIL CONTINUES

The Marconi Trail, which eventually leads to the Fortress of Louisbourg, was named after the Italian inventor Guglielmo Marconi, a genius in his own right who sent the first transatlantic wireless message from Nova Scotia to England on December 15, 1902. Out of Glace Bay follow the trail along Big Glace Bay Lake to Donkin and Port Morien. This is a lovely coastal drive that leads all the way to Louisbourg, and the pristine quality of the route is well worth the extra time and effort. In Port Morien, a pastoral fishing community, you'll see a cairn that commemorates the site's importance as the first coal-mining operation in North America. Port Morien has a beautiful harbor, with brightly painted Cape Island boats reflected in the still water. The route continues to Mira Bay, a perfect place for swimming or picnicking on the beach. At Mira gut, where the Mira River meets the sea, I saw a gang of kids jumping off a steel suspension bridge into the river water. It seemed like a great thing to do on a hot summer afternoon.

The road continues around to Main-à-Dieu, a very small town that was almost destroyed by a huge forest fire in June 1972. You can still see where the fire scorched much of the town, including a Roman Catholic church. Main-à-Dieu (French for "hand of God") has one of the largest fishing fleets on this coast. As a local man said to me, "Those who don't fish usually get out and move to Toronto or Halifax for work."

From Main-à-Dieu, the Marconi Trail connects with Little Lorraine, a beautiful village with a small harbor. There is a detour five miles south of Main-à-Dieu, just before Little Lorraine, which leads to Baleine. Baleine has two claims on history. It was in July 1629 that Sir James Stewart attempted to settle this land. But the Baleine encampment, known as the Barony of New Galloway, was captured by a Frenchman, Captain Charles Daniel Dieppe, who changed its name to Port aux Baleines ("Whale Harbor"). More recently, Baleine was the place where the British adventurer Beryl Markham crash-landed her plane during her remarkable solo flight across the Atlantic in 1936. Markham records her crash-landing (a nosedive into a bog) as an "Atlantic flight from Abingdon, England, to a nameless swamp in Cape Breton—nonstop." While her goal was to reach New York she ended up in a bog near Louisbourg,—but was fortunate to escape the crash with few injuries.

Baleine is close to the headland called Cape Breton, a name that originated with Basque fishermen in the early 1500s, making it one of the oldest geographical names in North America. From here, the Marconi Trail passes the inlets of Gooseberry Cove and Wild Cove and ends at the town of Louisbourg.

LOUISBOURG

Famous for the Fortress of Louisbourg, the largest historical reconstruction project in Canada, Louisbourg is also a busy fishing town with a large fish-processing plant. The town's attractions include the old Sydney-Louisbourg Railway Station Museum, the Atlantic Statiquarium Marine Museum and the Louisbourg Craft Workshop on the waterfront. There are some good restaurants here as well. You'll see a lighthouse on the eastern end of Louisbourg Harbour. The original was built around 1730, making it the second oldest lighthouse in North America.

The Fortress of Louisbourg

The real attraction of Louisbourg is some distance from town, but you can see it well in advance from the long road that approaches the Fortress of Louisbourg National Historic Park. There is a visitors center off Route 22 that carries tourists by bus to the site. As you approach the fortress, you can easily allow your mind to slip back to the 1700s, when the fortress was originally built. It was once the headquarters for all French activity in the maritimes, having taken the French more than 20 years to build it—from 1720 to 1744.

The vast size of this fortress posed a threat to the New England colonies, who finally attacked Louisbourg in 1745. William Pepperell, from Kittery, Maine, was in command of the New Englanders who laid siege to the fortress for 49 days. The siege is famous in North American colonial history, for it seemed impossible that a crew of untrained volunteers could outmaneuver the French military as they did. However, Louisbourg was handed back to the French in 1748 under the Treaty of Aix-la-Chapelle. In 1758, Louisbourg was again taken, this time by the British navy led by Brigadier General James Wolfe. Assuming that any attack would come from the harbor, the French were caught unprepared when the British attacked from the rear, coming ashore at Kennington Cove. Louisbourg was defeated, and the majority of the French settlers were deported back to France. Some French settled on the islands of St. Pierre and Miquelon, which belong to France even today.

Louisbourg was dismantled and the site crumbled into ruins, but it did not fade from the minds of the local residents. The reconstruction began in 1961, after years of pressure from local groups, and it is now a National Historic Site. With the decline of the mining and steel economy, the government commissioned the many talented men of Cape Breton to rebuild the fortress. Archeologists, masons, historians and others spent two decades perfecting what is today a re-creation of a thriving French colony just as it appeared at the height of its influence in North America. As you wander about the fortress community, volunteers in period costume will be making candles, singing songs or talking of the hardships of being a soldier. Try as you might, you will not get them to break with their "moment in time" and acting as if it were still 1774. From their perspective, France is still looking towards a glorious future in this new land, with Louisbourg at the center of all her power.

I arrived very early in the morning at the fortress, before the endless stream of tourists showed up, and I wandered about, watching women and children in period costume pick daisies. I said *"bonjour"* to the soldiers, smiled at the monk in his long, dark robe and began to enjoy living in the 1700s when fish and game were plentiful and the world beyond Louisbourg was still an unexplored mystery. It's a beautiful site, undertaken at great expense to the Canadian government; a day here is well spent. The guard at the gates will be sure to ask if you are French or English. He jokingly informs all English people that if they are not out of the fort by 4 P.M., they'll be locked up for the night!

Be sure to try the restaurant, with its traditional food served on pewter plates, and frothing beer served in pewter mugs. At 2 P.M. every day, the battle of Louisbourg is re-enacted—amidst clouds of smoke, battle cries and falling men. Costumed presentations take place at the fortress from June 1 to September 30. Walking tours are offered in May and October, although some of the buildings are closed.

Accommodations

Louisbourg has nice bed & breakfasts and smaller-scale hotels. It's a pleasant town to stay in. The **Louisbourg Motel** (1225 Main Street, 733-3155, $45 single, $50 double) has 45 units and a licensed dining room and lounge with wheelchair accessibility. Other options: **Elizabeth Hall Bed & Breakfast** (Route 22, three miles before Louisbourg, 733-3044, $30 single, $35 double). Full breakfast. **The Manse Bed & Breakfast** (17 Strathcona Street, 733-3155, $30 single, $35 double). Overlooks the harbor. **Peck Manor Bed & Breakfast** (Main Street, 733-3268, $30 single, $35 double). Full breakfast.

Campgrounds

Stonewall Trailer Park and Campground (on Route 22, six miles from the Fortress of Louisbourg, 733-2058, $12) has a wooded campground, swimming pool and canteen. **Louisbourg Motorhome Park** (on harborfront, for vehicles only, $12) is open in summer months only.

Dining

An all-time favorite spot in Louisbourg is **The Grubstake Restaurant** (1274-1276 Main Street, 733-2308) with its nineteenth-century decor, fresh baked pastries and traditional meals of lobster, scallops and swordfish. The **Anchors Aweigh Restaurant** (Main Street, next to the tourist bureau) is cheaper than the Grubstake and makes a good cheeseburger. Also try the **Fortress View Restaurant** (Main Street, 733-3009) for specialties like lobster, haddock and scallops. At the Fortress of Louisbourg, there is also a restaurant serving popular foods of the eighteenth century.

THE FLEUR-DE-LIS TRAIL

To return to Sydney on the Fleur-de-lis Trail, you should take Route 22. If you do not want to return to Sydney, take the route as far as Albert Bridge and nearby Mira River Provincial Park. The Mira

River is a highly popular summertime destination for Nova Scotians. From here you can travel the Fleur-de-lis Trail to Fourchu Head and on to Victoria Bridge, St. Peter's Bay and the Strait of Canso.

Another option is to return to Sydney along Route 327 and then head south down Route 4 to St. Peter's Bay. You'll pass the town of Johnstown, where the Sacred Heart Church, built in 1891, houses the French altar from Port Toulouse dating back to 1717. Loch Lomond, off Route 4, was named after the beloved Loch Lomond in Scotland by settlers who arrived in 1827.

This entire area of southern Cape Breton is worth exploring, with its myriad islands, rivers, lighthouses and campsites. The Fleur-de-lis Trail, offering a more off-the-beaten-track route, may be just the remedy you need after the crowds along the Cabot Trail and at Louisbourg. Be sure to stop at St. Peter's Canal before leaving Cape Breton via Port Hawkesbury. This historic site, called Port Toulouse by the French, was a fortified harbor used to defend Isle Royale (Cape Breton) against the English. A museum on the west side commemorates one of the area's first settlers, Nicholas Denys, a trader who recorded the comings and goings of the Micmac people, whom he came to know and trust. Much of what historians know about the Micmac is due to Denys's careful note-taking.

The area around St. Peter's is lovely. Most of the residents fish in Chedabucto Bay, where large oil tankers often pass on their way to Port Hawkesbury. If you talk to local fisherman, you'll find them very disgruntled about the oil spills that have led to the decline in fish. Richmond County, the last county before crossing the Strait of Canso, boasts of holding 22 festivals during the summer months in the varied communities that thrive here.

Accommodations

At St. Peter's, there's the **MacDonald Hotel** (Route 4, near the Irving Garage, 535-2997, $30 single, $35 double), which offers complimentary breakfast. **Inn on the Canal** (St. Peter's, 535-2200, $65 double) has rooms and cabins that overlook St. Peter's Bay. At Arichat, on Petit-de-Grat Island, try **L'Auberge Acadienne** (High Road, 226-2200, $60 single, $75 double) for its nineteenth-century-style Acadian atmosphere. Open year-round. At Grand River, **Salmon View Housekeeping Log Cabins** (fifteen miles from St. Peter's, 587-2725, $50-60 single/double) has fishing-boat rentals.

Campgrounds

Acadian Campsite (Arichat, 226-2447, $12) has wooded sites and lake swimming. **Battery Provincial Park** (five miles east of St. Peter's, 525-3094, $8) is a wooded campground with a view of the locks. In St. Peter's, **St. Peter's Campground** (intersection of Routes 4 and 247, 535-3333, $12) has views of the Bras d'Or Lake.

Dining

In St. Peter's, **Heritage Tea Room** (Main Street, 535-2089) has lobster suppers, plus all the mussels you can eat. Available every day at 4 P.M. in summer. **La Cuisine Acadienne** (Louisdale, 345-2817) has home-cooked Acadian meals, including rappie pie, plus fish and steak. The **MacDonald Dining Room** (St. Peter's, 535-2338) features home cooking, gourmet-style. **L'Auberge Acadienne** (Arichat, 30 minutes from Canso Causeway, 226-2200) is a well-known inn with an exquisite dining room. Also try the **Inn on the Canal** (St. Peter's, 535-2200) for their licensed dining room featuring traditional Canadian food.

THE MARINE DRIVE

Following Nova Scotia's Marine Drive along the Eastern Shore between the Strait of Canso and Halifax is a nice alternative to the Trans-Canada Highway when returning from Cape Breton. The rugged Eastern Shore has some wonderful rivers for trout fishing, quiet coastal villages, dense forests and long, sandy beaches with plovers, sandpipers and other shore birds scurrying against the tide. The road along the Eastern Shore, formerly called the "old Guysborough Road," passes through some of the most rustic parts of Nova Scotia.

STRAIT OF CANSO TO SHIP HARBOUR

If you're leaving Port Hawkesbury after touring Cape Breton, cross the Strait of Canso and turn southeast to Mulgrave. As the Marine Drive enters Guysborough County, it passes through the town of Boylston, settled by New England Loyalists in 1786. A visit to the wooded Boylston Provincial Park offers a good spot for a picnic. The village of Guysborough is situated at the head of Chedabucto Bay. In 1650, it was started as a fishing station by Nicholas Denys, the French settler who went on to write about his experiences with the Micmac Indians. The community later became a French garrison town until the English arrived in the 1760s. By 1784, Guysborough was a prosperous Loyalist town, where lumber was the main export. The name *Chedabucto* is a Micmac name meaning "the great long harbor." But during the 1800s, the harbor ebbed away and it became impossible for ships to come and go here.

Continue along the Marine Drive to Cape Canso and the historic fishing town of Canso, founded in 1605. The name *Canso* came from the Indian word *Kamsok*, which means "opposite the lofty cliffs." Canso was an important fishing station for the French and Portuguese during the 1500s and was later frequented by New Englanders. By 1720, it had become a British garrison built to protect the community from the French threat at Louisbourg. In Canso there is a Seamen's Memorial that is dedicated to the many Canso fishermen who have lost their lives at sea.

Getting back on the Marine Drive, you'll reach the small town of Larry's River, originally an Acadian community settled in 1797. The town was named after Larry Keating, a man from Halifax who lived here one winter hunting moose. Farther along the Marine Drive, you pass New Harbour, with its abundance of foxberry and cranberry barrens. The road then curves around a headland into picturesque Isaac's Harbour and Stormont. Stormont was a French fishing station as far back as 1607. The first English settlers were from North and South Carolina regiments who arrived here in 1783, after the American Revolution. It was at the mouth of Country Harbour that the ship *Saladin* was stranded in 1844, with a murdered captain and part of the crew still aboard the mutinous ship. If you decide not to go to Stormont, take the seven-minute ferry ride from Isaac's Harbour to continue on to Sherbrooke. The ride offers brilliant views of Country Harbour. At Sherbrooke, you can take Route 7 inland to Antigonish or continue south on the Marine Drive. Sherbrooke is situated on the banks of the St. Mary's River, one of the area's best rivers for salmon and trout. There is a heavy run of salmon in spring and early summer from a chain of five lakes called the Sherbrooke Lakes.

Sherbrooke started out as a fur-trading post, founded by a French trader named La Giraudière in 1655. English settlers later named it after Sir John Coape Sherbrooke, lieutenant-governor of Nova Scotia. The town now draws tourists who visit the many restored buildings that represent the 1860 to 1980 era. This living museum has costumed guides who take you through a blacksmith shop, post office, woodworking shop and tea room. The guides are local residents who tell stories of their forebears. In all, there are 25 restored buildings to visit.

Just to the south, don't miss the tiny town of Goldenville, population 16. It was the scene of a major gold rush in 1862 when hundreds of millions of dollars worth of gold was excavated. The mines shut down over 40 years ago, but mining companies are now considering reopening them. Nearby is the beautiful Liscombe Lodge at Liscombe Mills, a lodge built in a rustic setting overlooking the Liscombe River at the foot of a small waterfall. The lodge is massive, with 65 rooms, cottages and chalets. The main lodge has a large stone fireplace.

The Marine Drive moves on to Port Dufferin, named in honor of the Marquis of Dufferin who was governor-general of Canada from 1872 to 1878. The Marquis of Dufferin Lodge here was built in 1859 by Henry Balcom, a sea captain and prosperous merchant. People come to this registered historic property to spend weekends salmon fishing at nearby Salmon River, which is also abundant with trout. The coastal drive from here to Sheet Harbour is rustic and peaceful. You'll pass Beaver Harbour, supposedly named by the legendary Indian Glooscap, who threw one of the large shoreline rocks at a large beaver. Sheet Harbour is at the junction of Routes 7 and 224, where you have the option of heading inland towards Upper Musquodoboit and Pleasant Valley. Originally settled by Loyalists after the American Revolution, Sheet Harbour was the site of the first sulphite pulp mill in Canada. Just south of Sheet Harbour is the uniquely named town of *Mushaboom*. This Micmac word means "hair of the dead lying there." The Indians believed that fairies used to gather here and pull each other's hair, leaving the tufts lying on the ground. Nearby Spry Harbour and Spry Bay are lovely towns, very typical of Eastern Shore fishing communities. Taylors Head Provincial Park is adjacent to Spry Harbour. There is a series of boardwalks leading out to the sand dunes and the long stretch of beach. From the parking lot, you can begin a walk along various trails to Mushaboom Harbour and the edge of the peninsula.

Moose River, south of Spry Harbour, is the location of the Moose River Gold Mines. In 1936, during a hunt for gold, three men were caught in a cave-in here while inspecting an abandoned mine. After ten days underground and a dramatic rescue attempt, two of the three men were found alive. Tangier, which comes next, is the site of Nova Scotia's earliest gold mines. They opened in 1860 and were prospected for 30 years. The calm waters along the coast here are ideal for canoeing.

SHIP HARBOUR TO THE MUSQUODOBOIT VALLEY

Ship Harbour is the site of abundant marine life. Thousands of white buoys mark North America's largest cultivated mussel farms. Research and spawning activities draw marine biologists as well as the curious to visit the farms. Tours are available by calling Little Harbours Fisheries (423-6610). Nearby Clam Bay, which is reached by taking the road from Ship Harbour around the coast, was once called "the place of clams" by the Micmacs. It has a vast beach with flat white sand, perfect for clam digging.

Clam Bay is close to Lake Charlotte, an extremely popular destination for hunters and sports fishermen along the Marine Drive. And shellfish seekers can visit Jeddore Oyster Pond. There is a museum here at a site that once belonged to oysterman James Myers. The museum illustrates the life-style of Myers and his family who lived here at the turn of the century. The Marine Drive then passes Martinique Beach, one of the longest beaches in Nova Scotia, stretching three miles along the shore. There is a game sanctuary behind the beach that fills with migratory birds in the fall and early winter.

THE MUSQUODOBOIT VALLEY

The Musquodoboit Valley is both a rich dairy farming area and a productive region for fish and wildlife. The valley was first settled by Europeans in 1692 and later populated by New England Loyalists and Northern Irish immigrants around 1784.

At Musquodoboit Harbour, the largest town along the western part of the Marine Drive, there is a yacht club, restaurants, a tourist information center and banks. Visit the Musquodoboit Railway Museum situated in the former Canadian National Railway Station. The station was built around 1918. The old railcars can be boarded, and a guide will fill you in on the details about the railroad.

Continue along the Marine Drive towards Halifax passing the unusually named towns of West Chezzetcook and Grand Desert. These towns were settled by Acadians, who cultivated the salt marsh here. Be sure to see the large baroque church in the center of Grand Desert. Just before pulling into the Dartmouth area, visit the coastal community of Lawrencetown and the Lawrencetown Beach Provincial Park. Just off Route 207, the town of Porter's Lake is also worth visiting. You'll pass the district of Preston, named for Captain Preston of Boston Massacre fame. Preston is the oldest black community in Canada, settled in 1796 by Jamaicans and later by freed slaves who arrived from the Chesapeake Bay region of the United States in 1816. Finally, the Marine Drive passes Cole Harbour, with its Cole Harbour Heritage Farm Museum, open year-round. The site had strong ties with the commerce in and around Halifax, and the old farmhouse was a center of trade between the village and the city. There are plenty of farm animals here, and a weekly farmer's market.

Accommodations/Dining

Accommodations are not abundant along the Marine Drive, but there are enough bed & breakfasts and campgrounds to suit most visitors. Starting in Guysborough, there's the **Belmont Resort** (exit 37 to Route 16, 533-3904, $55 single, $60 double) near a golf course, canoe rental area and boat launch. In the small community of Bickerton West in Guysborough County, the highly recommended **By-the-Sea Bed & Breakfast** (Route 211 east, 364-2575, $35 single, $45 double) has light evening meals and views of the sea. In Sherbrooke, there's **Marine Motel and Cabins** (522-2235, $50 single, $55 double, weekly rates available). Or try **St. Mary's River Lodge** (522-2177, $40 single, $45 double) within view of historic Sherbrooke Village. At Liscomb Mills, the highly popular **Liscomb Lodge** (on Route 7, 779-2307, $90 single, $100 double) has a licensed dining room, tennis courts, a marina, freshwater fishing, guides and equipment. Also popular with Canadians is the **Marquis of Dufferin Seaside Inn** (Port Dufferin, eight miles east of Sheet Harbour, 654-2696, $65 single, $75 double) with a licensed dining room, sun lounge and deck, fishing, rowboats and sailing. At Sheet Harbour, the **Cousins Motel and Marina** (827-3451, $45 single, $50 double) has a licensed dining room overlooking the harbor, boat rentals and harbor cruises. In Musquodoboit Harbour, the highly recommended **Camelot Inn** (on Route 7, 889-2198, $45 single, $50 double) has a licensed dining room serving breakfast and dinner.

Campgrounds

Boylston Provincial Park (between Guysborough and Boylston, 533-3326, $8) is situated in a wooded campground with harbor views. **Salsman Provincial Park** (on Route 316, south of Goshen, 387-2877, $8) is located on the west side of Country Harbour. In Sherbrooke, **Riverside Campground** (on river off Route 7, 522-2913, $8) has 20 sites, a laundromat, canteen, restaurant and fire grills. At Elderbank, 17 miles north of Musquodoboit Harbour on Route 357, **Dollar Lake Provincial Park** (384-2770, $9) is situated along a white sandy beach on the shore of a large lake. West of Sheet Harbour, at Murphy's Cove, **Murphy's Camping-on-the-Ocean** (772-2208, $9) is in a wooded campground by the sea. At Porter's Lake, **Porter's Lake Provincial Park** (three miles south of Route 7 on West Porter's Lake Road, 827-2250, $8) is set on the lake, with wheelchair-accessible sites.

PRINCE EDWARD ISLAND

Mileage Chart for Prince Edward Island

Charlottetown to Summerside	38 miles
Charlottetown to Alberton	55 miles
Charlottetown to Souris	50 miles
Charlottetown to Murray Harbour	35 miles
Charlottetown to Mount Carmel	50 miles
Charlottetown to Tignish	75 miles
Charlottetown to Halifax, NS*	201 miles
Charlottetown to Yarmouth, NS*	389 miles
Charlottetown to Saint John, NB*	194 miles
Charlottetown to Calais, ME*	256 miles
Charlottetown to St. John's, NF*	880 miles

*By ferry

East Point

Souris

Panmure Island
Provincial Park

Murray Harbour

Montague

Murray
River

Eldon

Charlottetown

Prince Edward
Island Nat'l Park

North
Rustico

Cavendish

Malpeque

Summerside

Mount Carmel

Tignish

Alberton

The Blue Heron Drive

The King's Byway

The Lady Slipper Drive

PRINCE EDWARD ISLAND
GREEN HILLS AND GREEN GABLES

Y ou never know what peace is until you walk on the shores, fields or along the winding red roads of Abegweit on a summer twilight when the dew is falling, the stars are peeping out and the sea keeps its nightly tryst with the little land it loves," wrote Lucy Maud Montgomery, author of *Anne of Green Gables,* about Prince Edward Island. And indeed, this is an island that lives up to all encomiums.

According to Micmac Indian legend, all the beautiful places on earth were painted by their mythical hero Glooscap, who then dipped his brush into the myriad of colors and created Abegweit, or Prince Edward Island, his favorite place of all. There is no denying the beauty of Prince Edward Island, called simply P.E.I. by most locals. The green hills resemble Ireland, the quiet farms tucked into valleys look like western England and the rugged bluffs and distinct accents of the islanders remind one of Scotland.

This crescent-shaped island situated in the Gulf of St. Lawrence is justly called the "Garden of the Gulf." There is such a clean, crisp quality to Prince Edward Island that touring here is a joy as you drive amidst the fields, villages, farms and fishing towns that give this island its unsurpassed beauty.

Visitors often come to Prince Edward Island to swim at the beaches along the Northumberland Strait, where warm waters lap against sandy shores. Cyclists and walkers find the island perfect for their activities. And the abundance of campgrounds and farm tourist homes makes it easy to stay for days and days, sleeping under the stars on warm summer nights or in a barn if you like. The islanders, of course, know a different Prince Edward Island, whose wintertime isolation, when farming and fishing come to a halt, makes for rugged communities separated by miles of potato fields and back roads.

A BRIEF HISTORY

Prince Edward Island was originally the home of Micmac Indians, who had been living for thousands of years on Abegweit, which means "land cradled by waves." The Micmacs hunted for bear, caribou and moose and fished the rich waters of the Northumberland Strait and the Gulf of St. Lawrence. The Micmacs wore skins and furs, used simple tools and lived a seminomadic hunter/gatherer existence. The first European to set foot on Prince Edward Island was the French explorer Jacques Cartier who, in 1534, upon seeing the red soil and deep greens of the hills exclaimed that it was ". . . the fairest land 'tis possible to see!" The island was named Île St. Jean by the French who established a settlement at Port La Joye (now Fort Amherst) in 1720. As in the other Maritime provinces, the struggle for supremacy in North America between the French and English embroiled Prince Edward Island through the 1700s. Finally, in 1758, the British took over the island, deporting the Acadian settlers who, like their Nova Scotian brothers, were shipped to the swamplands of Louisiana and today are called Cajuns. Some Acadians avoided expulsion by hiding in the woods. As a result, there is still a bustling Acadian community on the island today.

The British named their new land St. John Island, and it was annexed to Nova Scotia. A British captain named Samuel Holland surveyed the land in 1764, dividing it up into 67 lots, or townships, which were sold to English gentry on a lottery basis. The colony grew, but the farmers and fishermen who actually lived on the land objected to absentee landlords and ruthless rent collectors. For almost 100 years, islanders protested against this absentee policy and were finally rewarded with the Land Purchase Act of 1853. The island government bought back the land for resale to the working tenants of the farms and fisheries.

With both Saint John, New Brunswick, and St. John's, Newfoundland, carrying the same name, the island's name was changed from St. John Island to Prince Edward Island in 1799.

While the population of Prince Edward Island grew with the arrival of Loyalists from the New England states who came here after the American Revolution, another large group of settlers came to the island during the late 1700s. Driven to leave Scotland because of highland clearances and English repression, the Scots first arrived in

1775. They found the dense forests of Prince Edward Island to be a bit daunting but soon prospered here building ships and exporting lumber. A second wave of Scottish immigration occurred in the early 1800s, when lowland Scots joined their highland brothers. This gave the island its unique Scottish flavor marked even today by Scottish music, dances and the distinct kilts and bagpipes. There is a Robbie Burns Day celebrated across the island, with traditional oatcakes and haggis, bagpipes and song.

Prince Edward Island was also settled by Irish immigrants who first came to the new land between 1767 and 1810. Then a vast, second wave of settlers came between 1810 and 1835 from places like Waterford, Kilkenny and Tipperary in Ireland. And from 1830 to 1850, some 4,000 Irish arrived from counties like Tyrone, Donegal and Monaghan. By 1848, there were 6,407 Irish-born residents living on the island. There were also an estimated 6,736 native Scots.

Because of the Charlottetown Conference held here in 1864, Prince Edward Island is recognized as the Cradle of the Confederation and birthplace of Canada. The new coalition government that was formed in 1864 included the three Maritime provinces, and Québec and Ontario. Newfoundland and Labrador did not join the confederation until 1949. The lovely city of Charlottetown was chosen as the location for the conference, although the people of the island were initially reluctant to join a confederation—the islanders met with other Canadian delegates but viewed them suspiciously.

A local newspaper described the gathering as "the most brilliant fete that has ever occurred in Charlottetown," for the meetings were accompanied by banquets and luncheons. At the end of five days, the delegates, perhaps after food and drink brought them closer together, reached a decision to form a Canadian Confederation, and conferences in Québec and London formalized the arrangement. By October 1867, Canada had become a nation.

Prince Edward Island went on to prosper as a potato-growing region, thanks to its rich red soil that seems to be perfect for this crop. Shipbuilding also took on importance to the island during the Golden Age of Sail. Much of the island is still dense woodland, which makes it an excellent habitat for bird life. The waters around Prince Edward Island are full of marine life, with delicacies like the Malpeque oysters, blue fin tuna and salmon in abundance. There are also plenty of opportunities to see whales, harp seals, grey seals and harbor porpoises.

The islanders of today still farm and fish but increasingly rely on the flourishing tourist trade in summer. They are particularly overwhelmed by Japanese visitors who come in droves to visit the home of Anne of Green Gables at Cavendish. Recently, residents of Prince Edward Island have begun to worry about the amount of real estate the Japanese are buying on the island and wonder what future changes this may spell for their beloved island.

GEOGRAPHY AND CLIMATE

Prince Edward Island was once humorously described as two huge beaches with potato fields in between. In fact, Prince Edward Island is a farming province, and a rural way of life does prevail here. Prince Edward Island is the smallest Canadian province, encompassing 2,184 square miles. Sixty-three percent of the land is rural.

The soil here is famous for its deep red color and productivity, and inland the island is covered with northern evergreen and hardwood forests. But it is also a Maritime community, and many island activities and characteristics come from a life lived close to the sea. There are some excellent clam-digging regions, for example, along the island's windswept beaches.

Divided into three counties—King, Queen and Prince—there is ample room on this island for the traveler to explore.

HIGHLIGHTS

Although Prince Edward Island is described as "a calm and peaceful island," any Atlantic island is susceptible to fierce storms in winter and some angry summer days as well. Fortunately, the island is sheltered somewhat by the mainland and the Northumberland Strait. In summer, temperatures average in the 70s, with low humidity and steady breezes. The evenings are cooler, with the average temperature in the high 60s on summer nights. Be sure to bring a light jacket or sweater for your trip. The hottest months are July and August, when the water is perfect for swimming. Many Maritimers agree that the best time to see Prince Edward Island is in September, when the tourists are gone but summer tends to linger on.

One high point of a visit to Prince Edward Island, particularly for Japanese visitors, is a tour of Anne of Green Gables home at Cavendish.

It is hard to figure out why Anne's fictional story is so beloved in Japan; this red-headed orphan girl who learns about right and wrong seems a strange symbol to be worshipped by these foreign visitors. But the Japanese love Anne, and they come to Prince Edward Island in huge numbers to see the stage performance of *Anne of Green Gables* in Charlottetown and then visit her fictional home at Cavendish. The house was actually the home of Lucy Maud Montgomery, whose stories about Anne of Green Gables were based on her love of the island and its beauty. Of Prince Edward Island she once said, "compressed by the inviolate sea, it floats on the waves of the blue gulf, a green seclusion and haunt of ancient peace." At Cavendish, I particularly enjoyed watching the Japanese families stretch out on the lawn of Anne's home while their children ran and played. The home and its pastoral setting appear in the film *Anne of Green Gables*. Both home and landscape typify the beauty of Prince Edward Island.

In June and July the wild lupine flower blooms throughout the island, covering the hillsides with a rainbow of purples, blues, pinks and yellows. Prince Edward Island also has its splendid National Park, with the stately hotel Dalvay-by-the-Sea and miles of beaches, sand dunes and rugged bluffs.

PRACTICALITIES

Getting There

BY AIR. Charlottetown is only 20 minutes by air from Halifax International Airport, and has connections to many major eastern cites in the United States and Canada. The island is serviced by three regional carriers: Air Atlantic, Air Nova IntAir, as well as by Air Canada. There are a number of tour agencies that can arrange your flight to Prince Edward Island, or you can do it independently through a local travel agent. Island Value Vacations of Charlottetown offers an interesting package-priced tour of the island. Call toll free in Canada and the eastern United States at (800) 565-0260.

BY LAND. The island must first be reached by ferry, but once there, driving is not only hassle free, it's fun. There are some great touring roads throughout Prince Edward Island. Gasoline stations are plentiful, though slightly more expensive than in the United States. Year-round bus service within the province is available through

Island Transit. Rates and schedules are available from the Island Information Center or from Island Transit, located at 308 Queen Street, Charlottetown, 892-6167.

BY SEA. There are two ferry services that operate between Prince Edward Island and the mainland. Marine Atlantic connects Cape Tormentine, New Brunswick, to Borden, Prince Edward Island. The trip takes 45 minutes, with departures every two hours. The round-trip fare is $25. Farther east, Northumberland Ferries travel between Caribou, Nova Scotia, and Wood Island, Prince Edward Island, in 75 minutes. This particular crossing is on a far smaller ferry than the *Abegweit,* which plies the waters between Cape Tormentine and Borden.

Because the Northumberland ferry is smaller, the lines to board are very long. I waited three hours to get on at Wood Island, after arriving at 11:00 A.M. on a summer weekday. Try to arrive for the crossing as early as possible during the peak season. The ferry leaves every hour and a half until 7 P.M. The round-trip fare is $25.

There is also an interesting ferry excursion from Souris, Prince Edward Island, in eastern King's County, to the Magdalen Islands, long sandbar-like islands that are officially part of Québec Province. Hundreds of seals have their babies on these islands each March. The white fur of these babies once made them a target of hunters, but today they are protected and becoming something of a tourist attraction. Tours run each March to the Magdalen Islands for seal-watching. From April 1 to June 15 and from September 16 to 30, ferry service from Souris departs every day at 2 P.M.

Tourist Information

As is customary in Canada, the tourist authority in Prince Edward Island is very well organized and helpful. There are Tour-the-Island visitor information centers in Charlottetown, Borden, Portage and Summerside in Prince County; at Brackley Beach, Cavendish, Stanhope and Wood Island in Queens County and in Montague and Souris in King's County. There are also information centers on the mainland at Caribou, Nova Scotia, and Aulac, New Brunswick. For more information, you can contact Visitor Services, P.O. Box 940, Charlottetown, Prince Edward Island, Canada C1A 7M5, (800) 565-0267 in North America or (800) 565-7421 in the Maritimes.

Time

Prince Edward Island is on Atlantic Time, one hour ahead of Eastern Time.

Telephones

The area code for Prince Edward Island is **902.**

THE BLUE HERON DRIVE

Because Prince Edward Island is divided into three counties, the tourism authority has mapped out the island with three scenic drives: the Blue Heron Drive, the King's Byway and the Lady Slipper Drive.

The Blue Heron Drive is central to Prince Edward Island, for it passes through the provincial capital at Charlottetown. Most of the drive is in Queens County, but it also cuts into Prince County. This loop covers 110 miles altogether and begins and ends in Charlottetown. The Blue Heron Drive also passes the Prince Edward Island National Park, with its vast beaches and sand dunes, and ends at the tourist town of Cavendish, the fictional home of Anne of Green Gables. Nearby New London Bay, habitat of the blue heron, is the inspiration for the drive's name. The herons are a common sight along this route and are quite beautiful to see. At Kensington, there is a turnoff that leads to the western route called Lady Slipper Drive, named after the island's national flower.

CHARLOTTETOWN

Charlottetown's place in history as the birthplace of Canada gives this quiet Victorian town a certain regal quality. But it still remains Canada's most sparsely populated provincial capital. Although the population of Charlottetown stands at 45,000 for most the year, it doubles during the summer months of July and August with tourists arriving from Europe, Japan, Hong Kong, Australia, western Canada and the United States. The capital is only 32 miles from the ferry at Wood Island (arriving from Nova Scotia) and 34 miles from the ferry at Borden (arriving from New Brunswick). Charlottetown is laid out in a triangular way; its central focus is the Confederation Plaza with its art center, museum, memorial to the members of the Charlottetown Conference and a theater featuring the play *Anne of Green Gables*. The tourist office for Charlottetown and the rest of the island is on the corner of University Avenue and Summer Street (368-4444). There are banks, restaurants, hotels, bed & breakfasts, pubs and shops throughout the city.

Attractions

This prestigious, red-brick and stone city has its historic monuments and edifices, but it also has an attractive waterfront with boardwalks, the Charlottetown Yacht Club and Victoria Park. This expansive park is at the west side of town, with footpaths along the edge that overlook the harbor. On the distant hillside, you'll see Port La Joye/Fort Amherst National Historic Site, where the French originally settled in 1720.

By 1758, the British had taken over the fort, and changed the island's name to St. John, with Charlottetown as its capital. The town grew slowly, bolstered by the arrival of United Empire Loyalists after the American Revolution and Scottish and Irish immigrants who came here throughout the nineteenth century. Today, one third of the island's population lives in Charlottetown. The main intersection is at University and Euston Streets, but it is also interesting to amble along Richmond, Queen, King, Prince and Water streets with their numerous pubs, coffee shops, craft stores and bookshops.

❖ Confederation Center of the Arts

This massive, modern structure at the foot of University Avenue was built in the 1960s, a time when architectural styles changed the look of many communities, including Charlottetown. The building seems a little out of place next to the Victorian brick and stone that characterize much of the town. The center houses an impressive art gallery, library, museum and theater. The art gallery and museum cost $1 to enter during July and August; for the rest of the year they're free. Tours of the center are conducted year-round.

❖ Province House

Next door is Province House, an old sandstone building built in 1843 as a courthouse. In front of the building, there is an impressive monument to the brave soldiers who fought in the wars. It was here that the historic Charlottetown Conference agreement, leading to the formation of a Canadian Confederation, was signed on September 3, 1864. The Province House is now a National Historic Site, yet the building remains busy throughout the day with meetings of the provincial legislature.

❖ St. Paul's Church

Located on Church Street, east of Province House, this red sandstone building is the oldest church on the island, built in 1747. Notice the elaborate interior woodwork.

❖ Beaconsfield House

This beautiful Victorian mansion overlooking the harbor was built in 1877 by architect William Critchlow Harris for shipbuilder James Peake, Jr. Today the house is the headquarters of the Prince Edward Island Museum and Heritage Foundation, and is also a center for genealogical research, housing numerous books on the heritage and history of the island.

❖ Victoria Park

A favorite of locals, this 40-acre park is used for jogging, summertime softball matches and strolling amidst the white birches. Bordering the grounds at the park, there is a regal, white, neoclassical building called Government House. This is the official residence of the lieutenant-governor of the island. The park area has excellent harbor views and an extensive walk along the water's edge, past an old collection of cannons from the days when the park was called Fort George.

❖ Fort Amherst/Port La Joye National Historic Site

Although it is some distance from Charlottetown, Fort Amherst is within easy view from the harbor and is easily reached from town. The site marks the first permanent European settlement on Prince Edward Island. Located at Rocky Point on Blockhouse Point Road, the site was established by the French in 1720. The British drove the French out in 1758 and built Fort Amherst over the site of the original French garrison. It was occupied by the British until 1768, after which it fell into disrepair. Today, mounds of earth, windswept fields and the strategic position of the site are all that remain. There is a visitors center here that offers insight into the early days of French and English settlement.

Accommodations

There are some nice bed & breakfasts in Charlottetown as well as a new hotel and convention center that caters to large tour groups, particularly the Japanese. The **Prince Edward Hotel and Convention Center** (18 Queen Street, 566-2222, $120-150 single/double) is located in Harbourside, Olde Charlotte Town, and features a sauna, restaurant, harbor cruises, a marina and waterfront park. It's popular with the Japanese en route to the Mecca of Cavendish. Another favorite with tourists is **The Charlottetown—A Rodd Classic Hotel** (corner of Kent and Pownal streets, 894-7371, $100 single, $130 double), featuring dinner-theater mid-June to early

September, conference facilities and suites. Also try **Dundee Arms Inn and Motel, Ltd.** (200 Pownal Street, 892-2496, $80 single, $90 double), which has rooms furnished with antiques. For simpler accommodation, try **MacInnis Tourist Home** (80 Euston Street, 892-6725, $28 single/double). It's run by a friendly family, and breakfast is included.

Other options: **McCloskey's Tourist Home** (28 Lilac Avenue, 894-9434, $25 daily, $155 weekly) located by the water with licensed dining room. **McNichol's Tourist Home** (20 Maplewood Crescent, 892-6381, $25-35 single/double). **MacKeen's Tourist Home** (176 King Street, 892-6296, $25 single, $30 double). Open year-round; continental breakfast included.

Campgrounds

In Churchill, 16 miles southwest of Charlottetown, try **Strathgartney Provincial Park** (675-3599, $13 daily) with nature trails, kitchen shelter and free firewood. In Charlottetown, the **Southport Trailer Park** (569-2287, $10) has phone and cable TV and a restaurant nearby.

Dining

For breakfast or lunch, there are plenty of nifty restaurants tucked away all around Charlottetown. Try **Pat's Rose and Grey Room** (Richmond Street, 892-2222) for burgers, subs and pizzas, or the **Richmond Street Diner** (Richmond Street, 892-8744) for breakfast or lunch. For seafood and steaks, try **Tradewind Restaurant** (189 Kent Street, 894-4291) or **Town and Country Restaurant** (219 Queen Street, 892-2282). The **Charlottetown Yacht Club** on the harbor off Water Street serves chowder, burgers and salads at lunchtime; open to the public. For more elegant dining, try **Marina Dining Room** (238 Grafton Street, 892-2461) or **Lobsterman's Landing** (Prince Street Wharf, 368-2888) for fresh lobster and seafood.

Crafts

The lovely craft stores in Charlottetown make it one of the best places to buy the work of craftspeople on the island. The best store I found was **The Island Crafts Shop** (156 Richmond Street, 892-5152), which carries a beautiful array of original work including pottery, weavings, silk screen, batik and jewelry made by members of the Prince Edward Island Crafts Council. Also on Richmond Street, try **Province House Gift Shop** (165 Richmond Street, 566-7626) and

The Two Sisters (150 Richmond Street, 894-3407) with its unique collection of country and Victorian styles. Also try **The Bird's Eye Nature Store, Inc.** (177 Queen Street, 566-DUCK), in the heart of downtown, north of the Confederation Center of the Arts and **The Croft House, Inc.** (Kent Street, 566-1606), for paintings, pottery, quilts and weavings.

THE BLUE HERON DRIVE FROM CHARLOTTETOWN

To reach the popular Prince Edward Island National Park and nearby Cavendish, it's best to begin in Charlottetown and head north along the King's Byway to the Blue Heron Drive.

The Blue Heron Drive travels inland through Brackley and Harrington and then reaches the shores of the Gulf of St. Lawrence at Brackley Beach. The beach is a favorite spot for Charlottetown residents who spend weekends here by the sea. There are plenty of cabins, tourist homes and beach houses to stay in. This area is part of the coastal Prince Edward Island National Park, which encompasses 25 miles of some of the finest white sand in North America, plus dunes and abundant bird life. The Gulf Stream passes by this northern stretch of land, so the water is warmer here than elsewhere on the island. There are wooden walkways at Brackley Beach that were built amidst the sand dunes to avoid disrupting the fragile marram grass, a nesting area for birds. More than 210 species of birds can be found here, notably the northern phalarope, Swainson's thrush, slate-colored junco and the piping plover. From Brackley Beach, there is a shore road that covers the length of Prince Edward Island National Park. The beaches at Stanhope, Brackley and Dalvay are extremely popular with wind surfers because of the steady winds and sheltered bays. In 1864, Stanhope was the scene of a beach party among the Canadian delegates who had attended the Charlottetown Conference.

If you head east along Route 15 towards Grand Tracadie you will see the elegant Victorian hotel called Dalvay-by-the-Sea. This was once a summer home for Alexander MacDonald and his family who arrived here in the late 1800s. MacDonald, a wealthy Scotsman who built his fortune with the Standard Oil Company in Cleveland, Ohio, was so intrigued by Prince Edward Island that he had his dream home built here in 1896. Furnished with antiques and artifacts gathered during a lifetime of travel, the home was an absolute palace in the eyes of many islanders. On summer evenings, the MacDonalds had dances and balls. It is said that when MacDonald was an elderly man and quite ill, he halted his horse and carriage at Long Point before leaving Prince Edward Island and looked back at his summer home for the last time, whispering "Good-bye Dalvay." The home was eventually sold to the federal government and was turned into a hotel in 1939. There is still a special ambience to the place, with its great stone fireplace in the living room, wide staircase and beautiful rooms overlooking the sea. This is the kind of hotel where you could spend an endless summer reading novels, swimming and just dreaming.

The beach road, Route 15, heading west leads to Rustico Island with its twisted spruce trees holding steady against the wind. This area was originally settled by Acadians, and French-speaking families continue to live in this area today. At South Rustico, you'll find an old Farmer's Bank, started in 1864 by Reverend Georges-Etienne Belcourt and a group of Acadian farmers. It used the credit-union principle long before this system was introduced elsewhere in Canada. When the bank closed in 1894, it was not due to lack of support or money. Rather, it was ordered shut by the Canadian government, under pressure from larger banks. As one islander put it, "So much for the Confederation." The two-story sandstone building is now a small museum that includes an exhibit of the bank's own $5 notes.

The Blue Heron Drive continues to the northwest, reaching Cavendish, also situated near the sea. Green Gables House, the fictional home of Anne of Green Gables, is located here and has been made into a museum. If you have read Lucy Maud Montgomery's 1908 book, *Anne of Green Gables,* or seen the film about Anne, you will appreciate visiting the special places in Anne's life, such as the Babbling Brook, the Haunted Woods and Lovers Lane. Montgomery, who died in 1942, is buried nearby at Cavendish Cemetery. It is said that Anne's fictional home is the tenth most popular travel destination for the Japanese.

The Blue Heron Drive really takes on a magic quality after Cavendish. The road winds and curves past Hope River and Stanley Bridge, where the views of New London Bay, the green hills, blue herons and white clapboard farmhouses seem untouched by the chaos of the twentieth century. At Stanley Bridge, there is a marine aquarium with live seals and fish and a display of mounted birds and butterflies from all over the world. From Stanley Bridge, you can take a detour south on Route 254 to see Devil's Punch Bowl Provincial Park. The story goes that in 1771, a man hauling a wagonload of liquor met the devil here. He was so shocked by the sight that his liquor fell off the wagon, forming a huge crater in the earth. While the man was able to get back "on the wagon," he had to leave his liquor behind.

Next you'll pass New London, the birthplace of Lucy Maud Montgomery. From New London, the Blue Heron Drive crosses Southwest River and passes through Springbrook, French River and Malpeque. Malpeque is famous for its flower gardens, featuring 400 colors and varieties of the dahlia, among many others. At one time, Malpeque was an important port for schooners and was slated to be the "capital" of Prince County. But when the railroad was built across the island, it stopped in Kensington, not Malpeque. As the schooner trade faded, so did Malpeque's importance. One relic to its past is an old gabled house that was once a hotel for merchants, sea captains and traders.

From Malpeque, you can reach Cabot Provincial Park, which overlooks the Darnley Basin, Malpeque Bay and Hog Island. The drive then turns south, and reaches the town of Kensington, where there is a military museum with relics dating back to the Boer War.

From Kensington, the Blue Heron Drive heads southwest towards Bedeque Bay and Dunk River.

"The Dunk" is the largest fresh-water stream on the island and is the center of considerable attention among the island's marine biologists, naturalists and others. It is also the best salmon and trout fishing river in all of Prince Edward Island.

The Blue Heron Drive then reaches Borden, where a tour of the island's South Shore begins. Borden is the site where the ferries arrive from Cape Tormentine, New Brunswick. The town was named after Sir Robert Borden, Prime Minister of Canada in 1918, the year that the community was established as a ferry terminal for services to the mainland. In the 1900s, prior to the advent of modern ice breaker vessels, islanders wanting to reach the mainland in winter had to use iceboats—rowboats reinforced with iron runners.

At nearby Cape Traverse, you'll see a replica of one of the old iceboats on display. At the border of Prince County and Queens County you'll pass through the small town of Victoria. The harbor and nearby provincial park are quite picturesque. It is said that from Victoria wharf, a phantom ship has been sighted at night, burning in the Northumberland Strait. The South Shore of Prince Edward Island has a network of provincial parks, most notably the Argyle Shore

Provincial Park. The Argyle Shore is characterized by sandstone cliffs and layers of bedrock that are multicolored. At Argyle Shore, Victoria and Chelton there are facilities for swimmers and picnickers and ample room to wander along the beaches. Inland, visit the town of Strathgartney and the provincial park here. You'll find nature trails and a picnic site. Farther inland, you'll reach Bonshaw Provincial Park where the river is popular with sports fishermen searching for speckled trout, rainbow trout and Atlantic salmon.

As you approach Rocky Point along the Blue Heron Trail look for the cliff-top church of St. Martin's in Cumberland. Built of red island sandstone to withstand the winter winds, it is the smallest stone church east of Québec. Rocky Point and Cape Tyron are the site of the first white settlement on Prince Edward Island. In 1720, 200 French settlers arrived here, shortly before the onset of winter. The Micmac Indians were generous, helping these early settlers survive through the winter. The French built up their defenses at Port La Joye and hoped to develop the island as a "breadbasket" of agriculture to feed the French settlement at Louisbourg. But without much assistance from the French government, the settlement did not last. It was taken over by the British in 1758 and renamed Fort Amherst. The British used the fort until 1768, when they relocated and let the fort crumble to ruins. Unlike the Fortress of Louisbourg, no reconstruction of the site has ever been attempted. There are some artifacts from the British and French settlements here, unearthed during the 1970s. The site is open from June 1 to Labor Day every day between 10 A.M. and 6 P.M. Admission is free.

From Fort Amherst, the Blue Heron Drive turns eastward across the West River past Cornwall, North River and back to Charlottetown.

Accommodations

Brackley Beach has plenty of accommodations for visitors to the Prince Edward Island National Park. On the upper scale, try **Millstream Cottage and Motel** (672-2186, $55-65 single/double) or **Shaw's Hotel and Cottages** (672-2022, $135-160 single/double). For a cozier atmosphere try the **Windsong Farm Bed & Breakfast** (672-2874, $65-70 single/double) complete with hearty breakfast, common sitting room and nearby ocean beach. **North Shore Bed & Breakfast** (672-2242, $40-45 single/double) has lovely rooms with complimentary farm breakfast. For rustic cottages, try **Brackley Beach on the Bay Cottages** (19 Centennial Drive, Sherwood,

892-9762, $70 per day) close to the island visitor information center.

At Grand Tracadie, also along the Prince Edward Island National Park, try the grand **Dalvay-by-the-Sea** (Route 2 east to Route 6, 672-2048, $175-275 nightly). This lovely Victorian hotel has all the makings for a great holiday. The restaurant is open to nonhotel guests, and there is easy access to the beach. At Rusticoville, there's **The Breakers-by-the Sea** (on Route 6, five miles from Cavendish, 963-2555, $125 daily). On a less expensive scale, try **The Pines Motel** (Rusticoville, 963-2029, $80) with six cottages on the shore and a licensed dining room. At North Rustico, there's **Gulf View Cottages** (963-2052, $70) only ten minutes from the beach. Or try **MacLure Bed & Breakfast** (four miles from Cavendish, 963-2239, $45 nightly).

Cavendish is a popular place to stay for tourists who wish to visit the home of Anne of Green Gables. There is an endless variety of accommodations here starting with motor inns and ending with bed & breakfasts. **Cavendish Gulf View Motel and Cottages** (963-2181, $80-120) has spacious grounds, ocean views, a golf course and deep-sea fishing tours. For something different, try the **Island Wild Resort** (Route 6, just east of Cavendish, 963-2193, $80-150 single/double) with its cottages, ocean views and sun decks. For a more casual setting, there's **MacLure Bed & Breakfast** (Hunter River, Cavendish, 963-2239, $30-35) with continental breakfast and transportation on request. Also try **Avonlea Cottages** (963-2729, $50-70 single/double) with one- to three-bedroom cottages and licensed dining room.

As the Blue Heron Drive turns southward, you'll reach the **Captain's Quarters** (entrance to Cabot Provincial Park at Malpeque, 836-5169, $65 single/double) within walking distance of the ocean. Also **Duggan Guest Home** (Kensington, 836-3444, $30 daily, $200 weekly) is near the Malpeque gardens. At Borden, where the ferry from New Brunswick docks, try the **Carleton Motel** (five minutes from ferry, 855-2644, $40-70 single/double) with its licensed dining room. Or try the **Dutchess Gateway Bed & Breakfast** (855-2765, $40 daily) with a licensed dining room, tennis court and beach nearby.

Campgrounds

There are plenty of camping areas along the Blue Heron Trail, particularly near the Prince Edward Island National Park. At Brackley Beach, try **Dunwurkin-by-the Sea** (between Brackley Beach and Oyster Bed Bridge, 672-3390, $15). It's only 20 minutes from Charlottetown, complete with waterfront sites, washrooms and laundry facilities.

On Rustico Island, **Rustico Island Campground** (three miles west of Brackley Beach, 672-2211, $10) features summer evening theater and slide shows. At Stanhope, **Stanhope Campground** (on Gulf Shore Parkway, 672-2211, $17) has a licensed dining room and is close to a golf course and the beach.

Cavendish Campground (one mile west of Cavendish on Gulf Shore Parkway, 672-2211, $15) is run by the National Park service. At **Cavendish Sunset Campground** (National Park entrance, 963-2440, $16) there is an amusement center, licensed dining room nearby and kitchen shelters. In Prince County, along the Blue Heron Trail, the **Cabot Provincial Park** (Malpeque, 836-5635, $14) has a supervised beach, kitchen shelters and laundromat. At Eldon, try **Lord Selkirk Provincial Park** (659-2427, $14) with its recreation program with evening activities.

Dining

The whole Prince Edward Island National Park area has plenty of seafood, lobster and special suppers. **Lobster Trap Lounge** (Route 15, 672-2769) has sandwiches, salads, and mussels. Also try **North Winds Motel** (Route 6, 672-2245) for fish and chips and burgers. At Grand Tracadie, treat yourself to an excellent meal at **Dalvay-by-the-Sea** (Route 6, 672-2048). The licensed dining room is open to non-hotel guests for seafood, lobster and steaks. The **Rustico Resort** (Route 242, South Rustico, 963-2357) has excellent seafood and steaks. In North Rustico, try **Idle Oars Restaurant** (Route 6, 963-2534) for seafood.

In Cavendish, the **Galley Restaurant** (Route 13, 963-3383) has good seafood and steaks. For lobster, try the **Lobster Plate** (Route 6, 963-3312).

At Malpeque, try **Cabot Fisheries Co-op** (836-3062) with unusual features like snow crab (in season), eel and shellfish. At Victoria, near the Argyle Shore Provincial Park, try **Victoria Seafoods** (658-2018) for fresh scallops and seafood.

THE KING'S BYWAY

O n arriving in Charlottetown, I asked a local what his favorite part of the island was. He said, "undoubtedly, eastern Prince Edward Island. It's beautiful, untouristed and uncluttered." I found his judgment to be absolutely true. The eastern part of Prince Edward Island is hilly and rugged; its fields are the deepest green and the island's finest white sand beach is here at Panmure Island. In summer, the landscape is carpeted with purple, pink and yellow blooms of lupine. It's well worth a tour, and the 234-mile-long King's Byway Drive—which covers much of Eastern Prince Edward Island and King's County—is the ideal way to experience it.

NORTH TO THE GULF

Eastern Prince Edward Island is almost entirely separated from the rest of the island by the vast Hillsborough River that stretches from Charlottetown to northern Prince Edward Island, stopping at tiny Head of Hillsborough. Take Route 2, the King's Byway, north from Charlottetown through the tobacco-growing regions to St. Andrew's. Here at St. Andrew's National Historic Site you'll see the restored church that honors the Scottish-born Reverend Angus McEachern, the province's first Catholic bishop. The church was built in 1805 and has since been renovated. During summer there is a schedule of concerts and a lecture series.

A monument here marks the site on which McEachern founded St. Andrew's College—the island's first institution of higher learning— in 1831. St. Andrew's is just north of Mt. Stewart, a very small town quite possibly of very little significance to other travelers—-but important to me because my great great-grandfather, a descendant of early Loyalist settlers, lived and is buried here. I went to the small cemetery at Mt. Stewart and found his aged tombstone. His surname was Clark, and he was buried next to his wife, whose maiden name was Coffin. I then went to the post office and asked a woman if there were still Clarks living in town. She said yes. Then I told her that my great great-grandmother was a Coffin. "Well, my last name is Coffin!"

she said. I later noticed throughout my travels in Prince Edward Island that other people were scanning cemeteries, looking for the names of their Loyalist, Scottish, Irish or French ancestors.

Continue north from Mt. Stewart past Savage Harbour and St. Peter's Bay, two areas where it's possible to join a deep-sea fishing tour of the Gulf of St. Lawrence. St. Peter's Bay was named for a French nobleman, Comte de St. Pierre, who, in 1719, received a grant from the king of France to develop the colony on Île St. Jean (Prince Edward Island). At one point, St. Peter's prospered as the island's chief fishing center, but with little assistance from the French government this settlement eventually failed. In 1865, St. Peter's Lighthouse was built and is still in use today. The nearby village of Morell was named for Jean-Francois Morell, who lived here in 1739. The Morell River crosses King's County from north to south and is one of the island's wilder rivers. The Micmacs once referred to this area as *Pogoosumkek,* which means "clam ground river."

The area from St. Peter's to Naufrage is fairly flat terrain, but you'll pass plenty of fishing shacks and rugged shoreline before reaching Naufrage Harbour and Shipwreck Point. There is an old lighthouse here at the tip of the busy Naufrage Harbour. Continue on to Shipwreck Point, a site where many ships and sailors were lost at sea. Locals have been known to share a few stories about sighting ghost ships or finding sunken treasure here.

Continue on the King's Byway to North Lake. A relatively quiet lobstering village for much of the year, the area becomes the "Tuna Capital of the World" from August through October. Although North Lake has long been a prime destination for sports fishermen, in recent years the tuna seem to have moved elsewhere; they are not caught as often as they used to be. Be sure to check with a deep-sea fishing outfit to see how the tuna are running before heading out. A North Lake fisherman caught a 1,469-pound tuna in 1979, said to be the largest tuna in the world.

North Lake is also close to Campbells Cove Provincial Park. From here, Route 16 heads to East Point, so named because it's the most eastern point on the island. At East Point, you can visit the last manned lighthouse on Prince Edward Island, a wooden structure built in 1867. This area was once called *Kespemenagek* by the Micmac, meaning "the end of the island." You can park at East Point and walk to the lighthouse and the edge of the shore. In the distance you'll see Nova Scotia.

From East Point, follow the King's Byway to Basin Head. This beautiful bluff overlooking the Atlantic is the site of the Basin Head Fisheries Museum. Built like an old-style fish factory, the museum overlooks a small natural harbor that has a narrow entrance marked by a small arched bridge. In the early mornings, you can watch the fishermen heading out of this coastal inlet to the open sea, as their boats putter beneath the bridge leaving hardly a wake. The museum features plenty of photographs and artifacts depicting bygone fishing days on Prince Edward Island. In August the museum hosts a Harvest of the Sea festival. Basin Head is close to Red Point Provincial Park, which has grassy sand dunes leading out to fine beaches for picnicking or swimming. The beaches here are characterized by their singing sands. Well, not singing, exactly—actually, they make a squeaky sound as you walk.

SOURIS

This pleasant little town's name means "mouse" in French. Apparently, the early French settlers were overrun with field mice that destroyed their crops. The mice had most likely arrived on an incoming ship from Europe, and they multiplied quickly in the nearby forests. Souris is best known today as the ferry departure point for trips to the Magdalen Islands. The trip from Souris to Cap-aux-Meules is very popular with French Canadians because the Magdalen Islands are officially a part of Québec. With their magnificent sandbars, dunes and beaches, they serve many Canadians as a summer holiday spot. The Magdalen Islands are also attracting the attention of seal lovers and naturalists. Each March, thousands of harp seals are born in the Gulf of St. Lawrence, particularly on these islands. These white baby seals were once clubbed to death for their fur, but this practice is banned today. Now, you can join a tour out of Halifax and observe them in their natural environment. If you're interested, contact Natural Habitat Wildlife Adventures, One Sussex Station, Sussex, New Jersey 07461, (800) 543-8917.

There are regular ferry crossings from Souris at 2 P.M. in summer, except on Tuesdays. There are also regular flights from Charlottetown. For more information about the Îles de la Madeleine (Magdalen Islands) write to Association Touristique des Îles de la Madeleine, C.P. 1028 Cap-aux-Meules, Îles de la Madeleine, Québec,

Canada G0B 1B0, or phone (418) 986-2245. Overlooking the harbor at Souris, you'll see St. Mary's Roman Catholic Church, an impressive structure built of island sandstone in 1901.

The King's Byway continues to Rollo Bay, site of the annual outdoor Scottish fiddling and step-dancing festival staged in July.

Continue from here past Bay Fortune and Abells Cape. Once an actor's colony, Abells Cape was a favorite summer home for the stars who came from both Canada and the United States. There is a strange legend that tells of a man's last request to be buried at Abells Cape. When he eventually died, his family could not afford to send his body to Prince Edward Island and so he was buried in the southern United States. The cemetery where he was buried bordered the sea and during a storm, the actor's grave was overwhelmed by the ocean and swept out to sea. Months later a coffin washed up on the shores of Abells Cape containing the body of the actor!

By turning inland onto Route 4, you'll reach the town of Dundas. In late August, Dundas is the scene for the Prince Edward Island Plowing Match and Agricultural Fair. The fair features highland dancing, country music and home cooking. There are prizes awarded for the best beef and dairy cattle and produce.

BAY FORTUNE TO GEORGETOWN

The King's Byway takes this beautiful coastal route overlooking Boughton Bay, where the road then turns inland. If you have time, follow the coast to the small fishing village of Newport and on to Georgetown. Georgetown is a deep-water port and has one of the finer harbors along Canada's east coast. Once a thriving fishing and shipbuilding community, the town's industries have entered a period of decline. Georgetown's theater on Main Street is the oldest in Canada and the site of national theater festivals. This may explain the formation of an actors' summer colony in the 1800s at Abells Cape. Near Georgetown, you can visit Brudenell River Provincial Park, where there are plenty of swimming, camping, canoeing and horseback-riding activities available. Connected to the park by a natural causeway, you'll see Brudenell Island, which has a stone memorial commemorating the Scottish immigrants who settled here in the late 1750s.

At Montague, a pretty town situated along the Montague River, be sure to stop at the Lobster Shanty North for its excellent seafood.

In the guest book, look for the names of Queen Elizabeth II and Prince Philip, who dined here on July 1, 1973, which happens to be Canada Day. At Montague, you can join a boat tour along the Montague River and out to Cardigan Bay. It's not uncommon to sight seals on these tours. From Montague, you are within reach of Panmure Island. The island boasts of having the whitest sand in Prince Edward Island, found at Panmure Island Provincial Park. The island is joined to Prince Edward Island by a natural sandspit causeway. This area is very picturesque, a perfect place to picnic on a summer day. The island has a few elegant homes overlooking St. Mary's Bay and Panmure Head lighthouse, which was built in 1853. From Panmure Island, it's a quick drive to Murray Harbour and Murray River.

THE MURRAY RIVER AREA

Full of basking seals, sailboats, lobster boats and lovely craft shops, the Murray River area is a delightful place to visit. This picturesque area is close to the Wood Island ferry terminal, and it's worth stopping here for the night before taking the morning ferry to Nova Scotia. There are seal-watching tours that take in the beautiful Murray River and the Murray Islands. This is an ideal spot for yachtsmen and sports fishermen. Murray Harbour has a very active fishing fleet that catches lobster and hard-shell clams. It was once called *Esdwadek* by the Micmac Indians, which means "fishing place."

At Murray River, you'll see the old Northumberland Mill and Museum that recreates nineteenth-century life. Located near MacLure's Pond, this area is bordered by the Murray River Pines, the province's best stands of old red and white pine forest. The wood was once used for shipbuilding. For the kids, there's Fantasyland Provincial Park at nearby Gladstone, which has storybook characters and other treats. The King's Byway then runs along the southeastern shore of Prince Edward Island to Wood Island Provincial Park and ferry terminus. The trip to Caribou, Nova Scotia, takes less than an hour, but the lines can be dreadfully long here. Many people comment that the magic of being on such a great island as Prince Edward makes the arrival in Nova Scotia feel like a letdown. That feeling fades, but the notion to return to Prince Edward Island never does.

If you are continuing on to Charlottetown, the King's Byway

from the ferry is also the Trans-Canada Highway. After passing Pinette, a well-known area for clam digging, you'll see a turnoff onto Route 209 to Point Prim. Here you'll see the first lighthouse on the island, built on Point Prim in 1846. The electric light guides ships entering Hillsborough Bay and Charlottetown Harbour.

Just north of Point Prim you'll reach the historic area of Eldon and Belfast and nearby Lord Selkirk Provincial Park.

ELDON AND BELFAST

These two very small towns mark the area to which Lord Selkirk of Scotland led 800 highlanders in 1803. The small settlement of Eldon is still a farming village. Its proximity to Lord Selkirk Provincial Park and Orwell Bay make it a very scenic place to stop. Belfast is the site of St. John's Presbyterian Church, founded in 1823 by Lord Selkirk and the Scottish settlers. In the archives, you'll find the deed of land for the church and nearby cemetery signed by Lord Selkirk.

Orwell Corner is a tiny restored farm village depicting the life of the early Scottish settlers. There is a restored post office, keeper's house, church and barn. The planting and livestock-raising are done much the way they were 200 years ago. During the summer months, a traditional Scottish dance or ceilidh (pronounced kay-lee) is held every Wednesday evening for both locals and visitors. Nearby, there's Sir Andrew MacPhail Provincial Park where camping is permitted. MacPhail was a well-known Prince Edward Island writer and physician who was born here in Orwell in 1864.

For the last leg of the King's Byway, be sure to look east at Mt. Mellick and drive to the top of Tea Hill for a great view of Hillsborough Bay. Tea Hill and Alexandria are noted for their berry farms. From Tea Hill, follow the Trans-Canada Highway (King's Byway) to Charlottetown.

Accommodations

The King's Byway offers plenty of choices with either larger hotels and inns or farm guesthouses and bed & breakfasts. Heading north from Charlottetown, in Morell there's **Kelly's Bed & Breakfast** (Route 2, 961-2389, $35 single, $40 double) and **MoDhaicdh Bed & Breakfast** (Route 2, three miles east of Morrel, 961-2972, $30 single,

$40 double), both with licensed dining rooms and full breakfast. At St. Peter's, try **The Nor'Easter Lodge** (between Routes 2 and 16, 961-2613, $60 single, $65 double), set in the village overlooking St. Peter's Bay. At St. Peter's Bay, there's the **Crab n' Apple Bed & Breakfast** (west from junction of Routes 2 and 313, 961-3165, $30-35 single/double, including continental breakfast). At North Lake, at the far eastern end of Prince Edward Island, the **Bluefin Motel** (on Route 16, 357-2599, $50 single/$5 additional person) has a restaurant serving breakfast, lunch and dinner. Islanders are known to come here in the evening to sing songs and dance.

Around East Point, the **Sea Breeze Motel** in Kingsboro (Route 16, 357-2371, $50 single, $55 double) is set in a quiet area, surrounded by fields of lupine in summer. Licensed dining room, lounge and proximity to Basin Head. At Souris, try the popular **Matthew House Inn** (15 Breakwater Street, 687-3461, $50-70 single/double). This restored inn, overlooking Souris Harbour and one block from the Magdalen Islands ferry terminal, has eight charming rooms with bath.

The **Hilltop Motel** (Souris, 687-3315, $60-65 single/double) has a licensed restaurant and is also close to the Magdalen Islands ferry terminal. **The Inn at Bay Fortune** (Bay Fortune, 687-3745, $90-150 for a suite) is situated on 46 acres facing the sea and has an elegant dining room. In Montague, the very popular **Lobster Shanty North Motel and Cottage** (Route 17, Main Street, 838-2463, $60 double) is best known for its lobster suppers in the licensed dining room. Seal-watching cruises are nearby. Panmure Island is a great spot to stay, so try **Partridge's Bed & Breakfast** (838-4687, $50 single/double), which is close to a white sandy beach. Farther south in the Murray Harbour North area, **Lady Catherine's Bed & Breakfast** (Route 17, 962-3426, $40-45 single/double) is a nice, relaxing place to stay overlooking Northumberland Strait. At Murray River, **Fahlman Cottages** (Route 4, 962-3734, $40 single/double) is close to craft shops, museums and restaurants. Murray Harbour has plenty of accommodations for weekenders and tourists. Try **Forest and Stream Cottages** (Route 18, 962-3537, $50-55 single/double) with rowboating, bird-watching and nature trails. **Fox River Cottages** (Machon Point Road, 962-2881, $60) with its peaceful, scenic and secluded setting, is another good place to stay at Murray Harbour.

Campsites

At St. Peter's, try **St. Peter's Park** (Route 2 on St. Peter's Bay, 961-2786, $14) with kitchen shelter and free firewood. At the far eastern end of Prince Edward Island, try **Red Point Provincial Park** (Route 16, east of Souris, 357-2463, $14) with a supervised beach and a recreation program with evening activities. Panmure Island is a nice place for camping and offers plenty of facilities through the **Panmure Island Provincial Park** (Route 347, north of Gaspereaux, 838-4719, $14). Proximity to bay and ocean beach; fireplaces; canteen. At Murray Harbour, there's **Alpha and Omega Campground** (Route 18, 962-2494, $12) with rowboats, trout fishing and seal-watching cruises available. Murray Harbour North has **Seal Cove Campground** (30 minutes from Wood Island Ferry, 962-2745, $12) with dining room and nearby beach.

Dining

At Morell, the popular **Morell Legion Salmon and Lobster** (off Route 2, 961-2110) features seafood and steak. In North Lake, try the **Rod and Reel Restaurant** (Route 16, 357-2784), well known for its seafood, meat and vegetarian meals. It's a fun spot to come in the evening and meet Islanders.

Souris has plenty of restaurants, such as **Blue Fin Restaurant** (Feidel Avenue, 687-3271), with seafood and steaks, and **Hilltop Motel** (Lee Crane Drive, 687-3315), with sandwiches and burgers. At Souris West, try the **Platter House** (Route 2, 687-2764) for seafood platters and salads. In Georgetown, there's the **Drop Anchor Restaurant** (Georgetown Wharf, 652-2509) for seafood. Bay Fortune has a special dining place with a full menu, called **The Inn at Bay Fortune** (Route 310, 687-3745). Montague has the famous **Lobster Shanty North** (Main Street, 838-2463), featuring some of the best lobster and seafood on the southeastern shore.

In Murray River, try the **Terrace Heights** (Route 348, 962-2465) for seafood and Canadian cuisine. At Wood Island, there's **Crabby's Seafood** (Trans-Canada Highway, 963-3228), featuring (what else?) seafood. Visit the **Lighthouse Tea Room and Art Gallery** (Route 209, Point Prim Lighthouse) at Point Prim. At Eldon, **Selkirk Lobster Suppers** (Route 1, 659-2435) specializes in all-you-can-eat lobster.

Excursions

At Murray River, seal-viewing excursions are very popular. One of the better tours is **Garry's Seal Cruise** (962-2494). The tours depart at 1:00 P.M. 3:30 P.M. and 6:30 P.M. in summer and cost $12.50 for adults and $6.50 for children. Seal cruises from Montague are conducted by **Cruise Manada** (Montague Wharf, 838-3444, adults $12.50, children $6.50). For fishing, contact **Johnnie's Deep Sea Fishing** (Route 16, Naufrage Harbor, 961-2260), which takes three trips daily in summer. At North Lake, contact **Bluefin Tuna Charters** (357-2785). The boat departs daily at 9 A.M., 1 P.M. and 4:30 P.M. An eight-hour charter costs $300; a three-hour tour costs $15 per person. Also at North Lake, try **North Lake Tuna Charters, Inc.** (357-2055, eight-hour charter for $300).

THE LADY SLIPPER DRIVE

Western Prince Edward Island's low-lying terrain is less dramatic than eastern Prince Edward Island, and this region is certainly less visited than central Prince Edward Island. But there is still plenty to see and do. Along the Lady Slipper Drive, which is named after the island's official flower, you'll see twin-spired churches in seaside villages like Egmont Bay and Mount Carmel and hear the French language spoken among the Acadians living there.

The explorer Jacques Cartier landed on western Prince Edward Island near Alberton in 1536. He named the island Île St. Jean, leading the way for French settlement. The Acadians arrived in the early 1600s and farmed the land, fighting off plagues and the threat of starvation. During the British purges of 1758, when thousands of Acadians in Nova Scotia and New Brunswick were driven off their land, many Acadians on Prince Edward Island went into hiding in the woods. The 15,000 Acadians living on the island today are the descendants of these early settlers. Much of the woodlands in western Prince Edward Island were later used in the shipbuilding industry that prospered here in the nineteenth century.

Today, Prince County produces half of the island's potato crop. The sandy, red soil and temperate climate make Prince Edward Island an ideal spot for potatoes, which were introduced by early settlers in the 1700s. It's not unusual to hear other Maritimers refer to Prince Edward Islanders as "spuds" from "Spud Island." Of course, Islanders refer to Nova Scotians as "herring chokers" or "bluenosers," and to Newfoundlanders as "newfies." Western Prince Edward Island is also the location of a thriving Micmac Indian community—the Lennox Island Micmac nation. It has been home to the remaining Micmac people in Prince Edward Island since the late 1800s.

Although the Lady Slipper Drive officially begins at Summerside, if you are coming from the Blue Heron Drive, pick up the new route at Kensington. The route then dips down to Summerside to Cape Egmont and the Acadian Pioneer Village, then heads north to the fishing centers of Tignish and Alberton. Also along the north coast is Malpeque Bay, famous for its Malpeque oysters. After making a large loop, the route returns to Summerside.

SUMMERSIDE

This town, built along the shore, is marked by wooden homes and stores and an old town clock. It is sometimes referred to as the island's western capital. The town center has the appeal of a bustling turn-of-the-century community, lacking some of the sophistication of Charlottetown but very appealing to the eye. Closer to the waterfront, there are some new shops and restaurants being developed—this makes the area more attractive to pedestrians who want to shop and dine. Nearby is the Summerside Yacht Club with its splendid views of Bedeque Bay and Holman's Island. The latter was the site of a 125-room hotel destroyed by fire in 1904. Summerside is the home of the Canadian Forces Base (C.F.B.) that functions as an airborne search-and-rescue headquarters for Atlantic Canada. It is not uncommon for Maritimers to hear on the news that "the ship's crew were rescued by helicopter from C.F.B. Summerside." For people who make their living from the sea, these are very reassuring words.

From Summerside, head west to Cape Egmont, site of a recreated Acadian Pioneer Village based on an 1800 to 1820 settlement. The nearby town of Mount Carmel, overlooking Egmont Bay and marked by two tall-spired churches, is also authentically French—a thriving Acadian community of today. At the Historic Site, there is a restaurant called the Étoile de Mer serving traditional dishes like *fricot au poulet* (a hearty chicken stew) or *pâté à la rapure* (chicken and potato pie), which should be sampled.

From Mount Carmel to Egmont Bay, you can savor the Acadians' way of life, with their neatly kept homes and gardens, and the Acadian flag flying in front of the houses as an ever-present symbol of their identity. The baroque- and gothic-style churches, more commonly found in Europe, enhance the unique landscape. By traveling along Route 11, you'll reach Cape Egmont, with its aged lighthouse. Lobster is plentiful here; you can buy it fresh in late summer and early fall from the Acadian Fishermen's Co-operative at Cape Egmont.

Rounding the point and heading north, you'll reach Abram-Village where Acadian handcrafts, livestock and farm produce are on display. Each Labor Day weekend, the annual Egmont Bay and Mount Carmel Exhibition is held here in conjunction with Le Festival Acadien. This event features Acadian music, dance and cuisine.

The Lady Slipper Drive follows the coast a bit farther and then turns inland to Mt. Pleasant. You'll find that the area north from here

---

has less of the Acadian feel to it. By turning west you can reach West Point and Cedar Dunes Provincial Park. This is the westernmost point of Prince Edward Island. At the park, you'll see West Point Lighthouse, a century-old wooden structure that was manned until 1963. This lighthouse, now equipped with a modern electric lamp, is a crucial navigational aid to the huge freighters and oil tankers that ply these waters. The lighthouse was recently restored and now features a museum, licensed dining room, handcraft outlet and ten guestrooms. You'll learn at the museum that of the 76 lighthouses covering the island, only 16 are still in use and only 1 is still manned.

The north shore from West Point to North Cape is rich in "Irish moss," a type of seaweed that is harvested, processed and used as a thickener in yogurts, cosmetics and paints. Western Prince Edward Island's North Shore is the world's richest source of this product. After a storm, farmers and fishermen come down to the shore and rake in the dark purple seaweed. If you're lucky, you can observe the practice of "gathering the moss."

The area from Cape Wolfe (named for General James Wolfe who anchored here in 1759 on his way to lay siege to Québec) to Christopher's Cross is ideal for exploring. There are fishing villages, provincial parks and a strong sense of remoteness and unspoiled beauty that you only get from being on the shores of Prince Edward Island.

From Christopher's Cross, travel north to Seacow Pond and North Cape. Seacow Pond was named for the walruses that once bred and lived here by the thousands. They were hunted to near extinction by the early settlers and privateers. At windy North Cape, where the Gulf of St. Lawrence meets the tides of the Northumberland Strait, you'll see the Atlantic Wind Test Site, an international laboratory that uses windmills to experiment with alternative sources of energy.

From the northernmost tip of Prince Edward Island, ramble eastward down the other side of the Lady Slipper Drive to the bustling community of Tignish. This town is the center of activity along Prince Edward Island's far northwestern shore and is the western terminus for the Canadian National Railway on the island. Tignish has long been a fishing community whose proximity to both the Tignish River and the rich Gulf of St. Lawrence assured its prosperity. Vast quantities of cod and lobster are shipped out of Tignish each year; the town is one of the largest producers of processed lobster products worldwide. In 1923, the fishermen of Tignish formed the Tignish Fishermen's Co-op, the first organized union of fishermen in Canada.

Farther south is Jacques Cartier Provincial Park, which encompasses a 30-mile chain of sand dunes and beach all the way to Malpeque. Islanders consider it their province's best park. The islands just off shore along this stretch of beach are accessible by canoe or on foot at low tide. The protected bays are excellent sites for oysters and clams.

Alberton was the site of a bustling silver fox-raising industry, cofounded in 1894 by Charles Dalton and Robert Oulton. As a young man, Dalton was a trapper and woodsman on Prince Edward Island. He often noticed the Indians catching the occasional silver fox amidst the usual red foxes. These rare pelts were in big demand, so Dalton and Oulton captured two silver foxes and began breeding them. The industry thrived for 40 years, and at its peak, breeding pairs were worth $15,000. By the 1920s, many other entrepreneurs were breeding silver foxes, and with the onslaught of the depression, the company folded. Dalton went on to be lieutenant-governor of Prince Edward Island from 1930 to 1933.

The Lady Slipper Drive continues south towards the Tyne Valley. Here, follow Route 163 towards Lennox Island, which is home to the remaining Micmac Indians. This active community operates a company called Mahemigew, Inc. (meaning "coming from Mother Earth"), which harvests peat moss and blueberries. Fishing is another important industry. The Micmacs have their own school and teach their own language, as well as English. They also operate a health clinic and recreational facilities. Lennox Island became the homeland of the Micmac people in the late 1800s. Although the Micmacs were forced to give up their nomadic way of life, the community today seems to have thrived here as well as can be expected. The Lennox Island Band Council has published *Micmac Legends of Prince Edward Island,* which is interesting and well worth buying.

From Lennox Island, you can rejoin the Lady Slipper Drive on Route 12 and travel along Malpeque Bay, renowned for the more than ten million Malpeque oysters that are harvested here annually. The best oysters are harvested in spring and early summer, and for those of us who are oyster-lovers there is no better taste than a cold, raw oyster bought at its source. Malpeque Bay oysters are shipped all over the world and command high prices at gourmet restaurants. Because of conservation restrictions, the oyster beds are carefully protected and not overharvested. Oyster farming is a real science; the beds are moved at various times in the oysters' growth cycle to enhance their survival rates. After five years of waiting, they are ready to be harvested.

At Port Hill, near the Green Park Provincial Park, you can visit the restored home of James Yeo, Jr., which was built in 1864. Yeo was involved in shipbuilding on Prince Edward Island. For more insight into this once-thriving industry, visit the Green Park Shipbuilding Museum nearby.

Continuing on Lady Slipper Drive along Route 12, you'll pass the interesting settlements called South West Lot 16 and Central Lot 16. These are not Orwellian names of an island gone mad, but remnants of days long ago when wealthy British noblemen owned much of the islands. They served as absentee landlords of lots divided up by Captain Samuel Holland, who surveyed the island in 1764. By 1853, this practice of absentee landlordism was abolished, and most of the 67 lots were given proper names. These two lots were never given names, however.

And finally, the Lady Slipper Drive meets up with Route 2 heading back to Summerside and the circular tour is complete.

Accommodations

Summerside, with plenty of rooms, is a good starting point for exploring western Prince Edward Island. **Best Western Linkletter Inn and Convention Center** (311 Market Street, 436-2157, $75-100 single/double) is a new complex featuring a licensed dining room, mini-bars and handicapped accessibility. **Cairns Motel** (721 Water Street East, 436-5841, $40 single, $45 double) has a licensed dining room, a drive-in theater and is close to shops. Also in Summerside, **Silver Fox Inn** (61 Granville Street, 436-4033, $60-65 single/double) is an historic inn built as a private residence in 1892 and has spacious rooms with fireplaces.

At Mount Carmel, **Cormier's Cottages** (Route 11, 854-2872, $45 doubles, $5 additional person) has a dining room and separate cottages. Farther north at Abram-Village, there's the expensive **Chalet de Par-En-Bas** (Route 11, 854-2562, $100 daily). On the northwestern shore, **Ocean Side Bed & Breakfast** (Route 14, 859-3300, $35 single, $42 double) at Campbellton is a good place to stay. Farther north at Skinner's Pond, there's **Harbour Lights Cottages** (Route 14, 882-2479, $35 doubles, $5 additional) and **Keefe's Farm Tourist Home** (Route 14, six miles southwest of Tignish, 882-2686, $25). **Murphy's Tourist Home and Cottages** (Route 153, tel 882-2667, $35 single, $45 double) is another good place. Alberton also has some good inns and bed & breakfasts including **Poplar Lane Bed & Breakfast** (Main Street onto Poplar Street, 853-3732, $40 single, $45 double) and **Westerner Motel** (Route 12 at entrance to Alberton, 853-2215, $50-55 single/double). The Tyne Valley has some good accommodations at the **Tyne Valley Inn** (Route 12, 831-2042, $55-80 single/double) and the **West Island Inn** (Route 12 at Route 167, 831-2495, $40-55 single/double). At Grand River, the **MacLellan Homestead** (Richmond, RR 1, 854-2270, $80 double, $5 additional) is a five-bedroom country home on spacious grounds.

Campgrounds

At Cape Egmont, try **Moonlight Camping** (854-2746, $12) in the Acadian region of Prince Edward Island. West Point has the **Cedar Dunes Provincial Park** (Route 14, 15 miles south of O'Leary, 859-2711, $14), which overlooks a beach and has plenty of nature trails. On the northwest shore, try the **Harbour Lights Trailer Park** (Skinners Pond, Route 14, 436-2479, $10) where the center of the Irish moss industry is located. On the northeastern shore of Prince County, the highly recommended **Jacques Cartier Provincial Park** (Kildare Capes, 853-3232, $14) is on the beach, with kitchen shelter, canteen and camper's store. Port Hill has the **Green Park Provincial Park** (Route 12, four miles east of Tyne Valley, 831-2370, $15) with its shipbuilding display center and museum.

Dining

In Summerside, there is a stretch of fast food restaurants along Water Street ranging from **Pizza Delight** to **McDonald's.** For more traditional Canadian food, try **Estey's Fish and Chips** (148 Pope Road, 436-3459) or **Cosy Corners** (499 Water Street, 436-6550) for soups, roast beef and burgers. For licensed dining, try **Regent Restaurant and Lounge** (12 Summer Street, 436-3200) for seafood, steaks and salad bar.

Along the Lady Slipper Drive, **Étoile de Mer** (Mount Carmel, Acadian Village, 854-2227) features traditional Acadian cooking. At West Point, **West Point Lighthouse** (Route 14, 859-3605) is a restaurant within a lighthouse, featuring excellent chowders, seafood and steaks. In Miminegash, there's **Deagle's Holding, Ltd.** (Route 14, 882-2781), for fast food. At North Cape, **Wind and Reef** (Route 12, 882-3535) has seafood. Tignish, on the northeastern side of Prince

County, has the **Hitching Post Restaurant and Take-Out** (Route 2, 882-2172), and farther south there's the **Tyne Valley Inn** (Route 12, 831-2042) for home-cooked foods. At Malpeque, there's **Cabot Reach Restaurant** (off Route 20, 836-5597) for seafood and burgers. In Kensington, the **Pioneer Room** (21 School Street, 836-3547) has seafood, burgers and steaks.

Excursions

Prince County is not as well known for its deep-sea fishing as the rest of Prince Edward Island, but there are plenty of trout and salmon in the many rivers. Oysters and clams are plentiful too. At Cape Wolfe, go to **By-the-Sea Fish Farm** (on Route 14, 859-2701) where a well-stocked pond makes fishing rewarding. For deep-sea fishing, there's **Mel's Deep-Sea Fishing** (Tignish Shore, 882-2983). The price is $15 for adults for three hours. The many provincial parks in Prince County provide free activities for visitors organized by the park's staff. Camping, day-use activities and supervised ocean swimming are also available.

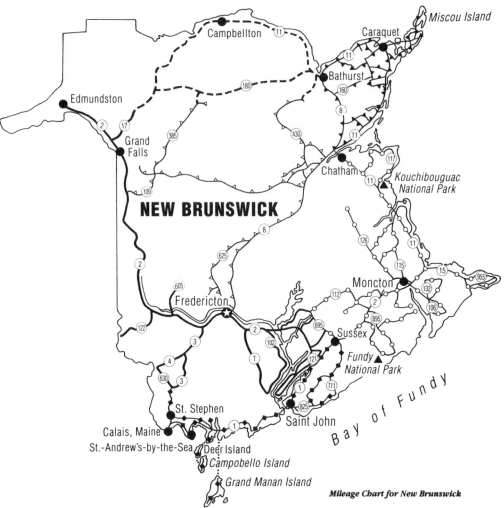

NEW BRUNSWICK

Campbellton
Miscou Island
Caraquet
Bathurst
Edmundston
Grand Falls
Chatham
Kouchibouguac National Park
Moncton
Fredericton
Sussex
Fundy National Park
St. Stephen
Calais, Maine
St.-Andrew's-by-the-Sea
Deer Island
Campobello Island
Grand Manan Island
Saint John
Bay of Fundy

The Fundy Tidal Coast

The Saint John River Valley

Southeast Shores

Miramichi Basin

The Acadian Shore

The Restigouche Uplands
and Central New Brunswick

Mileage Chart for New Brunswick

St. Stephen to Saint John	66 miles
St. Andrew's to Saint John	60 miles
Saint John to Fredericton	64 miles
Saint John to Moncton	94 miles
Saint John to Bathurst	221 miles
Saint John to Sackville	127 miles
Saint John to Edmunston	237 miles
Fredericton to Edmunston	171 miles
Fredericton to Grand Falls	134 miles
Fredericton to Campbellton	225 miles
St. Stephen to Cape Tormentine	224 miles
Woodstock to Sackville	205 miles
Grand Falls to Fredericton	134 miles
Grand Falls to Saint John	198 miles
Saint John to Chatham	177 miles
Saint John to Halifax, NS	265 miles
Saint John to Charlottetown, PEI*	201 miles
Saint John to St. John's, NF*	1,040 miles
Calais, ME, to Saint John, NB	71 miles
Bangor, ME, to Moncton, NB	285 miles

*By ferry

NEW BRUNSWICK
NATURE'S UNSPOILED REALM

Pretend we belong to a civilization, even a dying one.
Pretend. Pretend.
But there are woods and the rivers and the wind blowing.
There is the sea. Space. The wind blowing.
    —ELIZABETH BREWSTER
    FROM THE POEM "EAST COAST—CANADA"

This poet seems to capture the essence of New Brunswick, linked as it is to a rugged environment and historic past. New Brunswick is the Maritimes' least explored province, with more unspoiled wilderness area than the rest of Atlantic Canada combined. New Brunswick is characterized by forests and rivers but is also surrounded on three sides by the sea. Its Fundy Tides are world renowned, and its great rivers like the Miramichi attract canoers, kayakers and fishermen from around the globe. Yet despite its vast network of waterways from the Saint John River Valley (the Rhine of North America) to the channels and bays along the eastern coast, the settlements in New Brunswick are still sparse. Only 700,000 people live in a province that covers 28,354 square miles, 85 percent of which is forested.

Primarily made up of the descendants of Loyalists and Acadian settlers, two of the more prominent groups in Maritime history, New Brunswick has a rich cultural heritage. Immigration from Scotland and Ireland throughout the nineteenth century also added to the cultural makeup of the area. New Brunswick is the only official bilingual province in Canada; French-speaking people account for 35 percent of the population.

The province was one of the four original members of the confederation that created the Dominion of Canada, entering on July 1, 1867. New Brunswick has missed much of the industrial development that encroaches on most of North America. With 90 percent of all settlement huddled around the shores and rivers of New Brunswick, vast tracts of forests and a network of rivers and lakes remain virtually untouched. Because of its proximity to the Northumberland Strait, the waters in summer are quite warm, and the eastern shore is lined with beaches ideal for swimming and recreation. Steeped in culture and with a unique heritage, New Brunswick is an ideal place to spend the summer or fall, re-discovering the province's link to the past and enjoying its unspoiled natural areas.

The province has been divided into several regions by the tourist authority: the Fundy shore, the rugged Acadian coast, the interior with its vast river systems, the Saint John River Valley and the far northern regions of the Restigouche Uplands. Rushing tourists often zip right through these areas en route to Nova Scotia; they learn nothing of the Fundy Isles, the Miramichi River, Baie des Chaleurs or Chignecto Bay. But if you take time to explore this beautiful province, you'll certainly find reasons to return again and again.

A BRIEF HISTORY

Like Nova Scotia, New Brunswick was once a part of Acadia, and the early French settlers in this region also called themselves Acadians. In the 1600s, while the Micmac and Maliceet Indians still roamed the forests and fished the waters here, European fishermen began crossing the Atlantic in summer in search of cod. After a successful stint fishing the Bay of Fundy and the Northumberland Strait, the fishermen would head back to either France, England, Portugal or Spain with salted cod stacked high in their hulls.

Settlement of New Brunswick began after Samuel de Champlain landed at the mouth of the Saint John River in 1604, where there was already a large Indian encampment. Champlain later traveled north to present-day Baie des Chaleurs. The far northern island of Miscou had its first recorded French settler living there in 1627. Nicolas Denys, the French pioneer who recorded invaluable information about the Micmac Indians, also lived on Miscou in 1647. The area around northern New Brunswick continued to thrive as a fishing center, prompting the Acadian farmers to settle here around 1690. Like Nova Scotia, New Brunswick became a focus of dispute between the French and English governments, dragging the Acadians into the conflict. As in Nova Scotia, the Acadians were required to declare allegiance either to the French or to the English, and when they refused to comply, they were driven out of New Brunswick around the year 1755. Some Acadians who hid from the British in the woodlands or across the border in Québec eventually emerged from hiding. Others who had been deported later returned to the regions they once farmed. Today, Acadians make up a third of New Brunswick's population, living along the shores that they have cultivated for 300 years.

After the American Revolution of 1776, thousands of Loyalists, faced with the choice of staying in the newly formed United States or remaining loyal to the British crown, headed for the provinces of Nova Scotia and New Brunswick. While many went to the British garrison community at Halifax, others from New York and Massachusetts came to the Saint John River Valley. Towns like St. Andrew's, St. Stephen, Saint John and St. Martin's still maintain their Loyalist heritage. Loyalist settlement of the Saint John River Valley and the Bay of Fundy in 1784 marked the formation of New Brunswick as a separate province from Nova Scotia. The event was noted in London with the approval of a new seal, making the province "Provinciae Nov Bruns."

Throughout the nineteenth century, settlers arrived from Scotland and Ireland, primarily in the Saint John River Valley. The Gaelic heritage of New Brunswick is not as strong as elsewhere in the Maritimes, but the new immigrants helped the province become a fishing and farming power, a shipbuilding region and lumber-exporting area. The Irish brought their language, music and dances with them, giving the province its colorful Gaelic celebrations.

The flag of New Brunswick, depicting a golden lion on a red bar above an ancient oared galley on a blue ocean, is one of Atlantic Canada's most colorful. New Brunswickers strongly identify with their home province, and the tenacity of both the early Loyalist settlers and the Acadians carries over to today, giving the people an independent streak. It's fascinating to see these two "nations" coexist in the same province.

Because for nearly 300 years, the boat was the main mode of transportation in the province, 85 percent of the province is still forested. This inland wilderness was left to those who wanted the backwoods as a home; the civic-minded Loyalists and Acadians tended to stay within the confines of their hard-won coastal communities. Later, westward migration began to deplete the population of New Brunswick, as new generations headed west to the prairies, to California or the Pacific Northwest. Because the forests were bypassed, there is still plenty that is "wild" about New Brunswick.

GEOGRAPHY AND CLIMATE

With its beautiful forests and shorelines, New Brunswick remains a naturalist's dream. Rivers and lakes are numerous, and there is abundant marine life in the protected waters of Chignecto and Fundy Bays and the Northumberland Strait. The mountainous central highlands are marked by deep lakes, while the coastal shores are subject to some of the highest and lowest tides in the world. The Saint John River Valley provides some of the most dramatic scenery along its vast stretch, ending in Saint John with its reversing falls. Yachtsmen and mariners must wait out the tides to cross these falls, a feat that requires skill and patience. The Fundy Isles, another beautiful region, support an array of wildlife ranging from porpoises and whales to puffins and hawks. New Brunswick's climate is remarkably mild considering the varied geography of the province. Summers tend to be warm by day and cool by night, while winters are cold, snowy and long.

Because the best time to visit New Brunswick is in summer, the months of June, July and August are the busiest time of year. But September and October can also be nice. The first signs of frost usually appear in late September, but the days can still be pleasant. Plenty of visitors choose to come to New Brunswick in the autumn when fall foliage gives the area a riot of golden colors.

HIGHLIGHTS

A highlight of a visit to New Brunswick is the Fundy Trail, which encompasses the beautiful Fundy Isles of Grand Manan, Campobello and Deer. Along this coast the visitor will get a good glimpse of the Loyalist way of life: Be sure to view the beautiful homes of St. Andrew's and pause to soak in the European atmosphere of Saint John. The Saint John River, extending all the way to Fredericton, makes for one of the best river trips in North America. You can enjoy its pastoral beauty all along the riverbanks. Gagetown, in particular, seems set back in time. The Fundy tides at Hopewell Cape are phenomenal to watch, as their dramatic drop creates tidal bores along the Petitcodiac River. The Acadian Trail to the north follows a coast that is warmed by the Gulf Stream and offers beautiful beach resorts with a French ambience. The interior of New Brunswick has the magnificent Miramichi River with its abundance of fish and excellent waterways for canoers and kayakers. Finally, there's the Restigouche Uplands, a vast undeveloped area of rivers and forests, which is particularly popular with hunters and sports fishermen.

PRACTICALITIES

Getting There

BY AIR. Air Canada flies to both Saint John and Fredericton from major Canadian cities and some U.S. cities. Air Nova out of Halifax also offers flights to Saint John. New Brunswick has less air traffic from the United States than Nova Scotia does, due to its relatively easy accessibility by highway. Flights to more remote areas of this vast province can be arranged in Saint John or through your travel agent. There are airports throughout the province in areas like Grand Falls, Edmundston, Chatham and Campbellton.

BY LAND. New Brunswick is bordered by the State of Maine and is accessible from American highways at six points along the border. Typically, Americans from the New England states and New York cross the border between Calais, Maine and St. Stephen, New Brunswick, or they take Highway 95 to Houlton and cross into New Brunswick at Woodstock.

The crossing from Calais in Maine to St. Stephen is ideal because you are immediately at the Fundy shore—one of the most popular tourist regions of the province. You can also drive on to Saint John and take the ferry over to Digby, Nova Scotia. Be sure to fill up with gasoline before leaving the states, because the price for fuel is much higher in Canada.

The Trans-Canada Highway runs throughout the province, and major roads are well maintained. The back roads are also in good condition. The tourist authority can provide specific route and destination information throughout the province. New Brunswick's highways can offer a quick lesson in French, for all signs are written in both French and English.

BY SEA. There are toll ferries between New Brunswick and the provinces of Nova Scotia and Prince Edward Island. Within New Brunswick there are ferries from Blacks Harbour to Grand Manan and from Deer Island to Campobello. There are also several toll-free ferries operating between the Saint John River and Kennebecasis River and between Letete and Deer Island.

Taking the ferry across the Bay of Fundy between Saint John and Digby, Nova Scotia, provides a chance to look for marine life. The crossing takes two and a half hours and costs $18 for adults, $60 for automobiles one way. Departures are at 5:00 A.M., 1 P.M. and 8:15 P.M. The ferry from Cape Tormentine, New Brunswick, to Borden, Prince Edward Island, departs every hour on the half hour during the summer months and takes 45 minutes to cross. The rates are $6 for passengers and $16 for vehicles round-trip. As with all ferry links throughout Atlantic Canada, be sure to arrive early for your desired crossing because cars and trucks back up on both ends and lines tend to get very long.

Tourist Information

The Department of Tourism, Recreation and Heritage maintains tourist information centers at major entry points. These are indicated by road signs along provincial highways. Near Edmundston, there is an information center at St.-Jacques, just 15 miles from the city. After entering New Brunswick from Interstate 95, you'll find a center at Woodstock. There's also a center at St. Stephen, after crossing from Calais, Maine.

There are other information centers at St.-Leonard and Campbellton, as well as at sites sponsored by municipalities and service clubs in smaller communities throughout the province. For more information, write Tourism New Brunswick, P.O. Box 12345, Fredericton, New Brunswick, Canada E3B 5C3, or phone (800) 561-0123 from Canada and the United States or (800) 442-4442 from within New Brunswick. These numbers are for information only: Reservations cannot be made.

Language and Population

The population of New Brunswick is approximately 723,000, with the vast majority of the settlement along the coast. New Brunswick is Canada's only official bilingual province. The majority of the French-speaking population lives in the northern region along the Northumberland Strait and Baie des Chaleurs.

Time

New Brunswick is on Atlantic Time, one hour ahead of Eastern Time.

Telephones

The area code for New Brunswick is **506.**

THE FUNDY TIDAL COAST

T he Fundy Coast includes northern Maine and is often advertised as a "Two Nation Vacation." This region of New Brunswick was first visited by Samuel de Champlain and Sieur de Monts in 1604, when they wintered on the Île de St. Croix. The explorers claimed the area for France and called it Acadia, but the actual settlement did not last as the Acadians were expelled from their lands by the British in 1755. The most significant settlement of the area began after the arrival of the United Empire Loyalists in the late 1770s and early 1780s. The Loyalists had the greatest impact on this region and their presence is still felt today. This route is particularly interesting because it encompasses the Fundy Isles of Deer, Campobello and Grand Manan and the unique Flowerpot Rocks at Hopewell Cape. This route also includes the historic town of St.-Andrew's-by-the-Sea, the city of Saint John and Fundy National Park, with its dramatic tides.

ST. STEPHEN

The Fundy Tidal Coast route begins at the border town of St. Stephen, just across the river from Calais, Maine. During the War of 1812, while hostilities raged between the British and the Americans, the residents of St. Stephen, New Brunswick, and Calais, Maine, remained on peaceful, cooperative terms that continue to this day. In 1812, the town of St. Stephen loaned gunpowder intended for this war to their neighboring "enemies" in Calais for their Fourth of July celebration. Today, many New Brunswickers bordering Calais travel across the border to do their grocery shopping. You do notice a difference when crossing into Canada, however, not only with the new Maple Leaf flag and change in currency, but St. Stephen is an integral part of an era in history that shaped Canada. The United Empire Loyalists settled this town in the late 1700s, and the influence of the settlers is immediately noticeable when you see the lovely homes built originally for these early arrivals.

At St. Stephen, you can visit the Charlotte County Museum in the home of James Murchie. There are exhibits depicting the area in the late eighteenth century up to the early twentieth century. St. Stephen is also noted for being the place where the first chocolate bar was created at the Ganong candy factory in 1910. You can visit the Ganong factory (73 Milltown Boulevard, 466-6437, open daily), and sample some of the best chocolate bars in Canada. En route from St. Stephen you'll pass Oak Bay Provincial Park eight miles from the Canadian border. Turn south here along Route 127 towards St.-Andrew's-by-the-Sea. The outlying island here is Île de St. Croix, the site where Champlain wintered in 1604 and lost half his men to scurvy. Although the island is located in Maine there is a plaque there commemorating Champlain's landing. It reads: "To commemorate the discovery and occupation of this / Island by de Monts and Champlain / Who naming it L'Isle Sainte Croix / Founded here 26 June 1604 / The French Colony of Acadia / Then the only settlement of Europeans north of Florida."

Continue along the Trans-Canada Route 3 until you reach St.-Andrew's-by-the-Sea. This beautiful town is situated on Passamaquoddy Bay and is within view of the Maine coastline. It is one of the province's oldest towns, established in 1783 by the United Empire Loyalists. Its proximity to the United States caused quite a furor during the War of 1812 when Loyalists living in Castine, Maine, learned that the U.S.-Canada border had been moved to the other side of the St. Croix River. The entire Loyalist community packed up and moved to the other side of the river, present-day St. Andrew's, and those who could had their homes dismantled and floated across the river on a barge, which were rebuilt and still stand today.

St. Andrew's is an extremely popular resort area, where people come to enjoy the scenery as much as the history of the area. There are walking tours of the town organized by the Historical Society that begin at the famous Algonquin Hotel. The Algonquin Hotel sits on a hill overlooking the town, with red-tiled turrets that enhance the beauty of the landscape. In summer, one of the provinces' most popular events is the Festival of Arts, which offers orchestras, opera, ballet, film theater and workshops. While in St. Andrew's, visit the Juliette Ross Memorial Museum on Water Street, which has an excellent collection of furniture, Chinese porcelains and other objects gleaned from the town's seafaring past. Within walking distance from town, the Huntsman Marine Laboratory Musuem is well worth visiting. It is a laboratory that also serves as an oceanographic institute and aquarium featuring sturgeon, salmon, sea cucumbers and more. The money earned from the aquarium goes to nonprofit marine research and education.

Around St. Andrew's, you'll see five covered bridges, a trademark of a province that has a total of 133. The majority are along Route 127 on the way to St. George.

St. George is close to Letete, the departure point for ferries to beautiful Deer Island. St. George was settled around 1783 by a group of disbanded soldiers right near the Magaguadavic Falls. The falls are extremely popular with locals and visitors and in summer, salmon can be seen jumping the rapids on their upriver journey to spawn. The area was quarried for granite during the 1800s and used to build a cathedral in Boston and the Parliament Buildings in Ottawa. The Protestant Cemetery in St. George, next to St. Mark's Anglican Church, is one of the oldest in Canada. From St. George, you can catch the ferry to Deer Island. Continue south on Route 772 and you'll reach Blacks Harbour, the departure point for the ferry to Grand Manan.

THE FUNDY ISLES

The three Fundy Isles off the southern coast of New Brunswick are each unique and entirely unspoiled. Deer, Campobello and Grand Manan are very popular with yachtsmen and have their own unusual characteristics and lore. Accessible from different points along the coast, the largest island is Grand Manan, a haven for artists and writers dating back to the visits of Willa Cather, the novelist, and an increasingly popular spot with the international whale-watching set.

DEER ISLAND

Deer Island is one of the busiest of the three islands, and it is well known for its innovations in the lobster fishing industry and as the original salmon aquaculture site in North America. Ferries depart from the mainland at Letete to Deer Island on the hour. Once there, head for Point Park where you can get a look at the Old Sow whirlpool, one of the world's largest. There are inns and bed & breakfasts out here, as well as whale-watching tours, hiking/walking tours and plenty of scenery for the photographer.

CAMPOBELLO ISLAND

Campobello is linked to the mainland by a toll-free international bridge from Lubec, Maine, and to Deer Island by a small ferry that runs in summer. Campobello is best known to North Americans as Franklin Delano Roosevelt's "beloved isle" where he summered each year during his presidency. While the family lived in a lovely home that is now open to the public, Roosevelt, an avid sailor, was usually spotted offshore at the helm of his 56-foot schooner *Sewanna*. Because he was president, he was escorted by a naval destroyer, a power yacht and a press schooner during his sailing jaunts. Roosevelt took great pleasure in trying to outmaneuver his protectors, because it was said that the harder it was to navigate, the more he enjoyed sailing. He was known to change course, drop anchor or sail through shallow waters in an attempt to frustrate and confuse his escorts.

On Campobello, you can visit the 34-room "cottage" where the Roosevelts lived. There are many photographs, sketches and other mementos left by the former President. The house is open year-round and guides escort you through the rooms. In 1966, President Johnson and Lester Bowles Pearson, the Prime Minister of Canada, met at the Roosevelt house to dedicate a memorial to him. The island's history shows evidence of French settlement followed later by the Loyalists. The island was given to Captain William Owen in 1767 in exchange for an arm lost in battle. Benedict Arnold and his wife lived here for a while at Snug Cove. By the 1800s, the island had become a resort area for the wealthy.

GRAND MANAN ISLAND

Grand Manan is the largest of the Fundy Isles and is accessible by ferry from Blacks Harbour, the latter being a beautiful spot in its own right. The crossing takes about 45 minutes and it is common to see porpoises, whales and even sharks during the trip. The approach to Grand Manan by ferry first reaches North Head and the beautiful Swallowtail Lighthouse in the distance. The fishing fleet is very active here, and their main catch is sardines, which they process right on their boats. In summer, amidst these huge and expensive vessels, you'll see many yachts tied up alongside these boats, as anchorage or moorings at North Head are limited. At dusk or dawn on Grand

Manan, the sardine fleet is known to head out of the harbor at a moment's notice. I'll never forget watching a group of sailors aboard a fancy yacht, dressed regally with cocktails in hand, trying to disentangle themselves from the impatient sardine fishermen.

Grand Manan is also extremely busy in summer with whale-watchers, many of whom stay at the classic Marathon Inn, a highly recommended inn at North Head. Others come to the island for hiking, photographing fields of wild lupine or for bird-watching. Writers and artists frequent the island, too—Willa Cather was once a frequent visitor here.

From Ingall's Head Village on Grand Manan, there is a free ferry to White Head Island or a chartered boat to Three Islands. The latter is the home of the Bowdoin Scientific Station, a bird sanctuary harboring more than 240 species of birds. There are also tours to Machias Seal Island, where seals, puffins and whales are sighted.

Other places to visit on Grand Manan include Dark Harbor, a community built on the edge of steep cliffs whose main activity is gathering dulse, a form of seaweed. Dulse is sold in health food stores because of its high iodine content, and its popularity has given Dark Harbour the claim of being the "dulse capital of the world." You must travel along a dirt road to reach Dark Harbor. Seal Cove is a lovely town as well, accessible from Grand Harbor along a winding coastal road past old churches, fishing shanties and farms.

Accommodations

Starting with St. Stephen and continuing through the Fundy Isles call: **Bay's Edge Bed & Breakfast** (RR 3, St. Stephen, 466-5401, $40 single, $45 double), which is close to the beach and has an indoor and outdoor pool. The **Fundy Line Motel** (198 King Street, 466-2130, $50 single, $60 double) welcomes pets and is close to the beach. The **Old Victorian Bed & Breakfast** (30 Porter Street, 466-1483, $35 single, $40 double) and the expensive **Loon Bay Lodge** (RR 3, 466-1240, $130 single, $140 double) are both highly recommended. The latter is right on the beach.

In St.-Andrew's-by-the-Sea, accommodation is plentiful. Try the well-known but expensive **Algonquin Hotel** (184 Adophus Street, 529-8823, $125 single, $130 double), a resort with a licensed dining room, views of the harbor and proximity to town. Also recommended is the **Rossmount Inn** (RR 2, 529-3351, $70 single, $75 double) and the **Seaside Beach Resort** (339 Water Street, 529-3846, $50 single,

$55 double), which are popular summer resorts. The **Picket Fence Motel** (309 Reed Avenue, 529-8985, $50 single, $45 double) is a nice, family motel. On the cheaper side, try **Shady Maples Bed & Breakfast** (132 Sophia Street, 529-4426, $35 single, $40 double) and **Heritage Guest House** (100 Queen Street, 529-3875, $30 single, $35 double).

On the Fundy Isles, there are numerous inns and bed & breakfasts. On Deer Island, there's **Deer Island Log Cabin Guest-House by the Sea** (at Fairhaven, 747-2221, $40 single, $45 double) with its beachfront cabins. The **Clam Cove Farm Bed & Breakfast** (Fairhaven, 747-2025, $40 single, $45 double) and **West Isles World Bed & Breakfast** (Lamberts Cove, 747-2946, $35 single, $40 double) are relatively inexpensive and recommended. On Campobello Island, try **Friar's Bay Motor Lodge and Restaurant** (Welshpool, 752-2506, $30 single, $35 double) and **Campobello Island Club Lodge** (Welshpool, 752-2487, $40 single, $45 double) for rustic, family-style accommodation.

On Grand Manan, the absolute best place to stay is at the **Marathon Inn** (North Head, 662-8144, $50 single, $55 double) which was built in 1871, with its excellent dining room, common sitting room, lounge and views of North Head harbor. Also try the **Compass Rose** (North Head, 662-8570, $40 single, $45 double) overlooking the harbor. Other options: the **Ferry Wharf Inn** (North Head, 662-8588, $40 single, $45 double) and the **Grand Harbour Inn** (Ingall's Head Road, 662-3639, $35 single, $40 double).

Campgrounds

At St.-Andrew's-by-the-Sea, try **Island View Camping** (RR 1, Bayside, 529-3787, $12) and **Passamaquoddy Park** (Indian Point, 529-3439, $9) overlooking the Maine coast. On the Fundy Isles, try **Deer Island Point Park** (Fairhaven, 747-2423) near the beach. At Campobello, there's **Campobello Haven Campground and Restaurant** (Welshpool, 752-2360, $8) and **Herring Cove Provincial Park** (Welshpool, 752-2396), both with updated facilities. On Grand Manan, there's the **Anchorage Provincial Park** (Seal Cove, 662-3215) close to the beach, with hiking, showers and a kitchenette.

Dining

In St. Andrew's, the **Lighthouse Restaurant** (Lower Patrick Street, 529-3082) is set in a lighthouse with views of the Passmaquoddy Bay. Lobster is the specialty. **The Shiretown Inn** (Market Square, 529-8877) is an inn with an excellent licensed restaurant. Home-cooked food and elegant ambience; open year-round. Also try **Smuggler's Wharf** (227 Water Street) and **Rossmount Inn** (Route 127) for excellent seafood.

On the Fundy Isles, the best place to eat is on Grand Manan. The **Marathon Inn** (North Head, 662-8144) has nightly specials featuring fresh salmon, excellent desserts and a licensed dining room. Also try the **Compass Rose** (North Head, 662-8144) for home-cooked meals and afternoon tea, as well as complimentary breakfast.

Nature Tours

Grand Manan is the place to go for bird-watching, whale-watching and other nature tours. Contact **Island Coast Boat Tours** (P.O. Box 59, Castalia, Grand Manan, New Brunswick, Canada EOG IL0, 662-8181) for a 50-foot schooner trip to view puffins, razorbills, shearwaters and terns. Tour costs $60. Also try: **Sea Watch Tours** (Seal Cove, 662-8296) for a trip in a Cape Island boat to Machias Seal Island. **Don Baldwin's Island Tours** (Seal Cove, 662-8801) for a full-day birding and nature trip for $25.

FROM BLACKS HARBOUR TO SAINT JOHN

From Blacks Harbour you'll pass New River Beach on Route 1, which is close to Lepreau Falls. This entire highway is covered with fields of lupine during June and July when they bloom. It is also the site of New River Beach Provincial Park, with is beaches and camping facilities. Lepreau Falls are 80 feet high.

It's well worth taking your time to reach Saint John by exiting Highway 1 and taking Route 790 to Dipper and Chance Harbour. This lovely route reaches the protective shores of Dipper Harbour with its fishing fleet and excellent restaurant. Chance Harbour is also picturesque and the quiet coastal route prepares you for the more hectic entrance to Saint John, a busy city indeed.

SAINT JOHN

Saint John, called "The Loyalist City" is the largest in the province and a leading industrial center. Its vast harbor remains ice free year-round, making it an important port of call for large ships when the St. Lawrence Seaway freezes over each winter. Saint John has been a shipping center since the days of the Loyalists, and the city was able to make the transition from wooden ships to iron and steel. The first European to see Saint John was Jacques Cartier who arrived in 1534 and was welcomed by the great Micmac chieftan, Membertou. This chief was still around 70 years later when Sieur de Monts and Samuel de Champlain arrived in 1604.

In 1755, when 4,000 British Loyalists landed here, the region was mostly stumps and rocks and forests. They built Parrtown and Carleton, which later became Saint John. The city was incorporated in 1785, making Saint John Canada's oldest incorporated city. Its red-brick buildings, Victorian homes, clapboard Loyalist dwellings and well-known market have benefited from the city's recent renovation projects. The visitor will certainly be struck by the European feel of this city—with its gardens, historic streets, old waterfront and architectural styles. One main attraction for tourists is the reversing falls on the Saint John River. Twice a day, 50-foot tides race in from the Bay of Fundy, and the river current reverses, causing the water to flow upstream. This gives the river a whirlpool effect and it's difficult to discern which way the water is flowing. The powerful pull of tides and current can be very detrimental to yachts and small ships who must navigate under the Saint John Bridge, bordered on both sides by rocks. Vessels heading up- or down-river must time it just right when attempting to navigate through the reversing falls. As one yachtsman put it, "The fastest run (tide) is at the mill, with under the bridge a close second. If I can get by the mill, I can make it."

Another factor for yachtsmen cruising the Bay of Fundy is the notorious Fundy fogs that may not be discernable from the river but will hit the minute you enter the bay throwing a sailor into a choking bank of fog.

At the reversing falls, there is a large tourist information center, a picnic area and splendid views of the surging waters below.

OLD SAINT JOHN

In good weather, Saint John is a great city to explore on foot, and the city offers a variety of walking tours like the Loyalist Trail, the Prince William Walk and a walk along the waterfront. Don't miss the Old City Market, accessible from either Charlotte or Germain Street, which has been operating since 1876. In this huge vaulted building, with its old European feel, you can buy locally made cheeses, Mayflowers from the Micmac Indians, dulse harvested at Grand Manan and locally made crafts, along with meat, vegetables and fruit. King's Square, the site of the old market, is the area where most of the Loyalist homes are located. At the corner of Union and Germain streets, visit the Loyalist House, the city's oldest unchanged building dating back to 1810. This Georgian-style building is now a museum containing artifacts from the Loyalist era. It's open all summer from 10 A.M. to 5 P.M.

Nearby, you'll see the Old Country Courthouse, dating back to 1828 and the Old Loyalist Burying Ground. Also at King's Square, you'll see the Mallard house, site of New Brunswick's first legislative session.

The New Brunswick Museum (277 Douglas Avenue) has an excellent replica of the 1,625-ton ship *Marco Polo*. Originally built in the 1880s, it was one of the fastest-sailing ships of its time. Don't miss a walk along the waterfront, where Saint John's shipbuilding activities still thrive. The Loyalists began the tradition with their wooden ships, and while many Maritime communities lost importance after the Golden Age of Sail, Saint John continues to build iron and steel vessels.

THE SAINT JOHN RIVER VALLEY

Often referred to as "the Rhine of North America," the Saint John River is one of America's last great, unspoiled waterways.

Over 450 miles in length, it once served as a traveling route for the Maliceet Indians, a nomadic tribe that built canoes for travel and called the river "oa-lus-tuk," meaning "goodly river." In summer months, their canoes took them all the way to Nova Scotia. (The Maliceet canoe is a design that is still used today, but people commonly call it the Canadian canoe.) The Maliceet were described as being tall and sinewy with hazel eyes and copper-colored skin. They were said to have amazing speed and prowess on foot and by canoe. Their language is related to that of the Passamaquoddy Indians who once roamed the wilds of Maine.

There are three distinct regions of Saint John, where—thanks to limited development—the valley and tributaries still retain a pastoral quality. The regions are the Lower Saint John River Valley, the Upper Saint John River Valley and Madawaska, in the far northwest.

Originating in northern Maine, the river once flowed north to Baie des Chaleurs. But as centuries passed, it changed its course and now flows south to Saint John. A tour of the Saint John River Valley generally begins along the Trans-Canada Highway near Fredericton. From here, the river turns north at Meductic towards Hartland, site of the world's longest covered bridge. In the far northern town of St.-Leonard, you can reach the Restigouche River, one of the best Atlantic salmon and canoeing rivers in North America. The Saint John River route continues to Edmundston in the northwest region of Madawaska where the river then forms the border between Canada and the United States. The Lower Saint John River north of Saint John is actually easier to follow by boat; you capture the true feeling of the river by viewing it from the deck of a sailboat or ferry. So, if you have the opportunity to boat along this stretch of the river, don't pass it up. By road, there are a few travel options.

THE KINGSTON PENINSULA

This picturesque peninsula, with many of the province's 133 covered bridges, is a very popular detour. It's really one of the most attractive areas in New Brunswick, and there are ample opportunities for side trips to visit the bridges and have a picnic. You'll have two scenic toll-free ferry crossings, from Gondola Point to Belleisle Bay, and then to Evandale. From Evandale, you can follow Route 102 north for about 17 miles to Gagetown, site of the Queens County Museum and the Loomcrofters, a workshop of weavers whose tradition of excellence began in the late eighteenth century. With its fine craftsmanship linking it to the past, Gagetown seems to have gladly let the twentieth century slip by.

From Gagetown, the highway reaches Grand Lake, site of the Lakeside Provincial Park at Jemseg. There are plenty of campsites available here, and you'll easily find places to rent tackle and a boat for a fishing excursion.

FREDERICTON

The Acadians originally settled here during the early 1700s but were driven out by the British in 1759. By 1783, British Loyalists traveling upriver from Saint John established a permanent settlement here. Fredericton was dubbed the first "interior" settlement of the province, and it was designated the provincial capital in 1785. Smaller and less industrialized than Saint John, it has the ambience of a capital city and is called the "city of stately elms."

City Hall and the parade square are the center of historic Fredericton. Queen Street is noted for its Anglican Christ Church Cathedral built in 1853, one of the best examples of Gothic architecture in Canada. The Legislative building is the city's dominant structure. Inside, its Assembly chamber has two original Sir Joshua Reynolds portraits of King George III and Queen Charlotte.

The University of New Brunswick in Fredericton has a lovely campus with notable buildings like the University Library, the Playhouse, the Theater New Brunswick and the Beaverbrook Art Gallery. Much of the university owes its construction to Lord Beaverbrook, a self-made millionaire from northern New Brunswick whose original name was William Maxwell Aitken. Beaverbrook made his millions before the age of 30 through a Canada cement merger and went on to become the owner of London's *Daily Express* and a member of the British Parliament. He served on Winston Churchill's cabinet during World War II.

The Beaverbrook Art Gallery features works by Reynolds, Gainsborough, Turner, Constable and Hogarth. The popular "Santiago El Grande" by surrealist Salvador Dali is also displayed here. Just behind the gallery, you'll see the "Green," a massive park area between Queen Street and the Saint John River. Look out along the river for the many sculls that ply the waters. The rowers are generally university students who practice in spring and fall for national and international competitions.

Accommodations

The chain hotels are often well equipped to handle family or special needs, so try **Auberge Wandlyn Inn** (58 Prospect Street, 452-8937, $55 single, $60 double) with indoor/outdoor swimming pool, handicapped accessibility and licensed dining. The **Airport Inn** (2141 Lincoln Road, 458-9706, $40 single, $45 double) has basic rooms and a licensed dining room. There are plenty of reliable bed & breakfasts in Fredericton, including the **Chickadee Lodge Bed & Breakfast** (Kings Landing, 363-2759, $40 single, $45 double) and **Carriage House Bed & Breakfast** (230 University Avenue, 452-9924, $45 single, $50 double). Both are close to the river, offer full breakfast and have dining facilities. Also recommended is the **Appelot Bed & Breakfast** (RR 4, 472-6115, $30 single, $35 double) located by the river and offering a full breakfast.

Campgrounds

Near Fredericton, try **Hartt Island Campground** (near Silverwood, 450-6057, $12) and **Holyoke Motel and Campground** (459-7600, $10) with kitchen facilities, swimming pool and showers.

Dining

There's plenty of good dining in Fredericton, particularly near the university and in the historic part of the city. Try **La Vie en Rose** (570 Queen Street, 455-1319) for seafood, steaks and spit-roasted meals. **Terrace Dining Room** (Lord Beaverbrook Hotel, 659 Queen Street, 455-3371) has seafood and buffets, and the **Regency Room** (Fredericton Inn, 1315 Regent Street, 455-1430) has great steak and seafood. For less expensive fare, try the **Carelton Street Restaurant** (73 Carelton Street, 457-0518) for Canadian food. Also of note is **The Barn** (540 Queen Street, 455-2742) for chicken and ribs and the **Quarterdeck River and Roadhouse Restaurant** (363 Lincoln Road, 458-5801) for steak, seafood and chicken.

Nightlife

There are some nice pubs in Fredericton, and many feature live music and dancing in addition to game rooms and pub food. Try the **Club Cosmopolitan** (546 King Street, 458-5819) known as Fredericton's oldest and largest dance club. A popular pub is the **Dock Pub and Eatery** (375 King Street, 458-1254) with good tavern food in the heart of downtown. Also try the **Lunar Rogue** (625 King Street, 450-2065) for an old-world pub atmosphere.

Shopping

Fredericton has quite a few malls, but for more variety go downtown. For New Brunswick crafts, try **Aitkens Pewter** (375 King Street, 453-9474) for handcrafted pewter and jewelry. Also try the **Carriage House Studio** (136 Aberdeen Street, 455-2563) for copper enameling and enamel jewelry. The **Emporium** (Kings Landing Historical Settlement, 363-5805) has a large variety of books, crafts and souvenirs from around Atlantic Canada.

UPPER SAINT JOHN RIVER VALLEY

From Fredericton, proceed north along Route 105 to Mactaquac Provincial Park. This park is relatively new and very popular with Fredericton residents, particularly in summer. It has a golf course, two beaches, a marina and a pond for bass fishing. The facilities are excellent, and special events and activities are held all summer. Just opposite the entrance to the park, you'll see the Opus Craft Village. Locally made crafts are on sale here, featuring pottery, weavings and handmade candles.

The Mactaquac Provincial Park got its name from the nearby Mactaquac hydroelectric dam constructed in the late 1960s. The dam's development threatened an old Loyalist settlement at Kings Landing. To avert destruction, the town was made into the Kings Landing Historic Settlement and the old buildings were saved. Set on the riverbank, the settlement depicts Loyalist life from 1783 to 1900. Volunteers wear traditional dress and offer tours of more than 50 buildings, many of which were moved to higher ground after construction of the dam. At Kings Landing, the Kings Head Inn serves homemade meals using eighteenth-century recipes. There is also a daily performance during the summer by a Fredericton-based theater company.

Another area of interest is farther north on the Trans-Canada Highway at Meductic. This is the site of the Meductic Indian fort built by the Maliceet Indians for protection against the Mohawks. It is said that the Maliceets were terrified of the Mohawks and came here in summer to plant corn and seek protection in their fort. What little is known about this tribe comes from an Englishman named John Gyles, who as a boy was captured by the Indians in 1689. For six years, he was a reluctant member of the tribe, traveling all over Maine and New Brunswick. Despite the difficulties, he learned to love the Maliceets' way of life. Eventually he was taken in by a French family, and by the time he became an adult he spoke French, English and Maliceet fluently.

It was also at Meductic that Acadian settlers built the first chapel in New Brunswick in 1717. The chapel's bell was a gift from King Louis XV of France. It was later melted down into smaller bells. There is a cairn that marks the site of the church.

Route 2 then passes through Woodstock, a stately town with lovely old homes and a Loyalist past. The area is popular with bird-watchers and also draws Fredericton residents out for a weekend drive. There are shops and restaurants here as well as the Woodstock Walkabout, a self-guided tour of the historic town. Woodstock is the first major town you reach after crossing the Canadian border from Interstate 95 in Maine.

At the junction of Routes 2 and 105, you'll reach Hartland, site of the longest covered bridge in the world. Built in 1899, this engineering marvel has been preserved as an important historic attraction—stretching 1,282 feet across the Saint John River. Locals refer to it as the longest "kissin' bridge" in the world, for it took a horse and buggy an awfully long time to get through.

As you travel north along the river, the communities become far more spread out, and you begin to reach the region best known for its salmon rivers, provincial parks and wilderness. You also pass the Tobique Indian Reserve at Perth-Andover, where Indian handicrafts are on sale. At Perth-Andover, take the turnoff onto Route 385 along the Tobique River to Mt. Carleton Provincial Park.

MT. CARLETON PROVINCIAL PARK

This park, located between Restigouche and Northumberland Counties, is a recommended stop for seasoned campers. There are very few facilities for visitors. This is wild country, where moose, bear and deer roam the land, and otters, Atlantic salmon, brook trout and beavers ply the waters. Popular with hikers who climb Mt. Carleton (2,690 feet) and canoers who paddle along the Nepisiguit Lakes to the Nepisiguit River ("Angry River"), this park offers rugged isolation. Planning is required before setting out into its wilderness area. There are self-guiding booklets available at the park headquarters, located at Nictau Lake.

THE REPUBLIC OF MADAWASKA

The Republic of Madawaska begins near Grand Falls in northern New Brunswick and encompasses the cities of Edmundston and St.-Jacques as well as a wilderness region along the Maine border. The story of the origin of "the Republic" dates back to the early days of settlement. The French arrived first and settled near present-day Edmunston but were expelled by the English in 1783. They then settled in areas farther north, but the borders of Madawaska were disputed between Maine, Canada and New Brunswick for over 100 years. Finally, in 1842, the borders were drawn up and Madawaska became part of New Brunswick, although many residents here still refer to their home as the Republic of Madawaska. To this day, they have an honorary president of the republic and their own flag, decorated with an eagle and six stars. They consider Edmundston to be the capital of the Republic of Madawaska.

Grand Falls is an interesting stop; the 75-foot falls are among Canada's most impressive cataracts. The area was once an important logging center, and it has its share of lore. The story is told, for instance, of a big logger named Main John Glasier, who was the first man to drive logs over the Grand Falls sometime in the 1840s. At one time, it is said, Maine loggers dammed up the Allagash waterway, causing the Saint John River to be reduced to a trickle. Main John and a bunch of rugged lumberjacks marched 160 miles through the wilderness to destroy the dam. Locals still like to refer to the event as the "invasion of Maine."

From Grand Falls, you'll reach St.-Leonard with its St.-Leonard Church and internationally known Madawaska weavers, who make fine woven items for an international clientele. Farther along the Trans-Canada Highway, you'll reach St.-Basile, called the "Cradle of Madawaska," where a museum and original graveyard are worth visiting.

EDMUNDSTON

The city of Edmundston, the capital of the Republic of Madawaska, is predominately French-speaking. Driven from southern New Brunswick by the British in 1784, Acadians settled this rich region where the Saint John and Madawaska rivers meet. Because of a large pulp and paper mill, the rivers in the Edmundston area are polluted. Across the river from Edmundston, is the international border between Canada and the United States. In the city proper, look for the unique flag of Madawaska flying next to the Canadian flag at city hall. One of the best times to be here is in late July and early August, when the Madawaska natives, called the Brayon, enjoy a unique celebration called the Fête de Brayonne. The mixture of Acadian, Loyalist, Irish, French and Indian cultures makes this an ethnically diverse celebration. It's a wonderful opportunity to enjoy traditional food, dances and music.

Don't miss the Madawaska Museum (195 Herbert Boulevard), where you can gather information and look at artifacts representing the community's past. Nearby, at 145 Pine Street, the beautiful Roman Catholic Cathedral of the Immaculate Conception dominates the landscape with its twin spires. The Laporte Art Museum at the St. Louis Maillet College is also worth visiting. Take a side trip along Route 120 to Lac Baker, site of a provincial park featuring a beach, sailboat rentals, waterskiing and board sailing.

North of Edmundston is St.-Jacques, the first town you'll reach in the Republic of Madawaska if you're coming from Québec.

Accommodations

Woodstock is the first major town in New Brunswick. The **Auberge Wandlyn Inn** (328-8876, $50 single, $55 double) and the **John Gyles Motor Inn, Ltd.** (RR 1, 328-6622, $40 single, $45 double) are reliable motor inns for the weary traveler. Also try the **Queen Victoria Bed & Breakfast** (133 Chapel Street, 328-8382, $40 single, $45 double) with complimentary breakfast.

In picturesque Hartland, try **Campbell's Tourist Home and Bed & Breakfast** (375-4775, $30 single, $35 double), which is close to the river. Farther north at Perth-Andover, try the **Riviera Hotel** (Main Street, 273-2920, $25 single/double) or the **Valley View Motel** (RR 4, 273-2785, $30 single, $35 double). Grand Falls is a nice place to stay to view the falls. Try the highly recommended **Près du Lac** (RR 6, 473-1300, $55 single/double) with an indoor/outdoor pool, licensed dining room and handicapped access. The **Hill Top Motel** (131 Madawaska Road, 473-2684, $40 single, $45 double) is also good.

In Edmundston, there's the **Howard Johnson Hotel** (100 Rice Street, 739-8361, $65 single, $70 double) with a licensed dining room and indoor/outdoor swimming pool. Other options: **Motel Guy** (RR 3, 735-4253, $40 single, $43 double). **City View Tourist Home** (226 Rue du Pouvoir, 739-9058, $20 single, $25 double). **La Roma Motel** (RR 4, 735-3305, $40 single, $45 double).

Campgrounds

In Hartland, there's the **Bridgeview Campground and Gift Shop** (375-4388, $10) with washing facilities and shopping nearby. At Grand Falls, there's **Les Lacs Alma Camping** (RR 4, 473-5405, $10) with an indoor/outdoor swimming pool and proximity to the falls. Also try **Mulherin's Campground** (four miles south of Grand Falls, 473-3050, $12) and **Rapid Brook Camping** (one mile east of Grand Falls, 473-4536), which feature riverside campsites. In Edmundston, you can camp at **Les Jardins de la République** (Provincial Park, five miles north of the city, 735-4871) and **Rivière Iroquois River Camping** (1318 Rue Principle, 735-8169, $10). Both campsites are on the river. Mt. Carleton Provincial Park, mentioned earlier in this chapter, has ample room for camping but very few organized campsites.

Dining

In the Upper Saint John River Valley, Edmundston has the largest number of restaurants, but even here the selection is limited. All the major hotel chains have licensed restaurants. Try **La Praga Restaurant and Hotel** (127 Victoria Street, 735-5567) for steaks and seafood. Also try **Bel Air** (174 Victoria Street, 735-3329) for Canadian and Chinese food and **Maple Leaf Restaurant and Lounge** (359 Main Street, Clair) for home cooking. In Hartland, check out the **Riverview Family Restaurant** (Main Street, 375-4935) near the longest covered bridge in the world. For take-out, try **Dixie Lee** (Courtyard Plaza, 375-4877).

THE ACADIAN SHORE

The Acadian Shore route stretches from Sackville to Bathurst along the Chignecto Bay and Northumberland Strait all the way to the Baie des Chaleurs in northern New Brunswick. In the seventeenth century, the Acadians had been settled in southern New Brunswick for over 100 years when they were driven off their lands by the British during the Acadian expulsions of 1755. While the deportations sent the majority of the Acadians to the swamplands of Louisiana, many hid out in northern New Brunswick and Québec. Gradually, they returned to regain some of their lost land. Today, their cultural impact on New Brunswick is quite strong and you'll find this pleasant coast to be all the more interesting because of the unique heritage of the residents here.

THE TANTRAMAR MARSHES

The Tantramar Marshes make up the region from Sackville to Moncton including Cape Tormentine, where the ferry to Prince Edward Island is located. The Tantramar region is fertile marshland once farmed by the Acadians who were eventually expelled from this land. Many returned, however, and the Tantramar marshes are now populated by a mixture of Acadian families, Loyalists and later arrivals like the Scots and the Irish.

Geographically, the Bay of Fundy and the Tantramar, Petitcodiac and Gaspereau rivers created an area that was like a large seabed of alluvial mud and estuaries. The Acadians used a technique to dyke these marshes and reclaim good land from the sea. A description of their technique reads as follows:

They stopped the current of the sea by creating large dykes, called *aboideaux*. They planted five or six large trees where the sea enters the marshes, and filled the vacant places with mud so beaten down that the tide could not pass through it. In the middle they adjusted a flood-gate in such a way as to allow the water from the marsh to flow out at low water without permitting the water from the sea to flow in at high tide.

Fort Beausejour on the Nova Scotia border near Aulac is of historical interest and was built in the 1600s as a French fortification. After being defeated by the British in 1755 at Fort Beausejour under the command of Colonel Robert Monckton, the French relinquished their control over New Brunswick. In 1926, the site was declared a National Historic Site.

SACKVILLE

Sackville is a university town that was reclaimed by the sea with the Acadian system of dykes and aboiteaux and is situated in the center of the Tantramar marshes. Mount Allison University, a well-known New Brunswick institution, was founded in Sackville by Charles Allison in 1839. It was here that the first degree was awarded to a woman in the British Empire in the year 1875. Sackville is also home to many artists and the Owens Gallery on the university campus has an excellent fine arts department. Here, Alex Colville and Lorne Harris, among other Canadian artists, taught art. Sackville is also one of North America's major migratory bird routes and has a 50-acre waterfowl park with excellent viewing areas of the birds, wildlife and rare waterfowl. There is a tourist information center at the park, and each August the Atlantic Waterfowl celebration is held.

Sackville also boasts of having the only harness shop in North America that still produces handmade horse collars at the Sackville Harness Shop. The shop seems set back in time, where older craftsmen will sit stitching horse collars by hand. Orders come in from all over Canada and the United States where horse collars are custom-made for the size and shape of a particular horse's head.

AROUND SACKVILLE

From Sackville and nearby Fort Beausejour, you can travel along the picturesque Baie Verte to Cape Tormentine where the ferry departs for Prince Edward Island. This area is very green with low-lying farmland and Acadian homes. Look for the Acadian flag flying outside of the quaint, well-kept homes. From Cape Tormentine, you can travel along the Northumberland Strait to Shediac. The route here is dotted with beaches particularly around Cap-Pelé, a community founded by Acadian fishermen in 1780. The fishing is still good here, and the fish markets sell the freshest fish you can find. The route to Shediac marks the beginning of the Acadian Trail that stretches to Bathurst.

FROM SACKVILLE TO MONCTON

On the way to Moncton you'll reach St.-Joseph, the site of an Acadian mission. By 1854, an Acadian institute of higher learning was built here that is now called St.-Joseph's College. At the college, visit the Survival of the Acadians National Historic Site where 200 years of Acadian history is portrayed.

MONCTON

Moncton was named in honor of Colonel Robert Monckton, who commanded the British forces at Fort Beausejour in 1755. The "k" in his name was accidentally omitted when the city was named by the provincial legislature. Moncton today is a mixture of French and English cultures, with a historic downtown area. It has been an important railway center for connections throughout the Maritimes since it was designated the Maritime headquarters for the Inter-Colonial railway in 1872. The University of Moncton is located here, the only French-language university in New Brunswick, built in 1821. On the campus, there is an Acadian Museum and Art Gallery.

Of interest is the Tidal Bore that races up the Petitcodiac River from Chignecto Bay and the Bay of Fundy. It is best seen from Bore Park in downtown Moncton. Magnetic Hill, outside the city, is an unusual hill that gives cars the illusion of coasting uphill—backwards!

Near the hill is the Magic Mountain Water Park, excellent for children who need a break from driving and sightseeing. There is a game farm, wave pool, water slides and animals.

Accommodations

In Sackville, there's the **Marshlands Inn** (59 Bridge Street, 536-0170, $48 single, $55 double), which overlooks the marshes. The **Different Drummer** (82 West Main Street, 536-1291, $40 single, $42 double) is close to the Cumberland Basin and is handicapped accessible. In Moncton, there is plenty of accommodation to choose from.

Other options: **Beacon Light Motel** (1062 Mountain Road, 384-1734, $50 single, $55 double). **Bonaccord House Bed & Breakfast**

(250 Bonaccord Street, 388-1535, $35 single, $40 double). **Champlain Inn** (502 Kennedy Drive, 857-9686, $45 single, $50 double).

Camping

At Cape Tormentine, where the ferry leaves for Prince Edward Island, there's **MeriMist Acres Trailer Park** (Cape Tormentine, 538-7591, $12) and in Sackville, there's **Marshview Trailer Park** (536-2880, $10). At Moncton, try **Green Acres Campground** (within walking distance of Magnetic Hill, 384-0191, $10) and **Steeves Mountain Provincial Park** (eight miles west of Moncton, 372-5933, $12).

Dining

In Moncton, there's **Judson's** (130 Westmorland Street, 859-9099) featuring excellent char-grilled steaks, prime rib and Atlantic seafood. Also in Moncton, **Cy's Restaurant** (East Main Street, 857-0032) has seafood, and **Pizza Delight** (1315 Mountain Road, 859-8500) has excellent pizza. In Dieppe, try **McGinnis Landing Restaurant** (499 Paul Street, 856-6995) for Mexican, Italian and Canadian food.

SHEDIAC

The route between Moncton and Shediac is still part of the Tantramar marshes and was originally settled by Acadians and later by Loyalists, Scots and Irish. The town of Shediac is only 20-minutes driving time from Moncton and is called the "lobster capital of the world." The best time to find out if this claim to fame is true is during the five-day Shediac Lobster Festival held in mid-July. Because of the Gulf Stream, the beaches at nearby Parlee Beach Provincial Park boast of having very warm water for summer swimming. Temperatures reach 75 degrees Fahrenheit and there is a free trolley service from Shediac to the beach. For a brief time in the 1840s, Shediac was a port of some importance. But with the arrival of the stagecoach around 1850, people began moving elsewhere. However, when the railway came through in the 1900s, Shediac became a beach resort with some lovely Victorian inns that still stand today. Be sure to visit the Pascal Poirier Historical House in downtown Shediac. There is an art gallery here in the former home of the first French Acadian senator.

Continue north along Route 134 to Cocagne, at the mouth of the

Cocagne River. Here and at nearby St.-Antoine, it's possible to join a deep-sea fishing excursion. Cocagne was settled by Acadians who were expelled from Nova Scotia in 1767. The area is still French-speaking today and is noted for its *poutine rapée*, a typical Acadian dish. Farther north you'll reach Bouctouche, a seaside village that is the birthplace of the Acadian authoress Antoinine Maillet and industrialist K. C. Irving, owner of the Irving Gas Stations and considered one of the wealthiest men in Canada. While in Bouctouche, visit the Sacred Heart Chapel, considered to be a masterpiece of the craftsman and ornamentalist Leon Léger (1848-1918). Bouctouche is also famous for its oysters, so try them fresh while you're here. By turning inland you'll reach Richibucto, where an old church was built as a testament to the sea. The steeple is modeled on a lighthouse and the roof represents the waves rolling into the coast. There is a lovely fishing wharf on Richibucto River and the excellent Jardine Municipal Park with a beach and camping.

The coastal town of Rexton was settled by Scottish immigrants and was the home of the Jardine brothers from Dumfriesshire, Scotland. They developed an important shipbuilding industry here and built Kent County's first square-rigger in 1820. Nearby Richibucto has a small museum that tells of the county's shipping days.

KOUCHIBOUGUAC NATIONAL PARK

A Micmac word meaning "river of long tides," the Kouchibouguac Park is the largest and most popular National Park on the Acadian coast. While it doesn't have the dramatic tides of the Fundy National Park, it is made up of extensive lagoons and salt marshes that protect it from the storms of the Northumberland Strait. These sandbars resemble the coastline of Cape Cod in Massachusetts, minus the hordes of tourists.

There are three rivers that flow through the park into Kouchibouguac Bay, forming tidal estuaries. It's a great area for canoers and there are ample campsites along the way. There are extensive walking trails throughout the park where it is not uncommon to see black bear, moose and deer. Many streams have beaver dams and clam beds abound at low tide along the shore.

There are over 140 campsites within the park with room for trailers, tents and vans.

En route from Kouchibouguac heading north you'll pass through the Acadian villages of Point Sapin, Escuminac and Baie-Ste.-Anne along the coast toward the Miramichi Bay. These communities rely on fishing for their livelihood and the coastal road around Point Escuminac is marked by lighthouses and rugged shoreline.

CHATHAM

This area was once an important lumber resource for the shipbuilding activities of Joseph Cunard's shipbuilding industry (son of the Jardine family of nearby Rexton). There is ample information about the Golden Age of Sail in Chatham at the Miramichi Natural History Museum on Wellington Street. The famous Miramichi River runs into the Miramichi Bay at Chatham and it is here that the French explorer Jacques Cartier landed in 1534. If you were to travel the length of the river by canoe, the beginning of the 80-mile trip starts in Doaktown, southwest of Chatham and ends nearby at the Enclosure Provincial Park. A highly worthwhile trip if you have the time, money and supplies. Outfitters in Doaktown can rent supplies and provide a guide if required.

Newcastle is on Route 8, just upriver from Chatham and is a pulp and lumber exporting city. This is the home of Max Aitken, alias Lord Beaverbrook who took that title from a stream north of Newcastle when he became a British peer in 1917. He was born in the Old Manse on 225 Mary Street, which was the parsonage of his father, a Presbyterian minister. He had the Old Manse restored in 1950 and donated it to the town as a library, with an excellent collection of books. He went on to donate the town hall, theater and town square.

The route from Newcastle heading north intersects Route 11 at Ferry Road. By continuing north on Route 11 to the shore of the Miramichi Bay, you'll reach the MacDonald Farm, a restored 1820s sandstone farmhouse containing period furniture and a small museum. Roughly 35 miles north of here you'll reach Burnt Church, an Indian reserve that was once the site of a French church burned in 1759 by British troops marching towards Québec.

Tracadie is on the coast of Gloucester County and is a Micmac word meaning "ideal place to camp." Although the town is part of a British-named county (like much of New Brunswick), this area is entirely French-speaking, settled by Acadians who returned to the area in the 1780s. This is salmon and trout country, particularly along the Tracadie River while deep-sea fishing charters are also available. The main livelihood of the residents here is fishing, as well as in the town of Shippagan. This town is also an important area for peat moss, which is mined from the earth and dried in the sun. On Lameque Island, there is actually a Peat Moss Festival held in late July. The area north of Shippagan Peninsula makes up the islands of Lameque and Miscou, whose history of European presence dates back hundreds of years.

MISCOU ISLAND

The discovery by Europeans of the island of Miscou dates back to the year 1546 when Cartier's explorers named it Cap Despoir (Cape Despair). It is believed that Basque fishermen also sailed around this region in the fifteenth century, and there is record of a Frenchman named Raymond de la Ralde wintering here in 1627. The well-known Frenchman Nicolas Denys is also thought to have lived on Miscou Island in 1645. It appears that for many years Miscou Island was more of a fisherman's paradise than a desirable place for settlement, and Europeans primarily fished the rich waters of the Baie des Chaleurs in summer, returning to Europe by ship in the fall.

This island was a difficult and inhospitable place on which to live, and although fishermen took shelter here and small settlements were attempted, many Acadians and later settlers did not build large communities here. Today, Miscou is nearly an abandoned island, consisting mainly of bogs and sand dunes. The barren and remote quality of Miscou Island is very appealing to some visitors in summer, but it is a difficult place to eke out a living and is thought of as a "remote outpost of the nation." There is a lighthouse on the far tip of the island that has been in operation since 1856.

From Miscou Island travel northwest towards Caraquet on Baie des Chaleurs, a fishing community founded in 1758 and called the "cultural capital of Acadia." The tranquility here is rarely disrupted except during the summer Acadian Heritage Festival held on August 15. The festival includes the traditional Blessing of the Fleet meant to protect the fishermen for the coming year. Here, locals tell a story of a ghost ship, seen in Baie des Chaleurs at night, with its four masts and sails ablaze. Sightings have also been reported across the bay on the Gaspe Peninsula in Québec.

HISTORIC ACADIAN VILLAGE

Close to Caraquet you'll find the Historic Acadian Village, a 500-acre complex built to commemorate the hardships endured by the Acadians at the hands of the British. The village features traditional costumes, early Acadian homes, a tavern, school and blacksmith shop. Much of the construction was taken from authentic dwellings and shops throughout the province and reassembled here. The staff wears traditional dress and goes about the premises as if it were living in the 1700s. The site was chosen because of the dykes that were built by the early Acadian settlers.

BATHURST

Bathurst was established long ago by the early settler Nicolas Denys and his followers. Denys became governor of the Acadian coast and recorded much about the area in a book published in France in the mid-1600s. There is a memorial to him in the center of Bathurst, an industrial city specializing in the mining of zinc and copper. The mines and factories give the town an industrial feel, but there are still attractive beaches nearby on the Nepisiguit Bay at Youghall, Caron Point and Baie des Chaleurs. The Micmac word for Nepisiguit means "tumultuous river."

Close to Bathurst you'll find Youghall Provincial Park where there is a nature preserve for the migratory birds that pass through this region. The area around Bathurst is scenic with towns like Beresford and its municipal park and Nigadoo with a fine arts and crafts center. Close by, you'll see Nigadoo Falls and Petit-Rocher with its Mining and Mineral Interpretation Center. The center offers visits into an authentic mine. Close by, Pointe-Verte is a favorite fishing and scuba diving area—but for the latter, be sure to wear a wet suit.

Accommodations

The Acadian Trail is quite long, but this list will begin at Shediac and continue to Bathurst. In Shediac, try the **Auberge Belcourt Inn** (112 Main Street, 532-6098, $40 single, $45 double) within walking distance of the beach. **Seely's Motel, Ltd.** (Bellevue Heights, 532-6193, $50 single, $55 double) is located by the harbor and has a licensed dining room. On the lower end, try **Chez Francoise** (93 Main Street, 532-4405, $45 single/double).

In Richibucto, which borders the beautiful Kouchibouguac National Park, the **Silver Birch Motel, Ltd.** (Richibucto, 523-9766, $45 single, $50 double) is within driving distance to the beach. Also try **L'Auberge O'Leary Inn** (101 Main Street, 523-7515, $40 single, $45 double) close to the beach.

North of the National Park, you reach Chatham and Newcastle. Recommended accommodations in this area are **Morada Motel** (64 King Street, Chatham, 773-4491, $35 single, $40 double); **Sunnyside Bed & Breakfast** (65 Henderson Street, 773-4232, $35 single, $40 double) and **Fundy Line Motel** (869 King George Highway, Newcastle, 622-3650, $45 single, $50 double). Up north in Tracadie, there's **Motel Boudreau Ltee.** (395-2244, $38 single, $40 double) and **Motel Thomas** (Rue Principale, 395-9726, $37 single, $45 double). On the Baie des Chaleurs, try **Motel Bel Air** (Caraquet, 655 Boulevard St. Pierre Ouest, 727-3488, $35 single, $40 double) or **Hotel Paulin** (143 Boulevard St. Pierre Ouest, 727- 9981, $25 single, $30 double). In Bathurst, there's **Carey's-by-the-Sea** (Bathurst, Salmon Beach, 546-6801, $25 single, $30 double); **Atlantic Host Inn** (Vanier Boulevard, 548-3335, $65 single, $70 double) or **The Harbour Inn Bed & Breakfast** (262 Main Street, 546-4757, $30 single, $35 double).

Campgrounds

There are ample campgrounds all the way up the Acadian shore, particularly around the National Park area and the beaches along the Gulf of St. Lawrence. In Shediac, there's **Beausejour Camping** (Lino Road, 532-5885, $14) with swimming pool and proximity to the beach. Also in Shediac: **Parlee Beach Provincial Park** (Shediac, 532-1500, $12) and **Parc Chedik Camping** (East Main Street, 532-6713, $10).

At Kouchibouguac National Park and the surrounding area, there are plenty of campsites. There are three major areas for camping within the park run by the government of Canada. Try **Kouchibouguac National Park** (La Côte à Fabien Group Tenting, 876-2443, $11) or **Kouchibouguac National Park** (South Kouchibouguac, 876-2443, $12). Farther north, closer to Tracadie, there's **Tracadie Beach Camping** (Rivière-du-Portage, 395-4010, $12) on the beach and **Camping Cabestan** (Val-Comeau, 395-9425, $11) also along the shore. On the northern tip of Shippagan Peninsula, there's **Miscou Island Camping** (Miscou Center, 344-8638, $10), which offers splendid isolation. In Bathurst, **Hodnett's Camping** (RR 1, 546-4927, $8) has all the facilities as well as **Youghall Trailer Park and Campground** (747 Youghall Drive, 548-8370, $10).

Dining

Shediac is best known for lobster, so you can have your pick of lobster restaurants. Try **House of Lobster** (Parlee Beach Road, 532-6816) with both full and kid's menu or **Fisherman's Paradise** (Shediac Beach on Main Street, 532-6811) for lobster and steak. Also try the **Four Seas Restaurant** (762 Main Street, 532-1025) or the **Lobster Deck Restaurant and Lounge** (118 Main Street, 532-8737). **Fred's Restaurant** (400 Acadie Road, 577-4269) has family-style dining in Cap-Pelé. In Chatham, try the **Cunard Restaurant** (Cunard Street, 773-7107) for Chinese and Canadian cooking. Near Tracadie, try **La Fine Grobe by the Sea** (Nigadoo, 783-3138) for French cuisine and excellent seafood on an outdoor terrace overlooking Nepisiguit Bay. Many of Bathurst restaurants are part of the hotel or motel complexes such as **Danny's Inn and Conference Center** (Route 134, 546-6621) with its licensed dining room and coffee shop. There's also **Pizza Delight** (980 St. Peter's Avenue, 548-9434) for deep-dish pizza.

Undersea Exploration

Skin divers should contact **Leo Oursins, Inc.** (Caraquet Air Base, (506) 732-5238), to join an underwater tour of the Baie des Chaleurs.

THE RESTIGOUCHE UPLANDS AND CENTRAL NEW BRUNSWICK

The Restigouche Uplands encompass the vast uplands of Restigouche County extending from the Restigouche River to the Jacquet River. Central New Brunswick, which includes much of Northumberland and Victoria Counties, is also referred to as the Miramichi Basin because the Miramichi River flows through here.

THE RESTIGOUCHE UPLANDS

This region begins where the Acadian Coast ends, at Jacquet River Provincial Park. The islands just offshore are very popular with artists and photographers. This upland route covers a good deal of shoreline along the Baie des Chaleurs, including the town of Charlo with its waterfalls and scenic hiking trails.

At Eel River Crossing on Route 280, there is a fish culture station with tours available. This region was once popular with Scottish immigrants, and town names like Balmoral and Dundee attest to the Scottish influence here. Dalhousie is a nice town in a farming and fishing region that also exports processed wood products. Here you can visit the Restigouche Regional Museum in the center of town. There are boat tours available along the Baie des Chaleurs; guides tell the story of the alleged ghost ship that is seen burning in the bay at night. Nearby, the Chaleur Provincial Park has a beach and camping area. There is also a ferry route across the bay from Dalhousie to Québec.

CAMPBELLTON

This city of 9,000 is located at the western end of the Baie des Chaleurs. The region is popular with sports fishermen who come from around the world to fish for Atlantic salmon along the Restigouche River and its tributaries. Cambellton provides these sportsmen with the proper equipment and guides. This area, with its unspoiled beauty and abundant natural resources, is what folks call "God's Country."

Founded in 1773, Campbellton was named after Sir Archibald Campbell, who was once lieutenant-governor of the province. There is a cairn at Riverside Park that commemorates the Seven Years War, one of many battles between the English and French for control of North America, which took place in 1760. The Restigouche Gallery (39 Andrews Street) in Campbellton features an exhibit by regional artists and also has special displays from other Canadian cities. Nearby, at Atholville, visit Sugarloaf Mountain Provincial Park, which is a popular summer and winter recreation area, featuring tennis and hiking as well as skating and skiing.

At the junction of Routes 134 and 17, you'll reach Tide Head, where some of New Brunswick's best fiddlehead ferns can be found. Fiddlehead ferns are an edible delight, cooked in garlic or a bit of oil. There is also a great view of the surrounding countryside from Morrissey Rock Lookout.

Route 17 then turns southwest and heads inland to St.-Jean-Baptiste-de-Restigouche where Oliver's Historical Museum tells of the early settlement in this remote region. At Kedgwick, there is a replica of an old lumber camp that informs visitors of the region's forest heritage. St.-Quentin is popular with hunters and fishermen. From here you can follow an access road to Mt. Carleton Provincial Park. Beyond St.-Quentin you enter Central New Brunswick, commonly called the Miramichi Basin.

CENTRAL NEW BRUNSWICK

The vast Miramichi region in the center of the province is ideal for salmon fishermen, canoeists, explorers and modern pioneers. You can venture into this untamed region from different areas of New Brunswick. If you travel inland from the Acadian Trail you'll reach towns like Rogersville on Route 126 or Doaktown on Route 8. Rogersville was founded by Acadians but has been the site of a Trappist Monastery since 1904. It is also famed as the "Brussels Sprout Capital of Canada." Each year a festival is held here to celebrate this underrated crop. If you missed the Peat Moss Festival on the Acadian Shore, perhaps you owe the Brussels Sprout Capital a special visit!

DOAKTOWN

Doaktown is an outpost town with a museum that tells of its link to the salmon-rich Miramichi River system. It was named after the Scottish settler Robert Doak who arrived here in the early 1800s. Farther south is Boiestown, which is the geographic center of New Brunswick. This area's economy relies on lumber and fishing.

Boiestown is along Route 8, which leads to Fredericton and the Saint John River Valley. If you turn around and head north to the intersection with Route 108, you can then travel across the center of the province to the western town of Plaster Rock. The entire region is wooded, full of rivers and wildlife, but with very few settlements.

Accommodations

Campbellton has many lodging options, including places that cater to hunters and fishermen. **Ayelsford Inn Bed & Breakfast** (8 McMillan Avenue, 759-7672, $40 single, $45 double) has access to the beach, and pets are welcome. The **Auberge Caspian Inn** (26 Duke Street, 753-7606, $50 single, $55 double) has an indoor/outdoor swimming pool. Other options: **Auberge Braeston Inn** (RR 1, 753-7778, $30 single, $35 double). **Journey's End Motel** (3 Sugarloaf Street, 753-4121, $50 single, $55 double). **Idlewilde Cabins** (417 Mountain Road, 753-5576, $30 single, $35 double).

In Kedgwick, in the middle of the Restigouche Uplands, there's the **Windermere Motor Motel, Ltd.** (284-2015, $35 single, $40 double), and the **Motel R-17** (284-2196, $40 single, $45 double). The latter has a dining room. In St.-Quentin, south of Kedgwick, there's **Motel aux Quatres Vents, Inc.** (251 Rue Canada, 235-3129, $30 single, $35 double), and **Motel Hotel Victoria** (235-2002, $30 single, $35 double).

In Doaktown, part of the Miramichi Basin, try **Homestead Inn Bed & Breakfast** (RR 2, 365-7912, $30 single, $35 double) in a rustic setting near the river. Also in Doaktown: **River's Edge Cabin** (365-7917, $40 single/double) or **River View Cottages** (RR 2, 365-4555, $250 per week).

Camping

At Campbellton, there's **Idlewilde Trailers and Camping** (two miles east, 753-4665, $13) and **Sugarloaf Provincial Park** (753-7706,

$12). The latter is set in a park overlooking the water. In Kedgwick, there's the **Centre Plein Air de Kedgwick Ltee.** (284-2022, $10) and the picturesque **Kedgwick Provincial Park** (284-2295). In Doaktown, **Taylor's Campground** (365-4617, $10) is a good place to camp.

Dining

For good food in Campbellton, there's the **Braestone Inn** (RR 2, 753-7778) featuring home-cooked food in a licensed dining room. At Tide Head on the Québec border, try the **Country Kettle Dining Room** (Route 134, 753-4287) for down-home hospitality in a licensed dining room. For deep-dish pizza, there's **Pizza Delight** (13 Sugarloaf Street, 753-4444). Farther south in the Kedgwick and St.-Quentin area there's **Chez Carlo** (153 Canada Street, St.-Quentin, 235-3147) for Italian and Canadian cuisine. At Motel R 17, try **O'Regal Restaurant** (Kedgwick, 284-2196) for charbroiled steaks, fried chicken and homemade pie.

Deep-Sea Fishing

To join a deep-sea fishing charter or arrange a scenic tour, contact **Chaleur Phanton** (Dalhousie, 684-4722).

NEWFOUNDLAND
AND LABRADOR
ADVENTURES IN THE FAR NORTH

The sea there is swarming with fish,
which can be taken not only with the net,
but in baskets let down with a stone.

      —JOHN CABOT, IN 1497,
        REPORTING HIS DISCOVERY OF NEWFOUNDLAND

Canada's easternmost province of Newfoundland and Labrador has recently become, for Americans and Canadians as well as Europeans, a beckoning last frontier. There is a distinct feeling of adventure when you board the ferry in North Sydney, Nova Scotia, bound for Newfoundland and Labrador. You can't help but be dazzled by the sight of icebergs, the vast stretches of scenic coastline, the rare birds, the whales and seals, the Eskimo and Indian cultures and the sight of wild caribou herds roaming the tablelands of the province. In an era when tourists and travelers are becoming disillusioned with fabricated fun parks and crowded Old World cities, this vast province offers a reprieve from summer crowds and bus loads of retirees. It challenges you to bring your tent and hiking boots and explore amidst some of the best scenery in eastern North America.

Newfoundland and Labrador each have unique cultures. The distant tundra of Labrador is primarily inhabited by Innu and Innuit native people who have been living in the region for thousands of years. Newfoundland is primarily populated by rugged fishing and farming people of English, Irish or Scottish descent. Over the years, these hearty islanders have retained a very unique culture and outlook on life. Their stories, humor, music, festivals and traditions may have originated in the Old World, but Newfoundlanders or "Newfies" have put their own distinct touch into everything they do and say. Take the time during your visit to get to know these people. But remember, you won't be fully accepted by a Newfoundlander unless you "drink screech and kiss a cod." Screech is a strong rum that is

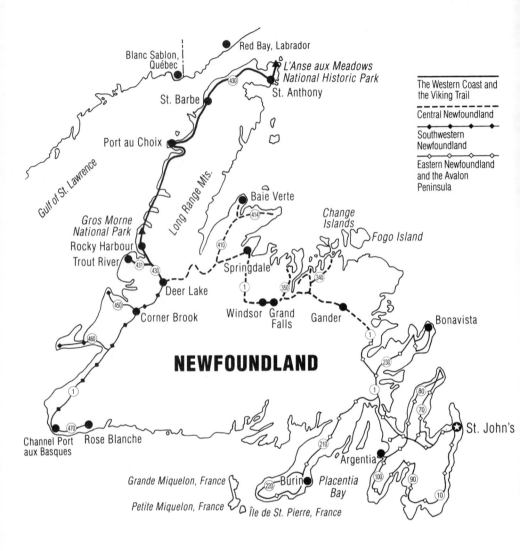

Red Bay, Labrador

Blanc Sablon, Québec

L'Anse aux Meadows
National Historic Park

St. Anthony

430

St. Barbe

Port au Choix

Gulf of St. Lawrence

Baie Verte

414

Change
Islands

Fogo Island

Gros Morne
National Park

Rocky Harbour
Trout River

431
430

Long Range Mts.

410

Springdale

1

350

340

Deer Lake

450

460

Corner Brook

Windsor Grand
Falls

Gander

Bonavista

230

1

NEWFOUNDLAND

80

70

1

Channel Port
aux Basques

470

Rose Blanche

1

210

St. John's

100

90

10

Argentia

Grande Miquelon, France

Burin Placentia
Bay

220

Petite Miquelon, France

Île de St. Pierre, France

The Western Coast and
the Viking Trail

Central Newfoundland

Southwestern
Newfoundland

Eastern Newfoundland
and the Avalon
Peninsula

Mileage Chart for Newfoundland

St. John's to Corner Brook	380 miles
St. John's to Port aux Basques	450 miles
St. John's to Argentia	45 miles
Corner Brook to Port aux Basques	100 miles
Corner Brook to Rocky Harbor	50 miles
Rocky Harbor to L'Anse aux Meadows	175 miles
St. John's to Grand Falls	200 miles
St. John's to Halifax, NS*	907 miles
St. John's, to Saint John, NB*	1,040 miles
St. John's, to Fredericton, NB*	1,065 miles
St. John's to Charlottetown, PEI*	880 miles
Grand Falls to Halifax, NS*	653 miles

*By ferry

made only in Newfoundland. And when they say "kiss a cod," they mean fish. Just that—kiss a dead fish on its fishy lips. Presumably, it takes plenty of screech-drinking to put one in the mood for cod-kissing.

A BRIEF HISTORY

Newfoundland and Labrador have a human history that dates back almost 10,000 years. Groups of North Americans such as the Innu, Innuit and Beothuk roamed the province hunting caribou, fishing and living peacefully at their own pace. The Beothuks were dominant on Newfoundland, traveling the island in snowshoes in winter and by canoe in summer. They hunted the now extinct great auk, as well as caribou, their main prey for food, clothing and shelter. Sadly, the Beothuk are also extinct; the last two Beothuk women were captured in the mid-1800s. What little is known of the Beothuk culture was learned from these two women.

The first white people to arrive in Labrador and Newfoundland came in 1000 A.D. when a small band of Viking explorers, led by Leif Eriksson, landed at what is present-day L'Anse aux Meadows on the Great Northern Peninsula on the west coast of Newfoundland. They had sailed for many days along the Labrador coast but settled on Newfoundland.

The Vikings stayed for two full seasons and called the land Vineland, meaning either "Land of Grapes" or "Land of Meadows." Once they were discovered by Indians living nearby, hostilities broke out. The much outnumbered Vikings sailed back to Iceland and Greenland in their open boats and did not return again. Before they left, the only woman among them had given birth to a son on Newfoundland soil. Knowledge of the Viking experience in this new land was recorded in Iceland in the thirteenth century, in volumes called the Norse Sagas. These are written accounts of the Vikings based on their oral history. In Indian legend, there is also a story of this encounter with white men with red beards. And in both the Sagas and the Indian legends, there is the story of a pregnant woman among them who gave birth to a son.

The exact location of this Viking settlement was not determined until 1964, when Norwegian explorer Helge Instad and his wife, Anne, followed an ancient Viking map sketched in the Norse Sagas. Their team discovered a Viking forge, an iron pin and a tiny stone wheel that led international scholars to agree that L'Anse aux

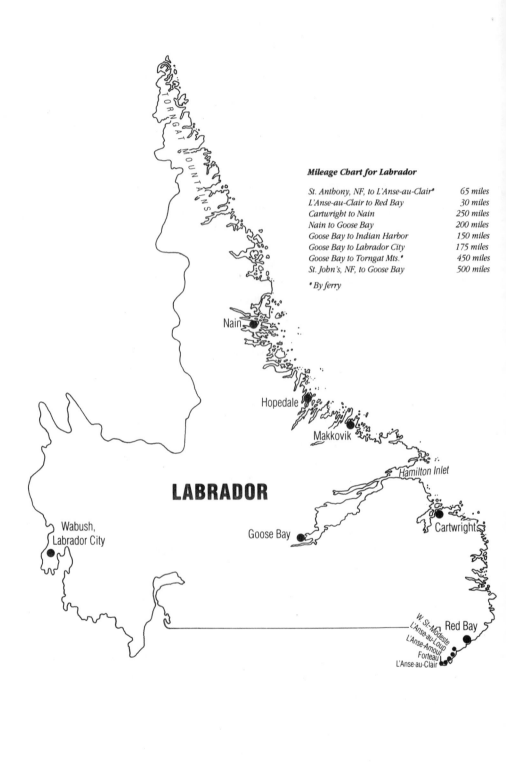

Mileage Chart for Labrador

St. Anthony, NF, to L'Anse-au-Clair*	65 miles
L'Anse-au-Clair to Red Bay	30 miles
Cartwright to Nain	250 miles
Nain to Goose Bay	200 miles
Goose Bay to Indian Harbor	150 miles
Goose Bay to Labrador City	175 miles
Goose Bay to Torngat Mts.*	450 miles
St. John's, NF, to Goose Bay	500 miles

By ferry

TORNGAT MOUNTAINS

Nain

Hopedale

Makkovik

Hamilton Inlet

LABRADOR

Wabush,
Labrador City

Goose Bay

Cartwright

W. St-Modeste
L'Anse-au-Loup
L'Anse-Amour
Forteau
L'Anse-au-Clair

Red Bay

Meadows was the sight of the Viking settlement. In 1991, a group of Norwegian adventurers repeated the voyage of the Vikings by sailing a replica of a Norse open boat to L'Anse aux Meadows. These modern-day explorers traveled across the Atlantic Ocean, stopping in the Faroe Islands, Iceland and Greenland. The aged Ingstad and his wife were present at L'Anse aux Meadows during the re-enactment of the Vikings' landing in July 1991.

The Vikings were not the only Europeans to reach North America before Columbus, although they had a 500-year head start. The island of Newfoundland was "officially" discovered in 1497 by the Venetian explorer John Cabot. Cabot and his crew sailed into a bay on the island's southeast shore. Because it was a holiday honoring St. John, Cabot unfurled his banner, claimed the land for England and named it St. John's. Even before Cabot's discovery, however, fishermen from Portugal, Spain, France and England were fishing the Grand Banks off Newfoundland. These men were not explorers but sturdy fishermen who were reluctant to tell of their rich fishing waters. So the discovery of Newfoundland was a well-kept secret until Cabot's claim. Cabot's voyage was funded by King Henry VII of England who ordered him to "seek out, discover and find whatsoever islands, countries, regions, or provinces . . . which before this time have been unknown to all Christians."

Upon his return to Bristol, Cabot's description of the abundance of cod lured more sailors to find this New Found Land, and further explorations were undertaken by the English, French, Portuguese and Spanish, including Jacques Cartier of France and the Corte Real brothers of Portugal. These early explorers, like John Cabot, were looking for ways to reach Asia, India and Africa. Cabot, among others, initially believed he had discovered the Orient. By 1502, the Portuguese had a map that identified Newfoundland as "the Land of the King of Portugal." The Portuguese dominated the harvesting of cod from the Grand Banks off Newfoundland for many years, shipping back tons of salted cod to Europe. Spanish, French and English fishermen also made the yearly voyage to fish the Grand Banks, and while many returned each year to Europe, others stayed on and began to settle this New Found Land.

In 1540, Basque whalers from northern Spain had set up a whaling station at Red Bay in Southern Labrador. The site was discovered by archeologists in 1977. The evidence of settlement included the wrecks of sixteenth-century ships, a cargo of barrels once full of oil

(North America's first oil spill) and compasses and navigational equipment. On shore, they discovered a kind of oil refinery, certainly the first ever on North American soil. Historically, these developments forced England to take decisive action and, with provisions and five ships, Sir Humphrey Gilbert was sent to Newfoundland. He landed at St. John's, where Portuguese and Spanish fishermen were living, and once again claimed the land for England in the year 1583.

For the next four centuries, Newfoundland struggled for an identity torn between French, English and native people, as well as privateers, pirates and rogues. The land was divided up in a feudal way, with certain powerful Englishmen like John Guy, Peter Easton, Sir William Vaughun and Lord Baltimore each holding a part of the island of Newfoundland, while Labrador on the mainland was left to the fishermen and Native Americans. In 1756, the Seven Years War broke out between the English and French. With an English victory, much of the lucrative fishing trade around the Grand Banks went to England. The British government did not want Newfoundland to be populated, preferring to exploit its rich fishing grounds. But settlers from England, Ireland and Scotland began to cross the Atlantic and eke out a living here farming, which was in violation of a British decree. In 1815, after a great deal of struggle and controversy, Newfoundland became a British colony and the way was paved for settlement.

By 1855, Newfoundland had become self-governing but reverted back to a colony after it went bankrupt during the Great Depression in the 1920s. It remained distant and uninvolved in Canadian affairs until 1947, when it finally joined the Confederation as one province—Newfoundland and Labrador.

With its long history of English, Irish and Scottish immigration and subsequent isolation, and its links to the Grand Banks, once the richest fishing lands in the world, Newfoundland developed a distinct culture. Newfoundlanders are among the most unique groups of Canadians, and are best known for their strong old-world brogues, hospitality, self-effacing humor (in the form of Newfie jokes) and fierce independent streak. Like islanders the world over, there is a sense of belonging that "come from aways" (visitors) cannot capture. Although the Newfoundlanders are glad to see visitors, they seem equally glad to see them go.

However, unemployment and the depletion of the fishing industry in Newfoundland is sending many residents away to search for jobs in Halifax, Toronto and other cities to the west. Even this trend has worked its way into Newfoundland humor with the observation that their southern neighbors, the Nova Scotians, are "just Newfoundlanders who couldn't afford to get to Toronto." Recently, offshore oil was discovered in the north of the province and big plans are afoot to build oil-drilling rigs. Although this will create jobs, the potential for damaging one of the richest fishing grounds in the world has divided Newfoundlanders about the proposed drilling. So changes are coming to this unique culture, too. Try to get here soon, just to appreciate Newfoundlanders' love for the land, expressed in Sir Cavendish Boyle's ode to Newfoundland, which ends in this stanza:

As loved our fathers, so we love,
Where once they stood we stand,
Their prayer we raise to heav'n above
We love thee wind-swept land
God guard thee, God guard thee,
God guard thee, Newfoundland.

GEOGRAPHY AND CLIMATE

Newfoundland is an island of mountains and forest marked by wild headlands and bays along the coast. Much of the development of Newfoundland and Labrador is focused along the shorelines, where the main industry has always been fishing. Labrador is particularly remote, and much of the region is inaccessible in winter due to icebergs and ice floes. While there is ferry service to Newfoundland year-round, icebergs are a real hazard to shipping. (It was off the coast of Newfoundland that the *Titanic* struck an iceberg.) It is not uncommon for the ferry from Nova Scotia to run into trouble getting to Newfoundland in winter.

Labrador is part of the oldest section of the Canadian shield, an underpinning of ancient rock that exists beneath the immense Hudson Bay. In Western Labrador, mining activities extract the bulk of Canada's iron ore.

Newfoundland's geography is also unique because of its inland fjords and unusual tablelands found at Gros Morne National Park. The tablelands, which have been declared a UNESCO Historic Site, support the theory of continental drift and plate tectonics. As you look over the tablelands, be aware that this was once a seabed and you'll begin to feel like you're at the bottom of a vast, dry ocean.

The climate in Newfoundland and Labrador is harsh all year long. Winters are bitterly cold, and summers can be rainy. Labrador's interior is plagued with flies during the summer, and much of it is inaccessible in winter. Newfoundlanders make the best of their harsh climate, spending winters skiing, ice fishing and enjoying snowmobile parties. The rugged climate hasn't spoiled the natives' sense of humor, as a popular expression like "May snow is good for sore eyes" can attest.

HIGHLIGHTS

One of the highlights of a visit to Newfoundland and Labrador is interacting with the people, particularly those who are unaccustomed to visitors. There is an openness that is surprising, considering how isolated the people have been from mainstream Canadian life. The friendliness of Newfoundlanders puts many cultures to shame, and their lively accents, their old world sensibilities and concern for others is unsurpassed in Canada.

Other highlights include a visit to Gros Morne National Park in western Newfoundland with its spectacular fjords and tablelands. At Gros Morne, it's possible to hike inland and see herds of wild caribou. Labrador, incidentally, has the largest wild caribou herds in Canada. While on the west coast of Newfoundland, travel to the Viking settlement at L'Anse aux Meadows, on the northwest tip of the island. To stand at this meadowed site and imagine a small band of Vikings landing here a thousand years ago is a very moving experience.

From western Newfoundland it's possible to take a ferry to Labrador, a remote, picturesque land that is still populated by Eskimos, Indians, missionaries and settlers seeking splendid isolation. Before the days of icebreakers, people used dog sleds to make the crossing in winter. Crossing the Strait of Belle Isle in this way was no easy task, and many a sled disappeared into the frigid waters. Ferry trips along Labrador's coast can be arranged, with glimpses of icebergs, whales and migrating birds making for an excellent adventure.

Finally, a visit to the city of St. John's, the oldest city in North America, and a tour of the surrounding Avalon peninsula are well worth your while. The peninsula, which has been settled for hundreds of years, is the cultural center of the island. Along the Newfoundland coast, where houses perch on rocks overlooking protective harbors, the village architecture is unlike any I've ever seen. All of Newfoundland was not linked by the Trans-Canada Highway until 1965, so many western Newfoundlanders are quite different from their eastern counterparts. But all islanders manage to make the trip to St. John's, at least once, and then they happily return to their side of the island, or to their ancient village.

PRACTICALITIES

Getting There

BY AIR. Getting to Newfoundland and Labrador by air is possible from most major U.S. and Canadian cities as well as northern Europe. The major airport in the province is at St. John's, with connections to Gander, Stephenville, Deer Lake and St. Anthony in Newfoundland and to Goose Bay in Labrador. Air Canada and Canadian Airlines International operate between regions of the province. For more information and reservations, contact Air Canada/Air Nova Airlines at (800) 4-CANADA or Canadian Airlines International at (800) 426-7000. Flights from Boston or Toronto to St. John's take approximately three hours; from Montreal, two hours.

BY LAND. To get to Newfoundland, you must take a car ferry. Ferries depart from North Sydney, Nova Scotia, and Goose Bay, Labrador. It is possible to travel through northern Québec on a partially paved highway to Labrador City and Wabush. This is a rugged journey that passes through the open-pit, iron-ore mining centers of western Labrador. From Labrador City/Wabush there is a partially paved road that traverses the interior of Labrador to Goose Bay. From Goose Bay, there is a ferry service to Lewisporte in northern Newfoundland.

On Newfoundland, the Trans-Canada Highway cuts across the center of the island all the way from Port aux Basques to St. John's. There is also trans-island bus and motorcoach charter service. Although bus service is fairly reliable, it is expensive and buses generally do not run more than once a day. In a pinch, many budget travelers hitchhike around Newfoundland, a reliable mode of transport on this hospitable island. For an interesting trip, there is train service between Sept-Isles, Québec and Labrador City provided by Iron Ore, Canada's railway. For more information, call (514) 871-1331.

There was once a railroad on Newfoundland, but sadly, the tracks have been torn up.

When driving in Newfoundland, be extremely careful of moose, particularly at night. The moose population is very high on the island, and they tend to wander across the highways. You may find yourself steering straight at an immobilized one-ton moose blinded by your headlights. Many moose are killed this way, but so are motorists, particularly tourists. It is advised that you drive slowly at night with headlights on low beam to avoid such a situation.

Winter driving in the province is particularly tricky. In the event that you must travel at this time of year, telephone the Department of Works, Services and Transportation in the following areas: Deer Lake (635-2162), Grand Falls (292-4300), Clarenville (466-7953) and St. John's (576-2381).

BY SEA. There is a year-round ferry service available from North Sydney, Nova Scotia, to Port aux Basques, Newfoundland, that takes six hours. Crossings are more frequent during the summer tourist season, with three departures a day from North Sydney at 9:00 A.M., 4 P.M. and 11:30 P.M. If you are crossing without a car, the price is $15.25; it's $46.25 for an automobile. There is also ferry service from North Sydney to Argentia, Newfoundland, operating from June through October. The crossing to Argentia is more expensive and time-consuming, but it lands you on the Avalon Peninsula within easy driving distance of St. John's. The tariff is $41 for individuals, $99 for automobiles. During the summer months, departures from North Sydney are at 4 P.M. on Tuesdays and Fridays and at 9 A.M. on Wednesdays and Saturdays.

To get to Labrador, you can take the ferry from Lewisporte in north central Newfoundland to Cartwright and Goose Bay, Labrador, from June 8 to September 10. The sailing time is 34 hours, and the boat departs from Lewisporte at 11 A.M. Mondays and 6 P.M. Thursdays. There is another ferry that departs from Lewisporte during the summer months that stops at St. Anthony in northwest Newfoundland and continues along coastal Labrador, stopping at hundreds of small settlements. This is basically a mail run, but it has become a popular journey for intrepid travelers. While some tourists find they must make reservations for this trip at least a year in advance, others have hopped on the ferry at St. Anthony with less than an hour's advance preparation. The latter do not get a guaranteed berth, however, and may end up sleeping in the lounge. It is advisable to plan this trip way in advance, although due to cancellations, you may find that there is room available at the last minute.

The drawbacks of traveling along the Labrador coast without a sleeping berth include having to sleep on chairs or in the hallway in a sleeping bag. The mailstops have become increasingly rowdy as the level of drunkenness increases among the berthless passengers. So it may be difficult to find peace and quiet. However, the trip offers the opportunity to view icebergs, Innuit villages, marine and bird life and much more. It's well worth it for the hearty traveler and gives one the feeling of being on an expedition.

There is also a ferry from St. Barbe to the Québec/Labrador border at Blanci Sablon and Île-au-Bois. This seasonal transport runs from June through September, departing on a first-come, first-serve basis, weather permitting. For up-to-date information on this ferry and other crossings contact Marine Atlantic Reservations Bureau, P.O. Box 250, North Sydney, Nova Scotia, Canada B2A 3M3, (902) 562-9470. For most vehicular ferry crossings, advance reservations are recommended. Travelers are reminded that Marine Atlantic requires that all fuel tanks be no more than three-quarters full when boarding the ferries.

There is also marine transportation along the southern coast of Newfoundland from Port aux Basques to Terrenceville reaching remote fishing villages like Little Bay, Grey River, Francois and English Harbour West.

Tourist Information

Tourist information is easily found in Newfoundland and Labrador, as in most of Atlantic Canada. The tourism bureau at Deer Lake in western Newfoundland has excellent information about Gros Morne National Park. There is so much to see in the park and inevitably so little time, that this information is really essential. For information about the Avalon Peninsula and St. John's, try the tourist information centers in St. John's and Whitbourne. For more information, write to Newfoundland Department of Development, Tourism Branch, P.O. Box 8730, St. John's, Newfoundland, Canada A1B 4K2, or phone (800) 563-6353.

Language and Population

English is the official language of Newfoundland and Labrador, but the province has strong dialects that are reminiscent of Ireland, old England and Scotland. Newfoundland has a dearth of sayings and a distinct vocabulary. A Newfoundlander would describe an ignorant person as a "blear," "oonshick" or "omadhaun." A "shooneen" is a coward. A person might also be described as "lonesome as a gull on a rock" or as "saucy as a crackie." If someone is being noisy, a Newfie might say "you are moidering my brains," while if someone is unreliable it might be said that "you can't tell the mind of a squid." If a Newfoundlander is wishing you good luck on your way, you'll hear them say "Fair weather to you and snow to your heels."

In Labrador, there is a strong native culture in regions with Innuit, Innu and other tribes of Eskimo and other North Americans. The "Livyers" are descendents of Europeans who settled along the southern coast of Labrador long ago.

The population of Newfoundland and Labrador is 568,000, making it the second smallest populated province in Canada. Yet the land mass covers 350,000 square miles. There is something unique to the people of this province, and any chance to visit them and the vast land they inhabit is a worthwhile trip.

Time

Newfoundland runs on Newfoundland Time, which is one-half hour ahead of Atlantic Time and one and one-half hours ahead of Eastern Time. Labrador is on Atlantic Time. Daylight Savings Time is in effect in Newfoundland and Labrador, beginning on the last Sunday in April and extending to the last Saturday in October.

Telephones

The area code for Newfoundland and Labrador is **709.**

THE WESTERN COAST

T he western region of Newfoundland extends from Port aux
Basques at the southwestern end of the island all the way to L'Anse
aux Meadows, the most northern point on the island. Although
many tourists travel only to St. John's and the Avalon Peninsula, the
western side of Newfoundland has some of the most dramatic
scenery and worthwhile excursions. There are two important World
Heritage Sites here: the tablelands at Gros Morne National Park and
the Viking settlement at L'Anse aux Meadows. There are fjords, rivers
and lakes to explore and some excellent hiking around Gros Morne.

The western shore has always been known for its high winds,
particularly around the southwestern tip of the island, so check the
weather report before traveling distances here. At times, usually during winter, the winds coming off the Long Range Mountains are so
strong that trucks are blown over. At one time, the railroad traveled
along the western shore to Corner Brook. On more than one occasion, the winds were so high that railcars were blown over. If you are
planning to travel towards Gros Morne National Park on the Trans-
Canada Highway, check with the local tourist office for an update on
weather conditions.

PORT AUX BASQUES

Port aux Basques is the first place you'll see if coming from Nova
Scotia by ferry. This town has typical Newfoundland architecture with
pastel-colored homes built on short stilts at the edge of the sea, surrounded by rock and a rugged harbor. Newfoundland immediately
gives you an impression of its extremes—in temperature, weather
and isolation—and Port aux Basques has the atmosphere that per-
vades all of Newfoundland. Once a fishing station for the French,
Portuguese and Basque in the sixteenth century, today Port aux
Basques is the principal terminus for the Marine Atlantic Ferry, which
operates year-round from here. Because the ferry leaves North
Sydney at 6 P.M. and 11:30 P.M., it is quite likely that you'll arrive at

Port aux Basques late at night, as I did. Without hotel reservations, I found that every hotel in the area (there are only a few) was booked. I spent the night in a campground. It was after midnight, and I couldn't see what I was doing when I pitched my tent. I was all alone, the wind howled and it rained hard, but, strangely, I felt safer in Newfoundland than I would have in my own backyard.

From Port aux Basques, there is a mail boat that travels along the southern coast to Terrenceville. It's possible to make this trip if there is room on the boat, but you should try to arrange a berth in advance. The boat stops in very remote regions where there are no roads connecting the townships. The majority of visitors skip this adventure and simply drive north along the Trans-Canada Highway towards Corner Brook. The route passes Cheeseman Provincial Park and Table Mountain. There is a trail that leads to the summit of this mountain where it is not unusual to sight caribou. Be sure to take precautions, though, if you plan to do any hiking in these remote and rugged areas.

Before striking out towards northern Newfoundland, take Route 470 east from Port aux Basques to Rose Blanche, where you'll pass towns like Isle aux Morts (Island of the Dead) and Burnt Islands. There is a real outpost feel to these small fishing villages in an area where numerous shipwrecks have occurred over the centuries. It is said that no fewer than 40 ships lie at the bottom of the Cabot Strait.

Back on the Trans-Canada Highway, the route continues north past towns like South Branch and Codroy Pond. This is the stretch of road that is most dangerous when there are high winds. About 20 miles out of Port aux Basques, there used to be a mountain home called Wreck House. A man living at Wreck House would report to the train conductors whether or not it was safe to pass. The train tracks are gone now, but the wind can still pose a threat, especially to trucks. You can get an update on current conditions from the tourist office in Port aux Basques before starting out.

Near St. George's, there is an information center. Just beyond, you can detour left to Stephenville and drive along the Port au Port peninsula, one of the prettier areas on the southwest side of the island. The peninsula is where the largest number of French-speaking Newfoundlanders live. This area, called the French Shore, was settled by deserters from the French navy. Stephenville is the largest community on St. George's Bay, and it has an airport, hotels and restaurants.

From Stephenville, continue along Route 460 to Cape St. George. There was once a lighthouse here, but now there is just a small park.

It's a good spot to take a photograph. If you backtrack to Route 463, you can travel into the French-speaking region to towns like Mainland. During August, the whole area of Port au Port peninsula celebrates *Une Longue Veillée* (meaning "A Long Evening"), a folk festival celebrating the French heritage of the region. The return drive to Stephenville gives you a chance to view both St. George's Bay and Port au Port Bay, so it's really a picturesque detour.

CORNER BROOK

The largest city on the western shore of Newfoundland, Corner Brook is built amidst the Blomidon Mountains. With a population of 25,000, it's an industrial center with a large pulp and paper mill, hotels and motels, restaurants and nightclubs. In July, there is a Hangashore Folk Festival featuring music, dance and food. Corner Brook is a good place to stop for lunch en route to Deer Lake and Gros Morne National Park. While you're here, tour along Route 450 to Lark Harbour or along Route 440 to Cox Cove. The drive along either shore of the Bay of Islands offers lovely views. On Route 450 stop at Blow Me Down Provincial Park where there are ample campsites and hiking trails into the Blomidon Mountains. The Humber River at Corner Brook, which empties into the Bay of Islands, is an excellent spot for salmon fishing. This river valley was explored by Captain James Cook in 1767 while he was charting the coast. While Corner Brook serves as a hunting and fishing center, there are also organized trips to the interior of the island, which can only be reached by small plane. North of Corner Brook you'll see Marble Mountain, the only ski resort in Newfoundland. Skiing at Marble Mountain is good from January to early April, and there are ample slopes for experts and beginners. Nearby Deer Lake has an excellent visitors center with ample information about Gros Morne National Park and the Viking Trail. Deer Lake was established as a logging community in the early 1890s.

GROS MORNE NATIONAL PARK AND THE VIKING TRAIL

A trip to *Gros Morne* (meaning "big gloomy") National Park and then on to the Viking settlement at L'Anse aux Meadows is a highlight of visiting Newfoundland. The park has some of the best scenery in eastern North America. Its natural history is so fascinating and unique, it was designated a UNESCO World Heritage Site in 1988.

Gros Morne National Park is accessible from Route 430 (marked as the Viking Trail) winding through the forest to Wiltondale. Here you can see the 2,644-foot slope of Gros Morne in the distance, with cliffs dropping off into the deep fjords. The climb is a half mile up but worth it: From Gros Morne the views from the summit of this mountain are spectacular. It is possible for the prepared hiker to walk inland for two or three days towards Silver Mountain. This hike into the mountainous interior traverses a vast tableland where caribou herds roam freely. It's a snow-covered route, even in summer, and park rangers have reported numerous hiking accidents. But if you have someone to hike with who's equally prepared, it's a great opportunity to see the wild side of Newfoundland.

The most rewarding way to reach the mountain is by taking Route 431 to Woody Point. This town overlooks beautiful Bonne Bay. There is a youth hostel at Woody Point where you'll meet some of the more adventurous visitors who come to hike, cycle, canoe or just explore the area by car. From Woody Point, continue to Trout River and you'll cross the tablelands, an area of special geological importance. The tablelands may have been the ocean floor billions of years ago. It's thought that when the continents rose and began to drift, this region of Newfoundland may have separated from mainland North America and collided with the Avalon Peninsula. The tablelands are best seen from the Trout River, where a tour guide explains the geological theories in greater detail.

From Woody Point, take the ferry across Bonne Bay to North Point where the road continues through the park. This is a beautiful little ferry crossing offering wonderful photo opportunities. From North Point the road reaches Rocky Harbour, a town with plenty of accommodations for tourists. Continue along the coast to Sally's Cove where you'll see a large parking lot on the right. It's about a one-hour walk from here to Western Brook Pond, where there is an excellent boat tour. You'll be rewarded with amazing views of these massive fjords that were formed over one million years ago. The lake, which is over 270 feet deep, was once fished for salmon and trout but is now off limits to fishermen. At the end of the lake, the boat drops off and picks up hikers touring Gros Morne's mountains. The boat tour takes about one hour.

Farther north along Route 430, you'll reach St. Pauls Inlet where boat tours are offered to those who want to see harbor seals. Seal sightings are literally guaranteed. Shallow Bay is an excellent spot to stop and walk along the beach. There is a great campground here where the staff puts on skits on summer nights, and campfires abound. In the distance you'll see Cow Head, where it is said that French explorer Jacques Cartier anchored in 1534.

THE VIKING TRAIL

The Viking Trail officially begins at Deer Lake, passing through Gros Morne National Park. After the beautiful scenery of the park, the long, flat drive to the Viking settlement at L'Anse aux Meadows is a striking contrast. It's a worthwhile trip, though, because you not only see the historic Viking settlement but you also catch a glimpse of floating icebergs. Icebergs seem to possess a real mystery, although as one fishermen put it after I gushed over their sculpted beauty, "I'd just as soon do without them."

The Viking Trail north of Gros Morne includes an interesting Historic Site at Port au Choix overlooking Ingornachoix Bay. Before reaching Port au Choix, though, stop at the Arches Provincial Park. There are two large rock arches here that have been carved by the sea through thousands of years of erosion. The surreal result is striking. The region around River of Ponds and Hawkes Bay is a favorite fishing area with abundant Atlantic salmon. At Port aux Choix, stop at the National Historic Site where, in 1967, an ancient cemetery was accidentally discovered. Archaeologists have identified the skeletons as belonging to the Maritime Archaic People, who were hunters and gatherers living along the eastern seaboard as early as 2000 B.C. There is an interpretive center at Port aux Choix that has information on this interesting find.

The coastal road from Port aux Choix to Eddies Cove passes numerous fishing communities. Look for the deserted St. John Island, where there is said to be buried treasure left by pirates who once harassed ships bound for Labrador. At St. Barbe, you'll reach the ferry departure point for trips to Labrador. The ferry runs seasonally, from May to December, on a first-come, first-serve basis. Continue through towns like Deadman's Cove, Nameless Cove and Savage Cove, which are all windswept, remote outposts overlooking the coast of Labrador. In the distance, you'll begin to see the bluish white shapes of icebergs.

On a stop at Eddies Cove, I asked a gas station attendant about the weather. "Didn't have much of a summer, but winters are plenty long here. That's when we get out our Skidoos and have Skidoo parties." The vast, flat land seems just right for snowmobiling, but the wind must really blow in winter up here. From Eddies Cove, the route turns inland toward the eastern side of the Great Northern Peninsula. The Viking Trail then splits and you can head south to St. Anthony or north to L'Anse aux Meadows.

L'ANSE AUX MEADOWS NATIONAL HISTORIC PARK

This World Heritage Site is believed to be the place where the Viking Leif Eriksson established a colony in 1000 A.D. The Norse sagas described this place as Vineland, "Land Of Grapes" or "Land of Meadows," where Leif, his son Thorvald and another Viking named Thorfinn Karlsefin once lived. Karlsefin was the father of a child named Snorri, who was the first person of European descent to be born in the New World. The final settlement had about eight Vikings, including one woman. It is recorded that during a fight with the *Skraelings* (Native Americans), who eventually drove the Vikings away, the Viking woman ran at the oncoming foe with her breasts bared, brandishing a sword.

Norwegian explorer Helge Ingstad and his wife, Anne Stine Ingstad, came to this site in 1960, following a hunch (and an ancient map taken from the Norse Sagas) that L'Anse aux Meadows was the site of the first Viking settlement. They were looking for mounds that might suggest a former house or dwelling, and they asked local people throughout their search if they had ever seen such mounds. At L'Anse aux Meadows, a local fisherman named George Decker had indeed seen mounds in the meadows, a place where local children often played. He led them to the site and the team set up camp here for six years, uncovering the evidence they needed. They found an old forge, an iron pin and a small wheel that were all documented as Norse objects. The blacksmith's forge used a technology that was only available to Europeans, refuting the possibility that it was an Indian settlement.

The full story of the discovery of L'Anse aux Meadows is fascinating. The excellent visitors center here has a film about the Norwegian couple's work. There is a replica of the sod house and the type of boats the Vikings used at the site. In July 1991, three replicas of the original Viking ships landed at L'Anse aux Meadows after crossing the Atlantic. They were greeted by a crowd of 15,000 spectators.

ST. ANTHONY

St. Anthony is another worthwhile destination with its beautiful harbor and magnificent icebergs. Visit the Greenfell House Museum overlooking the harbor adjacent to the Charles S. Curtis Memorial Hospital. The late Sir Wilfred Thomason Greenfell was a doctor and missionary who worked with many of Newfoundland's and Labrador's native Innuit people in the late 1800s and early 1900s. A fascinating and driven man, Greenfell once crossed a frozen stretch of ocean by dogsled to reach a patient in distress rather than wait and travel by road the following day. The ice broke up beneath him and most of his sled dogs perished. To prevent freezing to death, Greenfell killed his two remaining dogs and wrapped himself in their skins. He was rescued two days later.

Photographs at the museum give a good idea of how remote and risky life was in wintertime Labrador and Newfoundland. Also in St. Anthony, you can stop at Lighthouse Point to view the harbor and the icebergs offshore.

Accommodations

In Port aux Basques, accommodations are limited, and reservations should be made in advance if you're coming off the ferry from Nova Scotia at night. **St. Christophers Hotel** (Caribou Road, 695-7034, $50 single, $55 double) is open year-round and has 60 rooms. Another hotel open year-round is **Hotel Port aux Basques** (695-2250, $70 single, $75 double), within a mile of the ferry terminal. At Corner Brook, try the **Holiday Inn Downtown** (48 West Street, 634-5381, $80 single, $90 double) with a licensed dining room. The **Hotel Corner Brook** (Main Street, 634-8211, $45 single, $50 double) is a good deal in downtown Corner Brook.

Farther north at Deer Lake, there's the **Driftwood Inn** (3 Nicholsville Road, 635-5115, $55 single, $60 double) and **Deer Lake Motel** (Route 1, 635-3842, $55 single, $60 double) with its licensed dining room and easy access to Marble Mountain Ski Resort. Within

Gros Morne National Park, at Woody Point there's the **Woody Point Hostel** (Community Hall, 453-7254, $8 for members, $10 for non-members), which is open from June to September. There are more accommodations within the park at Rocky Harbour, including the popular **Ocean View Motel** (458-2941, $50 single, $55 double) with a licensed dining room. Organized boat tours of Western Brook Pond and Bonne Bay are organized through the Ocean View Motel. Also try **Bottom Brook Cottages** (Main Street, 458-2236, $50 single, $55 double) with a licensed restaurant and swimming pool. Boat tours are also arranged here.

There is a bed & breakfast near L'Anse aux Meadows in the far north at Gunners Cove called **Valhalla Lodge Bed & Breakfast** (623-2018, $35 single, $40 double). In St. Anthony, try the friendly **Howell's Tourist Home** (76B East Street, 454-3402, $28 single, $33 double), complete with full breakfast. The other alternatives in St. Anthony are the **St. Anthony Motel** (14 Goose Cove Road, 454-3200, $60 single, $65 double) with a licensed dining room and **Vineland Motel** (central St. Anthony, 454-8468, $50 single, $55 double) with a dining room and lounge.

Campgrounds

Between Corner Brook and Deer Lake, try the **Grand Lake Campground** (Route 401, Howley, 635-3628) or **Torrent River Nature Park** (Hawke's Bay, 248-5344, $11). All provincial and national parks in Newfoundland operate on a first-come, first-served basis.

It's possible to camp just about anywhere in Newfoundland, but the best bets are at the provincial campgrounds around Gros Morne National Park. These parks usually have a ranger on duty until 5 P.M. and there is a small fee. The main number for Gros Morne National Park is 458-2348. Individual campgrounds in national and provincial parks in Newfoundland do not have listed numbers. All the sites at Gros Morne are within walking distance of the beach or the mountains. One of the best is at **Shallow Bay**, ($6 per night) the northern-most campground in the park. There are 50 grassy sites near the beach, and on weekends there is a small outdoor theater where the staff performs skits and offers "lassie tea" (tea with molasses) to the audience after the performance. **Berry Hill** is also a large, centrally located campsite within the park, near the Lobster Cove Head lighthouse and the visitors center. Another favorite is **Lomond** ($6 per night) at the park entrance in Wiltondale. This is an exquisite spot with views of Bonne Bay and the Long Range Mountains. **Trout River Campground** ($7) is also very popular, situated along the Trout River. It has 35 wooded sites and is open from June to September. At nearby Rocky Harbour, try **Juniper Campground** (off Route 230, Pond Road, 458-2917, $11).

In the far north, there's **Viking Trailer Park** (Pistolet Bay, St. Anthony, 458-2917, $10) or the Provincial Park at Pistolet Bay off Route 437, four miles from Raleigh. The latter area has 30 sites, laundry facilities and day-use facilities.

Dining

Restaurants don't abound in Newfoundland; the better ones are normally part of a hotel or motel complex. The best deals for meals in Newfoundland are at the **Irving Gas Stations** where the old-style diners are still intact. The food is good and plentiful, and the people are friendly. Other alternatives include **Mary Brown's** (High Street, Port aux Basques, 695-3030) for fried chicken, **M & M Irving** (Stephenville), which is termed "a gas bar and restaurant" (i.e., eat here and get gas) and the **Seven Seas Restaurant** (16 West Street, Corner Brook, 634-6572) for Canadian and Chinese food. A nice place to eat in Rocky Harbour is **Fishermen's Landing** (458-2060) with fresh seafood. At Reef's Harbour, there's **Sam's Restaurant** (Reef's Harbour Junction) for seafood and home-baked breads. In St. Anthony, the **Vineland Motel** (5 minutes from the Viking Mall, 454-8843) has a good dining room. The **Viking Mall** also has take-out food and inexpensive eats.

Gros Morne National Park Boat Tours

There are three important boat tours at the park. The **Western Brook Pond** tour is arranged at the Ocean View Motel, Rocky Harbour (458-2730) and costs $23. Departure times are 10 A.M., 1 P.M. and 4 P.M. The **Tablelands Boat Tour** is arranged through the visitors center (451-2101) and costs $22. The 40-passenger Lady Catherine departs from the new wharf at Trout River Pond. The third tour is the **Seal Island Tours** on Bonne Bay. This can also be arranged by the visitors center. All three trips are highly recommended.

CENTRAL NEWFOUNDLAND

The center of Newfoundland is heavily wooded with one stretch of road passing from north to south, terminating in Harbour Breton. The most beautiful aspects of Central Newfoundland are the coastal communities scattered along its peninsulas and islands, like Baie Verte and the remote Fogo Island and Change Islands. Here, you'll see the quintessential Newfoundland, villages once inaccessible by highway that are still unaccustomed to the increasing influx of visitors each summer. Every little village is unique, its people separated by miles of coast but still able to come together every so often for a *time* (the Newfoundland word for party or get-together).

BAIE VERTE AND THE BEOTHUK TRAIL

This northern section of Central Newfoundland is beautiful and wild and is well worth exploring.

You must return to Deer Lake to begin an eastward tour across the island. Baie Verte peninsula is an area rich in mineral deposits including copper, gold, silver and zinc. On the way north you'll pass Sandy Lake where just a century ago, caribou herds 10,000 strong used to travel inland from here after migrating south from the Great Northern Peninsula. There are still small herds that can be spotted today. At nearby Howley, two moose captured in Nova Scotia were released in 1878 and four more were introduced from New Brunswick in 1904. From these beginnings, a moose population of 120,000 inhabit Newfoundland, and they roam the entire island. At Sandy Lake, there is an unpaved road that leads to Jacksons Arm. From here there is a ferry to Harbour Deep, the only community on this remote shore besides Englee. The ferry makes two trips a week, on Tuesdays and Fridays. This area was once busy with intensive whaling activity.

The road to Baie Verte and Fleur-de-Lys passes the Flatwater Pond Provincial Park, the site of a former logging camp. On Route 414, stop at Nippers Harbour to see the "Naked Lion," a rocky outcrop resembling a lion. At the tip, visit Fleur-de-Lys, where an ancient Dorset Eskimo site was discovered. The whole area of the Baie Verte peninsula had the first successful copper mine in Newfoundland. As you leave the peninsula, you'll pass Indian River Provincial Park along the Trans-Canada Highway. This river is the area where caribou hunters tracked their prey on the way to Birchy Lake. The road then diverges to Springdale, where there are hotel accommodations and restaurants.

At Roberts Arm, you'll find yourself in the middle of Beothuk country on the road called the Beothuk Trail. The now extinct Beothuk Indians lived in this area, and hunted the caribou herds as they migrated across Newfoundland. In 1823, the last two surviving Beothuk Indians, named *Demasduit* (called *Mary March*) and *Shanawdithit* (renamed *Nancy*) were captured near here at South Brook. These two women became invaluable to Beothuk researchers and offered insights into this dying culture. Nancy provided drawings illustrating the types of dwellings they lived in, their mythological beliefs and the stories of her people. Their language helped linguists form links between their society and those of other Indians in eastern North America. It is believed that the Beothuks inhabited Newfoundland for thousands of years, well before the Vikings dropped by and ages before John Cabot's "discovery."

At Badger, visit the Mary March Provincial Park where you can camp on the actual winter encampment of the Beothuk. The highway runs through a beautiful valley here, following Exploits River, a Beothuk water route to the open sea. Once on the ocean, the Beothuk hunted the Great Auk, a flightless bird that was hunted to extinction in the mid-1800s. Continue to Grand Falls, the largest city after St. John's and Corner Brook. It was at Grand Falls that the very last Beothuk Indian, Mary March, passed away. Visit the Mary March Museum on St. Catherine Street in Grand Falls. The museum offers insight into all that is known about the Beothuk and has information on other native peoples who lived in this region. Grand Falls is the site of Newfoundland's first pulp and paper mill, established by Lord Northcliffe and Lord Rothemere. Today it is a major supplier of the world's newsprint. Check at the visitor's information center in Grand Falls for details.

From Grand Falls you can take the southern Route 360 all the way to Harbour Breton. You have to turn around and come all the way back, however, unless there is room on the mail ferry that stops at Harbour Breton. The southern drive is like real outback travel, and you'll pass *Jipujikuei Kuespem* (meaning "little river pond") Provincial Park, formerly the hunting grounds for the Micmac Indians. Continue to the coast along Route 362 to Belleoram, a sea-swept community on the South Coast that has long been associated with the Grand Banks fishery. Nearby English Harbour West is famous as a supplier of excellent knitted goods.

THE BAY OF EXPLOITS AND ROAD TO THE ISLES

For those who've chosen to visit the remote northern islands of Newfoundland or to find out the meaning of the town Joe Batts Arm on Fogo Island, take Route 340 from the Notre Dame Junction towards Lewisporte. Lewisporte is the terminal for ferries to Labrador, effective from June to September. Ferries for Goose Bay depart at 11:00 A.M. on Mondays and for Cartwright at 6:00 P.M. on Thursdays. The trip takes 34 hours and returns the following day. There is another ferry that departs Lewisporte for St. Anthony and the coastal communities of Labrador. This is a popular trip for adventurous tourists and has a year-long waiting list. However, it may be possible to board at St. Anthony if you don't mind sleeping in the lounge. I met a traveler who simply showed up at departure time in St. Anthony and boarded the ferry, spending a week touring the Labrador coast.

From Lewisporte, you can reach Little Burnt Bay, a fishing community that has been unchanged for centuries. By backtracking, you are on Route 340 heading along the Notre Dame coastline to Campbellton, originally a Beothuk encampment. Pass through Loon Bay and Birchy Bay, settled in 1857 by fishermen who now rely on forestry and lobster fishing for their livelihood. At Boyds Cove there is a causeway that connects the Twillingate Islands to the mainland of Notre Dame Bay. The Twillingate area was established in the mid-1700s by families from Poole, England. Once the hub of the fishing industry in Notre Dame Bay, the town was so prosperous during the late 1800s that it had its own newspaper, *The Twillingate Sun,* and a winning cricket team. In July, Twillingate hosts the Twillingate Fish, Fun and Folk festival with some excellent West Country English dancing, music and songs.

CHANGE ISLANDS AND FOGO ISLAND

Return to Boyd's Cove for a drive along Route 340 and Route 355 to the village of Farewell, where you can catch the ferry to Change Islands. Located in Notre Dame Bay between Twillingate and Fogo, these two islands are joined by a causeway. This area was always popular with fishermen returning from Labrador, and by the beginning of the twentieth century, there were over 1,000 people living along the shores here. The numbers have dropped to 500 with the decline in the fishing industry. Change Islands did not have a motor vehicle on it until 1965, so as you can imagine very little has affected this remote outpost. The sunsets are dramatic and time seems to stand still. In winter, it's nearly impossible for these islanders to leave, so they hunker down and stay home.

From Change Islands or Farewell, catch the ferry to Fogo Island, one of the oldest settlements in Newfoundland. The people here arrived in the 1700s from England, and because of the isolation, little about their Elizabethan accents has changed. Fogo's villages include names like Seldom and Little Seldom, but the most notable is Joe Batts Arm, apparently named for a deserter from Captain James Cook's ship who sailed this coast in 1763. Joe Batt apparently lost an arm here, but nobody knows for sure. Fishing is the mainstay of the people on Fogo Island, and a church turned museum, called Bleak House, may attest to the grip the sea has had on the people here. As one local put it, "Oh, my dear, Fogo would be nothing at all without fishing." The fact that the fishing industry off the Grand Banks is in decline may indicate why so many young folk are leaving Fogo Island.

From Fogo Island, you can barely spot the remote Funk Island. This was formerly the nesting ground of the Great Auk, a large flightless bird that was hunted to extinction in the mid-1800s. Recently, a lone kayaker in search of the Great Auk (a bird shaped like a pelican that was hunted for its feathers and meat) paddled from Funk Island along the coast of Newfoundland, stopping in hundreds of small villages along the way. He had little hope of finding the Great Auk, but he raved about the great hospitality of Newfoundlanders.

After leaving Fogo Island and reaching Farewell, travel along Dog Bay to the unpaved Route 31. Here you can stop at places like Roger's Cove and Gander Bay South en route to Clarks Head and the beginning of the Gander Loop.

THE GANDER LOOP

This scenic loop around Hamilton Sound and northern Bonavista Bay begins in Gander, which may be a familiar name to those who know about the early days of aviation and World War II. With its proximity to Europe, Gander became a key air base for early transatlantic flights. In the 1930s it became known as the "Crossroads of the World." By World War II, it was developed into a major military air base, with factory-made North American planes being refueled and sent to the battlegrounds of Europe. After the war, many sophisticated travelers stretched their legs around Gander while their international flights refueled. Gander was also a favorite landing for defectors from the Soviet Union and Eastern Bloc countries. Gander is a little quieter today, but it is an excellent place to organize a fishing or hunting expedition, with small airplanes available to transport the group into the island's hinterlands. Caribou, black bear and moose abound in this area, as well as Atlantic salmon and trout.

From Gander, begin the Gander loop by heading north to Gander Bay and Carmanville. During the spring melt, you can see icebergs floating south with the Labrador current. Carry on around the sound past Musgrave Harbour where there is a Fishermen's Museum that was constructed by Sir William Coaker in the 1800s. Continue on to Deadman's Bay to do some beachcombing along the sandy beach here. Nearby is Lumsden, named for the methodist minister James Lumsden who worked in the community in 1885. At Windmill Bight Provincial Park, there is a story linked to a buried treasure hidden by a strange midnight phantom. There is a stream where a big rock is meant to conceal the treasure. Newtown is also on the Gander Trail, which was the home of Captain Joe Barbour who lost his way sailing home to Newfoundland in November, 1929. After 48 days at sea, the schooner landed at Tobermory, Scotland, where captain and crew were given a hero's welcome. The community helped refit the boat and installed an engine for the return trip. Farther south, an unpaved road leads to a causeway to Greenspond. A fishing community since the late 1600s, there is a Community Museum in the old courthouse that provides details about the lives of these early settlers. The Gander Loop passes through a number of small, picturesque villages ending in Gambo where there are camping facilities, gasoline stations and a hotel and restaurant.

TERRA NOVA PROVINCIAL PARK

This park is just south of Gambo and is the oldest of Newfoundland's two national parks. Its most appealing characteristics are its beaches, tidal flats and rich wildlife. The pitcher plant, a carnivorous yet beautiful plant that is the official flower of the province, grows here amidst the peat bogs. It's possible to see black bear, moose red foxes and the occasional lynx from the road here. Along the coast, you can spot whales, seals and icebergs in Bonavista Bay. There are ample campgrounds located at Dunphy's Pond, South Broad Cove and on Oldford's Island. Boat trips are available at Salton's Brook on Newman Sound. The Blue Hills, within the park, offer excellent views of the forests, bays and the distant points on the Bonavista peninsula. You can take a side trip along Route 310 to Salvage and Eastport on the Eastport Peninsula. At Salvage, the Lane house has been converted into a community musuem. At Burnside, there is a year-round ferry that reaches St. Brendan's at the tip of northern Bonavista Bay. This trip offers an excellent chance to view the rugged Newfoundland coast from the sea, where you can imagine the impressions the early settlers must have formed when they arrived from Europe.

Accommodations

Along Route 410 toward Baie Verte, try the **Baie Verte Inn** (White Bay, 532-8250, $50 single, $55 double) with its large dining room. At Roberts Arm, the **Lake Crescent Inn** (652-3067, $30 single, $35 double) is recommended, while the **Pelley Inn** (Springdale, 673-3931, $32 single, $37 double) is also good. Lewisporte has good accommodation at the **Brittany Inn** (535-2533, $50 single, $55 double), with boating and fishing nearby, and the **Sea Side Lodge Bed & Breakfast** (313 Main Street, 535-6305, $35 single, $40 double) is also good.

The remote islands of Change and Fogo have some accommodations. Try **Seven Oakes Tourist Home** (621-3256, $45 single, $50 double) and **Fogo Island Motel** (Fogo Island, 266-2556, $46 single, $50 double). The latter has a licensed dining room. Reservations in summer are recommended for these islands.

In Grand Falls, the **Mount Peyton Hotel** (214 Lincoln Road, 489-2251, $65 single, $70 double) has a large dining room. **The Carriage**

House (181 Grenfell Heights, Grand Falls, 489-7185, $45 single, $50 double) serves a full breakfast. At the far southern end of Central Newfoundland, there's **Breton Motel** (Harbour Breton, 885-2283, $50 single, $55 double) with coastal views.

At Gander, try the **Albatross Motel** (256-3956, $65 single, $70 double) or the **Cape Cod Inn** (66 Bennett Drive, 651-2269, $40 single, $45 double).

At Musgrave Harbor, along the Gander Loop, there's **Banting Motel** (655-2443, $50 single, $55 double) with a licensed dining room and facilities for campers at Banting Memorial Facilities. At Eastport, near the Terra Nova National Park, there's ample accommodation.

Other options: **Seaview Cottages** (on Bonavista Bay, 677-2271, $40 single, $50 double) or **Eastport Efficiency Units** (Eastport, 677-2458, $50 single, $55 double) with swimming pool, tennis court, boating, fishing and picnic tables.

Campgrounds

At Birchy Lake on Route 1, try **Fort Birchy Park and Campground** (between Corner Brook and Gran Falls on the Trans-Canada Highway, 551-1318, $12) with laundromat, restaurant, fireplaces and gas station nearby. At Botwood, there's **Botwood Municipal Park** (257-2479, $10) with salmon fishing nearby. At Lewisporte, try **Woolfrey's Pond Municipal Park** (Lewisporte, 535-2737, $5) with swimming and hiking nearby. The provincial and national parks in this area are also excellent, ranging from Beothuk Provincial Park to Indian River. **Terra Nova National Park** (Glovertown, 533-2706, $9 per night, $50 weekly) has 400 semi-serviced sites, with heated washrooms, showers and kitchen shelters. From mid-June to Labor Day, a National Park Motor Vehicle Permit is required. For further information, call or write the Superintendent, Terra Nova National Park, Glovertown, Newfoundland, Canada AOG 2LO, (709) 533-2801.

Dining

Before Grand Falls, your best bet for food on this route is at the Irving Gas Stations along the Trans-Canada Highway. Coffee-shop-style restaurants service the busy truck drivers, so the service is fast and the food is pretty good. In Grand Falls, there's the **Taiwan Restaurant** (High Street, 489- 4222) and **Loung's Garden Restaurant** (Trans-Canada Highway, 489-2440), both of which feature Chinese and Canadian food. In Gander, try the **Skipper's Inn** (118 Trans-Canada Highway, 256-2534) for lunch or dinner. There's a licensed dining room in Glovertown at the **Parkway Motel** (two miles west of Terra Nova National Park, 533-2222).

EASTERN NEWFOUNDLAND

T he southeastern section of Newfoundland—comprised of the Bonavista, Avalon and Burin Peninsulas—is the most densely populated region of the island. Each of the three peninsulas has its special history and natural attractions, and if you have the chance, you will most likely want to visit all three.

THE BONAVISTA PENINSULA

Cape Bonavista at the northeastern tip of the peninsula was the site of John Cabot's landfall on June 24, 1497. In 1500, the Portuguese explorer Gaspar Corte Real visited the east side of the peninsula near the present-day village of Trinity. Later, the peninsula was settled by the English, but battles with the French for land and fishing rights were not uncommon. During the eighteenth century, a fishing master named Michael Gill from Charlestown, Massachusetts, held off French raiders with two armed ships and the aid of local fishermen. There is certainly plenty of lore and history along this route, with some beautiful coastal views as well.

You can reach the peninsula from Terra Nova National Park along Route 233, an unpaved highway, or from Clarenville on the Trans-Canada Highway. Follow the northwest arm of the peninsula past Jiggin' Head Provincial Park to Kings Cove, one of the oldest villages on this road. Beyond that, you'll reach the spectacular Cape Bonavista, with its historic ties to John Cabot's voyage of discovery. Cabot actually sailed past here, continuing south to the area of present-day St. John's, which has grown into Newfoundland's largest city. Despite skirmishes throughout the 1700s between the French and English, Cape Bonavista endured as the most northerly English settlement in Newfoundland. While here, visit the lighthouse, built in 1843, that overlooks Bonavista Bay. It has been restored as a Provincial Historic Site and life-style museum. Tours are conducted by guides in period costume of the 1880s.

Throughout the peninsula, you'll notice half-underground, small sheds with sod roofs that are dug into the hills. These serve as community root cellars, where turnips, potatoes and squash are stored. For centuries, boiled root vegetables with salted meat—popularly called a "Jigg's Dinner"—has been a mainstay of the Newfoundlanders' diet.

Heading south along Trinity Bay, you'll pass Catalina and Port Union. It was here that Sir William Coaker formed the Fishermen's Protective Union, the first of its kind in Newfoundland. Continuing down Route 230, you'll reach the historic town of Trinity. The first court in North America convened here in 1615. Although this is one of the oldest settlements in the province, it was not until the eighteenth century that the West Country English arrived, bringing the strong accents and homespun traditions so characteristic of Trinity today. Trinity has preserved many of its historic buildings, including a Roman Catholic church, an Anglican church and the Society of United Fishermen's Hall, all built over 100 years ago. Two houses in town have been designated Provincial Historic Sites: the Hiscock House and the Garland House. At the Hiscock House, guides in period costume tell stories of the resourceful widow Emma Hiscock and her thrifty daughters. The Garland House was built for merchant Francis Lester in 1760. Lester, who came to Trinity in the early 1770s, made his fortune by creating a vast fishing empire. He returned to England to retire.

From Trinity, you can travel down Route 239 to Old Bonaventure with its views of the many coastal enclaves in Smith Sound. Return to Route 230 and travel to Georges Brook near Smith Sound Provincial Park. It was from here that islander William Epps Cormack set out in 1822 with a Micmac guide, Sylvester, to cross the interior of the island in search of the disappearing Beothuk Indians. They never found the elusive Beothuk, but the trip established Cormack as the first European on record to make the trek across Newfoundland.

From Clarenville, you can head for the Burin Peninsula where a ferry connects with the French-owned islands of St. Pierre and Miquelon, or you can travel down the Isthmus to the Avalon Peninsula, location of the city of St. John's. This narrow strip literally holds Newfoundland together. On either side lie Trinity and Placentia Bays, cut deep by melting glaciers. Some of the more interesting community names along the way are Come By Chance, Goobies, Tickle Harbour and La Manche. There are plenty of interesting inlets and coves to explore on the Isthmus before entering the Avalon Peninsula near Whitbourne.

Accommodations and Dining

On the Bonavista Peninsula, the **Schooner Motel** (Route 235 in Summerville, 545-2543, $45 single, $50 double) has a dining room and a nightclub. In Trinity East, the **Peace Cove Inn** (off Route 230, 781-2255, $35 single, $40 double) has a licensed dining room and good hunting and fishing nearby. Goobies, on the Isthmus, has **Welkomin** (Route 1, 542-3152, $40 single, $45 double) with a licensed restaurant.

Campgrounds

In Bonavista, **Paradise Farm Trailer Park** (Route 230, 468-2027, $10) has water and electrical hook-up. In Trinity, there's **Trinity Cabins Trailer Park** (Route 239, 464-3657, $10) with laundry facilities and a convenience store.

THE AVALON PENINSULA

Newfoundland's most easterly region, commonly called the Avalon, is an irregularly-shaped peninsula that is believed to have drifted over from the European continent 400 million years ago. Its rough, windswept landscape has been shaped by melting glaciers, then altered further by settlement and deforestation. With its precarious position on the edge of the North Atlantic, the Avalon is an important sanctuary for hundreds of species of seabirds who nest at Cape St. Mary's and Witless Bay. Cape Spear, the most easterly point of land in all of North America is a "must see" for visitors who drive here from historic St. John's. The cliffs of the southern shore and Cape Race are incredibly high, while inland caribou herds still roam the vast Avalon Wilderness Reserve. Within a few hours from any point on the Avalon, you can reach St. John's, the cultural hub of Newfoundland with entertainment, restaurants and shopping. From nesting gannets, black-legged kittiwakes and northern razorbills to great pubs, music and friendly people, the Avalon has an identity all its own that makes it highly popular with summer visitors.

ST. JOHN'S

St. John's is the hub of the Avalon. Its recorded English history dates back to 1497, when John Cabot sailed through its protective headland, called the Narrows, on St. John's Day. Fishermen have been coming to St. John's from many nations since the sixteenth century, and it's still possible to see the flags of many nations flying from the numerous vessels that enter and exit this harbor. The capital of the province bills itself as "the oldest community in North America," and there is still an old English feel to the city. Its dockside pubs of brick, the bustle of downtown Duckworth Street and the looming presence of the fortress on Signal Hill, site of the last battle of the Seven Years War between the British and French, all give the city its unique flavor.

The Victorian feel of the city is a result of rebuilding that occurred after a fire wiped out much of historic St. John's in the Victorian era. St. John's has an array of pastel-colored wooden homes hugging the hills above the harbor.

Attractions

Before setting out to see the sights, stop at the Tourist Commission's main office at City Hall, New Gower Street, or call 722-7080. The staff is very friendly and helpful. There's a booklet available describing self-guided walks and points of interest.

❖ *Newfoundland Museum*
Located on 285 Duckworth Street, this museum has some excellent displays, including the skeleton of a Beothuk Indian. There is also a Viking exhibit and a detailed history of St. John's. Open every day, free admission.

❖ *Murray Premises Museum*
Within this restored market building on Water Street, you'll find the second branch of the Newfoundland Museum. There is some interesting information here about the Basque whalers who came to Newfoundland in the early 1500s. Other displays focus on the marine, military and naval history of the province.

❖ *Cathedrals*
There are two beautiful cathedrals in St. John's that are both National Historic Sites. The Roman Catholic Basilica Cathedral of St. John the Baptist, on Military Road, is built to resemble a Latin Cross, with twin towers and a beautiful interior. Just south of this church you'll see the Anglican Cathedral of St. John the Baptist on Church Hill. Designed by Sir Gilbert Scott and built in 1849, it's considered to

be the best example of Ecclesiastical Gothic architecture in North America. Inside, there's a silver communion service presented by King William IV.

❖ Arts and Culture Center

Located on Prince Philip Drive, this impressive arts center built in 1967 is the scene of many performances and exhibits. During the Summer Festival of the Arts in July, many of the main events are held here.

❖ Signal Hill National Historic Park

Located east of town along Duckworth Street, this park is worth a visit, especially for the views. It overlooks the cliffs and St. John's Harbour with all its fishing and shipping activity. The final battle between the French and English was fought on Signal Hill, during the Seven Years War that ended in 1762. Also from this site, just beneath Cabot Tower, the first transatlantic wireless signal was received on December 12, 1901 by inventor Guglielmo Marconi.

❖ Quidi Vidi

At the eastern edge of St. John's, you'll reach the village of Quidi Vidi, one of the oldest in the province, settled in the 1700s. Nearby is Quidi Vidi Lake, site of the St. John's Regatta, a sailing contest that began in 1826. Considered to be the oldest sporting event in North America, the regatta is an annual happening that is thoroughly enjoyed by locals and visitors alike.

Accommodations

There are plenty of lodging choices in St. John's, ranging from tourist homes to major chain hotels. For all the amenities, the **Best Western Travellers Inn** (Kenmount Road, 722-5540, $60 single, $65 double) or **the Holiday Inn Government Centre** (180 Portugal Cove, 722-0506, $110 single, $125 double) are well-equipped places to stay. For a more rustic setting, **Parkview Inn** (118 Military Road, 753-2671, $45 single, $50 double) has fireplaces and a reading room. **The Prescott Inn Bed & Breakfast** (17-19 Military Road, 753-6036, $50 single, $55 double) is close to downtown. For inexpensive accommodation, the **Sea Flow Tourist Home** (53-55 William Street, 753-2425, $30 single, $35 double) is your best bet.

Campgrounds

The only campground within St. John's is **Pippy Park Trailer Park** (Nagles Place off Prince Philip Parkway, 737-3669, $12).

Dining and Entertainment

Much of St. John's dining and nightlife is centered around Duckworth and George Streets. Many of the large hotels have good, licensed restaurants. After this, the choices narrow down quite a bit. In historic St. John's, there's **Stone House Restaurant** (8 Kenna's Hill, 753-2380). Another good restaurant is **Chateau Park** (7 Park Avenue, 364-7725), which features seafood and steaks. Try **Haymarket Square** (223 Duckworth Street, 739-6676) for European and North American specialties. At the Arts and Culture Center, the **Act III** is an expensive but good restaurant. The pub food is good at **King Cod** (122 Duckworth Street). There's also a good Italian restaurant called **Sidestreet** (17 George Street, 739-9540). For evening entertainment, the place to be is George Street with its long line of English-style pubs. You're bound to hear both rock music and traditional Newfoundland tunes on a rowdy Saturday night. The area is popular with students, tourists and young professionals. **Graduate House** (112 Military Road) is especially popular on weekends and features free movies on Wednesday and Thursday nights.

Shopping

There are interesting craft stores in St. John's that feature work by many of the islands craftspeople and artists. The best shopping is along Duckworth Street. **The Cod Jigger** (250 Duckworth Street) has native bone and talc carvings, knitware and jewelry. **The Salt Box** (194 Duckworth Street) has excellent pottery, weavings and jewelry. For leather products, **Newfoundland Saddlery and Leather, Ltd.** (383 Duckworth Street), has good leather products and horse gear. **Newfoundland Weavery** (177 Water Street) has knitting, weavings and carvings.

THE NORTHEAST AVALON

There's a lot to see around Conception Bay from the tip of Pouch Cove to Bay de Verde. But first visit Cape Spear National Historic Park, east of St. John's. The Cape Spear Lighthouse served as a beacon for thousands of vessels heading towards St. John's from 1836 to 1955. It's now a life-style museum with information about the area. Head back to St. John's and then turn north towards Logy Bay and Middle Cove. For dramatic coastal views, this stretch is unrivaled. Historic Torbay was a strategic spot for the British forces in 1762, who under the command of Colonel Amherst, recaptured St. John's after it was briefly taken over by the French.

From Torbay you can drive north to Pouch (pronounced "pooch") Cove. The village is one of the original settlements on the island, dating back to 1611. Although permanent settlement in Newfoundland was forbidden in the seventeenth and eighteenth centuries, the treacherous harbor at Pouch Cove made it difficult for British ships to find the settlers and flush them out.

Cape St. Francis is accessible only by dirt road along the cliffs, so proceed with caution. It is believed that the cape was named by the Portuguese explorer Gaspar Corte Real in 1501. The lighthouse was built in 1887 and used during World War II as an antisubmarine operations outpost to monitor enemy U-boats in Conception Bay. Yes, they were that close! In fact, Bell Island, accessible by ferry from Portugal Cove, saw action during the war. On September 4, 1942, a German submarine sank two Canadian vessels, the *Saganaga* and the *Lord Strathcona*, that were docked to load iron ore from the Bell Island mines.

From here you can pass through Paradise (don't blink) towards Conception Bay South and Cupids. Explorer John Guy from Bristol, England, landed at Cupids in 1610 and attempted to establish a plantation. His efforts led the way for further settlement on Newfoundland.

From Cupids you can travel north to Harbour Grace, a village that gets its name from the French, who named it in the sixteenth century. Harbour Grace sheltered the pirate Peter Easton in the eighteenth century; the present day Community Museum was once his pirate fort. In 1919, the village was a departure point for early flights across the Atlantic. Harbour Grace's real heroine is Amelia Earhart, who departed from here in 1932 to become the first woman to fly solo across the Atlantic.

Just north of Harbour Grace, you'll reach Carbonear, a British settlement that was attacked by the French in 1696. The inhabitants were able to defend themselves, however, and the French could not capture it. There is a story told here about the "Princess of Carbonear." Supposedly, an Irish princess named Sheila Na Geira was captured in the English channel by a pirate named Gilbert Pike during the reign of Queen Elizabeth I. After the pirate and the princess fell in love, she persuaded him to give up his errant ways and settle in Newfoundland. They made their home at Carbonear and had a child, claimed to be the first European child born in Newfoundland. The Pike family continues to live in the village to this day, and beneath a tombstone at the west end of town, the ashes of the Princess of Carbonear and her pirate lover are said to be buried.

Continue north on Route 70 to a spit of land called Bay de Verde. This community was settled by English colonists in the 1600s, and its inaccessibility helped protect them from French raiders. Offshore you'll see Baccalieu Island, a notoriously treacherous area for ships. Dozens of ships lie beneath the ocean just off shore. From here you can coast down the Trinity Bay shore passing villages like Heart's Desire, Heart's Delight and Heart's Content all the way to Dildo, the latter being an excellent spot for whale-watching.

THE SOUTHERN AVALON

The route along the eastern and southern shores of the Avalon Peninsula stretches from St. John's to the ferry terminus at Argentia. There are two important bird sanctuaries here—at Witless Bay and Cape St. Mary's—plus an immense wilderness area featuring herds of wild caribou, moose and bear. You can take all this in easily as you're coming or going between the ferry and St. John's.

En route from Cape Spear National Historic Park, you'll soon reach Witless Bay, where a fantastic seabird sanctuary is located offshore. The sanctuary, which supports immense colonies of puffins, razor-billed auks, kittiwakes, guillemots and petrels, is world famous among bird-watchers and ornithologists. A permit is required if you intend to land on the islands, but you don't need one if you stay in a boat. Fishermen take sightseers out to see the birds nesting and flying around in vast numbers. The sight of these varied species is a real thrill, so don't forget your camera.

FROM WITLESS BAY TO TREPASSE

This stretch of coast has long been associated with pirates, rum runners and other sundry outlaws. Stories of the region's colorful past abound. At Aquaforte, south of Ferryland, it is said that a French fleet ran aground while avoiding the English and then buried their treasure before escaping on foot across the peninsula. Ferryland was established as a colony by Lord Baltimore in the early 1600s, when he fortified the cliffs with cannons. However, the Dutch destroyed the settlement during a battle in the year 1763. Farther along the coast, you'll pass Renews, where the English ship *The Mayflower* stopped for supplies in 1620 after 66 days at sea. This same ship landed at Plymouth Rock in the same year.

The Trepasse Barrens, which run along the southern tip of the peninsula, resemble Arctic tundra with heaths and barren ground. This is the summer range of the Avalon caribou herd, and you can see the animals along the highway. The rivers in this area, including North East Brook, North West Brook and Biscay Bay River, offer excellent trout fishing during July and August.

Pull out all the stops and stop at St. Shotts, where an old hermit called "the Sandcarrier" lived out his days in a little hut. His potato garden is still visible, overlooking the St. Shotts River. The most southern points on Newfoundland are nearby at Cape Freels and Cape Pine. Although the fishing has always been good off shore, this can be a very treacherous area for ships. Many a hulk lies in a watery grave here.

Around St. Peter's River on St. Mary's Bay you'll most likely spot whales, for they like to feed here in the summer months. St. Mary's is a community settled by Irish who speak a dialect called Newfoundland Irish. Be sure to visit Salmonier Nature Park north of St. Catherines to see caribou, moose and other wildlife indigenous to Newfoundland and Labrador. From St. Catherines, you can take Route 91 to Placentia, where the road then turns north to Argentia, and then the ferry to Nova Scotia.

One of the most worthwhile side trips, albeit along an unpaved road, is around the loop of southern Avalon to Cape St. Mary's Ecological Reserve. The reserve is the second largest nesting spot for the Gannet, a white bird with a long golden neck. You can sit right on the cliffs and watch the birds up close. This area's special meaning for Newfoundlanders was captured in the folk ballad "Let Me Fish Off Cape St. Mary's":

Let me sail up Golden Bay
With my oilskins all a'streamin'
From the thunder squall—when I hauled me trawl
And my old Cape Ann a'gleamin'
With my oilskins all a'streamin.' . . .

From Cape St. Mary's, travel north to Placentia, which was earlier named "Plaisance" in 1662 by the colonial French. This was an important French garrison in the 1690s. From here, they launched three attacks on St. John's. After the Treaty of Utrecht in 1713, the English moved into Placentia. At the ruins at Castle Hill National Historic Park, there is an Interpretation Center that tells of the French presence in Newfoundland. From Placentia, it's a short trip to Argentia, the Marine Atlantic terminus for ferries from North Sydney, Nova Scotia, during the summer months. In 1941, a famous offshore conference was held here between President Franklin Delano Roosevelt and Prime Minister Winston Churchill, which preceded the U.S. entry into World War II.

THE BURIN PENINSULA

You can get to the Burin Peninsula by leaving the Trans-Canada Highway at Goobies and following Route 210. The route runs inland from the peninsula's eastern shore, bypassing some of the beautiful coastline. Marystown is the largest community on Placentia Bay. It's here that many of the trawlers used in the Grand Banks fishery are built. There is a fish processing plant on the island across from Marystown. There are plenty of hearty shipbuilders and fishermen to be met around here with plenty of stories and songs about the Grand Banks fishery. The coastal area between Marystown and Burin is full of small, typical Newfoundland fishing villages. From Marystown as a starting point, you can tour the remote shores of the Burin Peninsula, called the "boot," stopping at St. Lawrence, Fortune and Grand Bank.

Fortune is the departure point for a little ferry trip to France, or more accurately, the islands of St. Pierre and Miquelon. These small islands are the last vestiges of French territory in the New World. Here, the tricolor French flag still flies, the rules and regulations come directly from France and in summer the cafés, the food, the music and the ambience are reminiscent of the French Riviera. Canadians and Americans must carry a driver's license or other identification, but passports are not required.

St. Pierre has the charm and atmosphere of a seedy French port, with its aged, wrought-iron balconies and winding, narrow streets. To reach the larger islands of Great and Little Miquelon, you can charter a boat through the St. Pierre tourist office. Prices are cheaper here than in Canada, particularly for wine and food. A visit to this little outback of France is highly recommended. As one native Newfoundlander put it, "It's like a slice of Paris without the traffic."

From Fortune and Grand Bank, take Route 213 to Frenchman's Cove Provincial Park where there's a freshwater lake for swimming. The route turns inland from here, heading away from the Burin Peninsula towards the Trans-Canada Highway and onward.

Accommodations

In Portugal Cove in northeast Avalon, **Beachy Cove Bed & Breakfast** (RR 1, 895-3120, $35 single, $40 double) is only 20 minutes from St. John's. At Carbonear, the **Carbonear Motel** (on Conception Bay, 596-5662, $40 single, $45 double) and **Fong's Motel** (Route 70, 596-5010, $60 single/double) are both good. The latter has a Chinese-Canadian dining room. On Avalon's southern shore, **The Downs Inn** (Route 10, 432-2808, $35 single, $40 double) has a licensed dining room featuring fresh seafood and home-cooked meals. At Trepasse in the far south, **Trepasse Motel and Tourist Home** (Route 10, 438-2934, $40 single, $45 double) features a dining room, and fishing and hunting nearby. At Placentia, try **Harold Hotel** (Main Street, 227-2107, $40 single, $45 double) or **Rosedale Manor** (near Argentia Ferry, 227-3613, $40 single, $45 double).

On the Burin Peninsula at Marystown, **Motel Mortier** (Route 210, 279-1600, $75 single/double) has a dining room and lounge. At Grand Bank, **Granny's Motor Inn** (Highway-By-Pass, 832-2180) is next to the St. Pierre Ferry Terminal.

Campgrounds

At Marysvale on Conception Bay, **Lakeside Trailer Park** (off Route 60, 528-4486, $10) has boating and fishing access. At Seal Cove, **Fish-a-Bit Trailer Park** (Route 60, 744-2196, $14) has canoe/boat rentals and a laundromat. There are numerous provincial parks in the area; camping is on a first-come, first-serve basis.

Dining

In remote areas such as the coast of the Avalon Peninsula, many hotels feature dining as well. In Carbonear, **Sal's Pizza, Ltd.** (596-8989), has eat-in or take-out Italian food. In Marystown, **Mrs. B's Cafe and Bakery** (Pen Mall, 279-2319) has home-baked goods. One excellent spot is **Rosedale Manor** (Placentia, 227-3613) located on the waterfront in a restored inn.

In Fortune, try **Central Restaurant** (minutes from St. Pierre Terminal) for fully licensed dining, including seafood platters.

LABRADOR

L abrador, which is three times the size of Newfoundland, is one of the last unexplored areas of Canada. Labrador's land is sectioned into the Québec mainland and separated by Newfoundland along the Strait of Belle Isle. The geological base of Labrador is the ancient Laurentian Shield, one of the oldest unchanged regions on earth. It is believed that Labrador looks exactly as it did before life on earth began. For nearly 9,000 years, it has been populated by the Innuit and Innu people who are Eskimo and Indian, respectively. Their villages are strewn along the eastern coast. European settlement on Labrador was sparse and began in the early 1800s when fishermen would cross the straits to fish in summer. Those who stayed livealong the Labrador Straits in the south and are commonly called "liveyers." The combined population of Labrador, with its native people and later arrivals, is only 29,000.

Labrador is characterized by its extremes: the weather, the dramatic scenery with its steep fjords and raging rivers and its remoteness. Large herds of caribou still roam the land and the rivers are abundant with fish. However, the rich mineral resources of Labrador have brought increasing development to interior areas like Labrador City and Wabush, where iron ore is the main industry. Churchill Falls is the site of an immense hydro-electric plant that provides power in Canada and the eastern United States. The Happy Valley–Goose Bay area was settled during World War II as an Air Force base and is also the terminus for the Marine Atlantic ferry from Lewisporte, Newfoundland. With a trend toward development of Labrador's interior, new roads are under construction. This is good news for hunters, fishermen and adventurers, as so much of the area is only accessible by small plane.

Although Labrador does not get too many visitors, an increasingly popular trip is by ferry along the coast. Travelers can stop in hundreds of small Eskimo and Indian villages along the route and get a real feel for the remoteness of the region. The popularity of this trip has increased over the years, and it is recommended that you reserve a berth on the Marine Atlantic mail boat at least a year in advance. Huge icebergs are a common sight as well as bird and marine life. One of the highlights of a visit here is Red Bay, an ancient Basque whaling site that was established in the 1500s.

THE LABRADOR STRAITS

The Labrador Straits at the southern end of Labrador make up the region from L'Anse-au-Clair to Red Bay, and they're accessible by ferry from St. Barbe on the Great Northern Peninsula of Newfoundland. During the spring and summer, you can take this short ferry trip across the Strait of Belle Isle to Blanc Sablon in Québec. From here you drive down Route 510 to the community of L'Anse-au-Clair in Labrador. Founded by the French in the 1700s, its meaning is "clear water cove." This spot gives you an excellent feel for life in remote Labrador and this is a very scenic fishing outport.

Farther north at Pinware River there is a provincial park. Here, archaeologists have uncovered burial sites of the Maritime Archaic Indians, which contain artifacts that date back 7,500 years. These people were believed to be nomadic caribou hunters and fishermen. They later migrated south along the Strait of Belle Isle and their remains are found throughout Atlantic Canada. You'll pass through other small European settlements like L'Anse-au-Loup and Capstan Island, which leads to Red Bay, at the end of Route 510. From here it is possible to continue along Labradors coast by mail ferry, if there happens to be extra room on the boat. There are no roads north of Red Bay except for an unpaved road between Happy Valley–Goose Bay and Labrador City.

Red Bay is a very interesting archeological find that provides evidence of the presence of Basque whalers on Labrador, who hunted whale from Red Bay in the 1500s. In 1977, archeologists uncovered the remains of a shore station where whale blubber was processed and sold as oil. Divers uncovered the remains of numerous whaling vessels with perfectly preserved hemp ropes, wooden blocks and a number of personal possessions. One large ship was found with a cargo of oil barrels. The ship was identified as the *San Juan,* which sank in 1565 just as it was leaving for Spain. This recorded find gives the *San Juan* wreck the distinction of being the cause of the first oil spill in North America.

Also at Red Bay, a whaler's cemetery was uncovered and more than 60 graves have been exposed. One of the best-preserved graves revealed the remains of an adult European male with a wooden cross embedded across his chest, suggesting that the man may have been a priest. This interesting find offers an excellent insight into the lives and possessions of these early visitors and once again links Atlantic Canada to an ancient past.

From Red Bay, you may want to inquire about the mail ferry along the coast. One traveler I met just showed up at the docks in St. Anthony, Newfoundland, boarded the ferry and took it all the way to Nain.

If you don't catch the ferry north, you have to retrace your steps back to L'Anse-au-Clair, as the highway ends at Red Bay.

WESTERN AND CENTRAL LABRADOR

The interior of Labrador is accessible from Goose Bay–Happy Valley, but you have to take the ferry from Lewisporte, Newfoundland, to get here. Once here, there is a rough and ready road to Labrador City that passes through Churchill Falls and the train depot at Esker. There is rail service from Esker to Québec that is called the Québec North Shore and Labrador Railroad.

From Goose Bay to Esker

For those attempting to drive from Goose Bay to Esker, it is possible to board the train (but not with your car) and travel through the very remote forests of Labrador and Québec. During my visit to southern Labrador, many adventurous travelers were planning to take this trip, but its the kind of journey you should be prepared for. For more information call the Québec North Shore and Labrador Railway at (709) 944-8205.

Happy Valley–Goose Bay

This is the Marine Atlantic ferry terminal for passengers coming from Lewisporte, Newfoundland. Goose Bay also has an airport that was established during World War II for transporting aircraft from the United States and Canada to Great Britain. It later became an important airfield for trans-atlantic flights and a major air base for the U. S. Strategic Air Force long-range bombers. Happy Valley is the civilian part of the area, while Goose Bay is manned by the Canadian Armed Forces and is used by the British Royal Air Force, U. S. Air Force, West German Air Force and Royal Netherlands Air Force for training and flying exercises. Increasing numbers of troops and aircraft are being sent here, which certainly helps Labrador's economy.

During the month of August, Happy Valley–Goose Bay is the site of the Labrador Canoe Regatta, which features a weekend of music, canoe races, food and drink. The gathering of native people and transients makes for an interesting glimpse of the people of Labrador. If you do make the trip all the way to Labrador City and Wabush, you'll find a mining city that has grown from rugged work camps to a modern town with all the necessary facilities and accommodations. The area is primarily involved in iron-ore mining, but it is also a favorite wintertime destination for downhill and cross-country skiers. The Nordic Ski Club has twice hosted World Cup events and Canada's national ski teams sometimes train here. In summer, people come to fish, canoe and camp. An alternative to driving here from Goose Bay is to drive through the forested regions of northern Québec along a partially paved road that runs from Baie Comeau through Gagnon, Fire Lake and Mount Wright on the Québec/Newfoundland border. The road than continues all the way to Labrador City and Wabush.

NORTHERN LABRADOR

Northern Labrador is still unexplored wilderness whose coast is populated by Innuit and Naskapi-Montagnais Indians. Because of the remoteness, they have managed to keep their traditions and life-styles intact. This area is very beautiful and wild, and many people attempt to explore the area by airplane. If you are lucky enough to get on the mail ferry from Newfoundland or Goose Bay, one of your first stops will be Makkovik, an interesting coastal community that was settled in the early nineteenth century by a Norwegian fur trader, Torsten Andersen, and his Labrador wife, Mary Thomas. The settlement became the Moravian Mission in 1896 and continued to function as a mission until 1948. The remote beauty of this region is inspiring and the native people continue to work on their bone jewelry, antler buttons and weavings as well as hunting and fishing.

North of Mokkovik, the ferry stops at the village of Postville, which was founded as a fur trading post in 1843 by a Québec merchant. It is believed that the Dorset Eskimo, who lived along these shores for 4,000 years, used to come to the Kaipokok Bay to hunt. Further up the coast at Hopedale you can visit the Hopedale Mission, the oldest wooden framed building existing in Québec, built in 1782. Now a National Historic Site, there is a preserved church, a store, a residence for missionaries and many huts. Again, native craftsmanship is in evidence here with skin mittens, carvings and weavings.

At remote Nain, you can visit the Nain Museum with its excellent collection of Innuit artifacts and relics from the Moravian Mission. A mission was also established in Nain in 1771.

One of the most northerly communities in Labrador is at Hebron, along the Kangershutsoak Bay. In 1829, another Monrovian mission was built here and the mission house is still standing today. You can tour the Hebron Mission National Historic Site to get a sense of how desolate these early missionaries must have felt. North of Hebron, at the tip of Labrador, you can see the wild and rugged Torngat Mountains, which draw mountain climbers from all over the world.

Wilderness travel in Labrador is both risky and exciting, but certain areas face restrictions. Try to contact the Provincial Department of Forestry prior to making vacation plans. If you're lucky enough to get to the Torngat Mountains, then you have reached the end of Labrador country. Just to know that this kind of wilderness is still out there, and that it's not that far from home, is an inspiring thought.

Accommodations/Dining

Due to the remoteness of Labrador, there are very few independent restaurants and most are part of a motel/hotel complex. In southern Labrador at L'Anse-au-Loup, there's **Barney's Hospitality Home** (Route 510, 927-5634, $25 single, $30 double). At Forteau, **Seaview Housekeeping Unit** (Route 510, 931-2840, $55 single, $60 double) is close to a restaurant. The **Northern Light Inn** (L'Anse-au-Clair, 931-2332, $50 single, $55 double) has a dining room and lounge and a craft shop.

In the Happy Valley–Goose Bay area, the **Labrador Inn** (Station C, 896-3351, $70 single, $75 double) has a dining room featuring Canadian and continental cuisine. The **Royal Inn** (5 Royal Avenue, 896-2456, $60 single, $65 double) has dining room and barbecue facilities. In Labrador City, **Carol Inn** (215 Drake Avenue, 944-7736, $75 single, $80 double) has a restaurant/lounge. In the far northern town of Nain, the **Atsanik Lodge** (922-2910, $60 single, $65 double) has a dining room and lounge. There's trout fishing and hunting nearby.

Campgrounds

Twenty miles north of Wabush, **Grand Hermine Park** (282-6218, $10) offers guided tours for hikers, boat rentals and a convenience store. There are provincial parks at Duley Lake, six miles out of Labrador City, that is popular with swimmers and boaters. Near Blanc Sablon in Québec, there is a camping site at Pinware River. Labrador is basically wide-open country and all villages along the coast would not object to campers. Watch out for polar bears, however.

Excursions

Labrador is one of those places that appeals to adventure travelers. The challenge of exploring this coast is well worth the cost, and there are some organized tours that will take you there. A group called **Inuilak Labrador** (P.O. Box 11, North West River, Labrador, Canada AOP 1MO, 497-8326) offers a Northern Sea Coast tour and a seven-day waterfall and Sub-Arctic tour. Wilderness canoes are provided and wilderness cabins can be rented. **Labrador Adventure** (P.O. Box 86, Churchill Falls, Labrador, Canada AOR 1AO, 925-3235) takes a tour of the largest underground power plant and a visit to the Labrador and Québec Indian Band at Esker.

PRONUNCIATION GUIDE

Nova Scotia

Acadia = ACADia

Amherst = AM-erst

Antigonish = anTIGonish

Baddeck = BAdeck

Berwick = BERwick

Bras d'Or Lake - bra-door lake

Brier Island = BRIer island

Cape Blomidon = cape BLOMidon

Cape Breton = cape Bretten

Cape Forchu = cape Forchew

Ceilidh = Kaylee

Cheticamp = CHETicamp

Dalhousie = DALhousie

Digby = digbee

Ecum Secum = EEkum seek-um

Evangeline = eVANgelin

Gaelic = GAILlic

Glace Bay = glayce bay

Glasgow = GLASgo

Glenholme = glenHOLMe

Glooscap = gloosCAP

Grand Pré = grand PRAY

Grosses Coques = GROSses KOKis

Hantsport = HANTSport

Ingonish = ingoNISH

Inverness = INverness

Judique = jewdeek

Kejimkujik National Park = kejimKUjik

La Have = la HAVe

Lunenburg = LOONenburg

Louisbourg = louieburg

Mahone Bay = maHONE bay

Main-à-Dieu = MAIN-a-doo

Margaree = MARgaree

Meteghan = MetEEGHAN

Musquodoboit Harbour = MUSquo-do-bit

Petit Étang = Peteet E tang

Petit-de-Grat = Peteet-de-GRAT

Petite Rivière = Peteet RIVier

Pictou = PICtow

Pointe de l'Église = point de leglaze

Pubnico = PUBnico

Pugwash = pugWASH

Shelburne = SHELburne

Shubenacadie = shubenACAdee

Ste. Anne du Ruisseau = saint Ann du russew

Tatamagouche = TATAmagoosh

Tidnish = tidNISH

Tracadie = traCAYdee

Truro = TRURo

Whycocomagh = whyCOcoma

Yarmouth = YARmuth

Prince Edward Island

Abegweit = ABA-jewit

Argyle Shore = ARgyle shore

Bedeque = bedEEK

Bideford = BITafurd

Bonshaw = BONshaw

Canceaux Cove = can-sew-cove

Cape Egmont = cape eggmont

Cavendish = CAVENdish

Charlottetown = CHARlottetown

Crapaud = crapODD

Cymbria = Simbria

Dalvay = dalVAY

Donagh = Donna

Dunstaffnage = dunstaffnagE

Ellerslie = ELLERslie

Gaspereaux = gas-per-o

Glengarry = glenGARRY

Grand Tracadie = grand traCAYdee

Keppoch = kep-Pok

Malpeque = Mal-peck

marram grass = MARram grass

Miminegash = mimINEGASH

Miniegash = mini-gash

Miscouche = MISkootch

Montague = MONTague

Naufrage = nauFRAG

Strathgartney = STRATHgartney

Souris = soree

Tignish = tigNISH

Tyne Valley = tine ValleyUigg = Wig

Panmure Island = PANmure island

New Brunswick

Aroostook = aROOStook

Atholville = ATHolville

Aulac = ALLack

Baie des Chaleurs = bay de CHALure

Balmoral = balMORal

Bathurst = BATHurst

Bouctouche = boocTOOCH

Campobello = CAMPobello

Cap-Pelé = cap PAYlay

Caraquet = CARAket

Chatham = Chat-em

Cocagne = Coke cane

Dumfries = Dumb-frees

Escuminac = es-kumin-ack

Foire Brayonne = for BRAYonNE

Fredericton = FREDricton

Grand Manan Island = grand maNAN island

Jacquet River = Jacket river

Jemseg = gem seg

Kedgwick = KEDGwick

Kennebecassis = kenneba-kasis

Kouchibouguac National Park =
    koogie-boo-guac

Lepreau = la pro

Madawaska = MA-DA-waska

Mactaquac Provincial Park = ma-ta-quock

Malecite = MALesight

Meductic = MEDatook

Miscou Island = MISsew island

Micmac = MICmac

New Brunswick *(continued)*

Miramichi Basin = MIRAmeechee basin

Moncton = MONKton

Nackawic = NACKawick

Neguac = nay-guock

Nepisiguit = neppis-a-quit

Oromocto = oroMOCto

Passamaquoddy Bay =

     pass-a-ma-quadie bay

Paquetville = PAketvil

Penobsquis = pen-OBsquis

Petitcodiac River =

     peteet-KOdeeack river

Pocologan = POco-LOgan

Pointe-Verte = point-vert

Point Escuminac = point esCOOManak

Quaco = QUACKO

Restigouche Uplands = rest-a-gooch

Richibucto = richiBUCKto

Saint-Antoine = saint ANToyn

Shediac = SHAYdeeack

Shippagan = shipPAGAN

Saint-Isidore = saint ISIdoor

Tetagouche Falls = TETgooch falls

Tracadie = traCAYdee

Youghall = yole

Newfoundland and Labrador

Avalon Peninsula = AValon peninsula

Argentia = are-gen-she-a

Bay d'Espoir = bay desPORE

Baie Verte = Bay Vert

Beothuk = beo-took

Burin Peninsula = BURin peninsula

Fleur-de-Lys = fleur-de-lees

Forteau = For Toe

Gros Morne = gross mourn

Guernsey = gurn zee

Isle aux Morts = eel a mort

L'Anse-au-Clair = lanz a clair

L'Anse aux Meadows = lanz a meadows

Makkovic = MAKkovic

Nain = nane

Placentia = PleSENsha

Port aux Basques = port a bask

Port aux Choix = port a shore

Quidi Vidi Battery = kiddee viddee battery

Torngat Mountains = TORNgat mountains

Twillingate = TWILLingate

Wabush = WAbush

INDEX

Tibetan Buddhist monastery, 112
Tignish, 159
Titanic, 209
Tiverton, 75
Tiverton Islands Museum, 75
Tobeatic Wildlife Management Area, 55
Tolmie Gallery, 81
Torngat Mountains, 248
Tracadie, 194-95
Train travel, in Atlantic Canada, 6
Transportation, in Atlantic Canada, 5-6
Travel, expense of in Atlantic Canada, 8
Traveler's checks, acceptance of in Atlantic Canada, 8
Trepasse Barrens, 240
Trinity, 233
Trinity Anglican Church, 54
Trotsky, Leon, 94
Trout River, 218
Truro, 91-92
Twillingate, 226

U

"Une Longue Veillée," 217
University of Moncton, 191
University of New Brunswick, 181
Upper Clements Park, 78
Upper Saint John River Valley, 183-88
Utrecht, Treaty of, 3, 13, 241

V

Victoria Park, 140
Vikings
    discovery of Atlantic Canada by, 2-3
    discovery of Labrador and
        Newfoundland by, 205
    settlements in Newfoundland by, 220
Viking Trail, 219-20
Volger's Cove, 52

W

Wabush, 247
Walter's Blacksmith Shop, 48
Welch, David, 76
West Berlin, 53
West Dover, 34
Western Head, 55
Western Shore, 40
West Point Lighthouse, 159
Westport, 76

Weymouth, 71
Weymouth North, 71
W.G. Earnest, 38
Whale-watching
    from the Avalon Peninsula, 239, 240
    in Bay of Fundy, 74
    from Brier Island, 74-76
    from Cheticamp, 109, 111
    near Digby, 72
    in New Brunswick, 2
    from Tiverton, 75
White Point, 57
Wildman, William, 61
Windsor, 39, 87-89
Witless Bay, 239
Wolfe, Brigadier General James, 121
Wolfville, 83-85
Wolfville Historical Museum, 84
Woodstock, 184, 187
World Pumpkin Festival, 88

Y

Yarmouth, 62-67
Yarmouth County Museum and
    Archives, 64
Yarmouth Light, 64-65
York Redoubt, 25
Youghall Provincial Park, 196
Young Teazer, 41, 42

Z

Zwicker house, 42, 48
Zwicker, Joshua, 42